MW00892125

DEAR CUSTOMERE

THANK YOU

FOR YOU ORDER

WWW.REALLYGREATSITE.COM

Preface

Hi talents! It is so glad to see you here and I would like to extend the warmest welcome to all the readers of my book. Your presence and interest in my work bring me immense happiness. It is my utmost desire to share my knowledge and experiences with you, and I am grateful for the opportunity to do so.

Thank you for joining me, and I hope you find inspiration, joy, and valuable insights within the pages of this book.

In this comprehensive exam preparation practice test, I am delighted to provide you with the carefully curated mock exam questions. These questions have been meticulously crafted to offer you a valuable opportunity to familiarize yourself with the format, style, and level of difficulty that you can expect during the actual exam.

This practice test goes beyond mere simulation; **it serves as a testament to your dedication in acquiring a widely recognized professional qualification, showcasing your competence and unwavering commitment to your profession and career. By choosing my book, I firmly believe that you are setting yourself apart from your peers, positioning yourself as a standout candidate throughout your lifelong career.**

Good Luck and All the Best

Walter

Important Message

*Important Message From Walter *

I am certain that you will find great value in the complimentary practice tests that I have meticulously created for your benefit. These tests offer a comprehensive glimpse into the authentic exam formats and simulate real-life exam conditions. Countless hours have been dedicated to their development, reflecting my unwavering commitment to excellence.

I would like to express my heartfelt gratitude for your support in purchasing my **FULL version exam practice tests book**. As a gesture of appreciation, I am delighted to offer you:

1. A **FREE COUPON** of the **exam simulation engine of this practice test at Udemy (udemy.com)**; and

2. A **FREE COUPON** of a **randomly selected practice test held by Walter Education at Udemy**

Once again, I am truly grateful for your support, and I look forward to having you in my future books & courses. If you believe that my work is deserving, kindly consider leaving positive comments and feedback.

Thank you,

Walter

FREE GIFTS

BUY A BOOK

Buy any Walter Education's Exam Practice Test Book

(Visit **WalterEducation.com**)

RATE A BOOK

Rate Walter's Book at Amazon and consider leaving a Positive Rating

See " How to Give a Rate "

GET FREE GIFTS

Send **Email** to Walter – Walter@WalterEducation.com with the purchase and review records, get **2 Free Gifts**

Up to 2 free gifts!

FOLLOW

 WalterEducation.com

 Walter@WalterEducation.com

HELP US IMPROVE!

TELL US WHAT YOU THINK

Kindly Requesting Your Valued Book Reviews

First and foremost, I would like to express my gratitude for choosing my book and your support as a valued learner. I am reaching out to you as I also publish this practice test in paperback and Kindle eBook format, and I kindly seek your support in taking a few moments to share your honest review of my books via the direct review links at the next page for the practice test.

As an author, reviews play a crucial role in shaping the success and recognition of my work. Your honest feedback and reviews not only help me improve as an author but also contribute to the credibility and visibility of the book for potential readers. Here are two important reasons why reviews are of significance:

1. Impact on Author's Growth: Reviews provide valuable insights and feedback that enable me to enhance future editions or create new study materials. Your constructive criticism, suggestions, and personal experiences can help me refine my content and make it even more beneficial for future readers.

2. Assistance to Fellow Customers: Your reviews are incredibly beneficial to other customers who are considering purchasing the book. By sharing your thoughts, you can help potential readers make informed decisions and gain confidence in the quality and relevance of the content. Your honest evaluation can guide them towards choosing a resource that aligns with their needs and goals.

To show my sincere appreciation for your time and effort in writing a review, I would like to offer you a free gift as a token of gratitude. Once you have submitted your reviews on the paperback and/or Kindle eBook versions of the book, please simply send me an email at **walter@waltereducation.com** with your review confirmation, and I will be delighted to provide you with the details of the free gift.

Please note that leaving a review is entirely voluntary, and I value your honest opinion above all else. Your feedback is instrumental in shaping the future of my work, and I genuinely appreciate your support in this endeavor.

Thank you once again for choosing my book and considering my request. If you have any questions or require further assistance, please feel free to reach out to me. I look forward to your valuable reviews.

Warm regards,

Walter

Direct URLs to visit all Walter's Practice Tests at Amazon

Visit Walter's author page:

http://WalterEducation.com

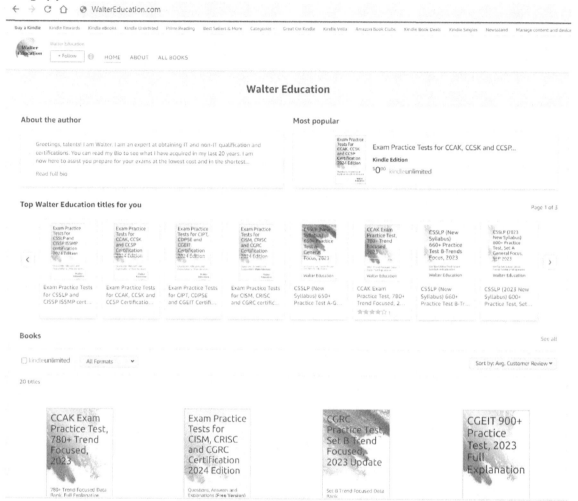

Or the **Links at Amazon Book Store:**

CCAK Exam Practice Test, 780+ Trend Focused, 2023	
Paperback Review URL:	- https://www.amazon.com/review/create-review?&asin=B0CJSXPYM7
Kindle eBook Review URL:	- https://www.amazon.com/review/create-review?&asin=B0CK9QQ44B

CERTIFIED DATA PRIVACY SOLUTIONS ENGINEER (CDPSE) 900+ PRACTICE TEST, 2023, FULL EXPLANATION	
Paperback Review URL:	- https://www.amazon.com/review/create-review?&asin=B0CGL3S5BH
Kindle eBook Review URL:	- https://www.amazon.com/review/create-review?&asin=B0CGL91NQ9

CGEIT 900+ Practice Test, 2023

Paperback Review URL: - https://www.amazon.com/review/create-review?&asin=B0CGW1Y1X9

Kindle eBook Review URL: - https://www.amazon.com/review/create-review?&asin=B0CJ83887B

CIPT, Certified Information Privacy Technologists, Practice Test

Paperback Review URL: - https://www.amazon.com/review/create-review?&asin=B0CJ4DLHG2

Kindle eBook Review URL: - https://www.amazon.com/review/create-review?&asin=B0CJ72MR4M

CRISC 1200+ Practice Test, 2023 (Exam Simulation and Core & Advanced Knowledge)

Paperback Review URL: - https://www.amazon.com/review/create-review?&asin=B0CJ43R78T

Kindle eBook Review URL: - https://www.amazon.com/review/create-review?&asin=B0CJ72JJLY

CISM 1050+ Practice Test,2023 Updated, Set B - Trends Focused, ISACA

Paperback Review URL: - https://www.amazon.com/review/create-review?&asin=B0CJSNR5Z2

Kindle eBook Review URL: - https://www.amazon.com/review/create-review?&asin=B0CJVWHJHW

CISM 1050+ Practice Test A - Core Focus, ISACA

Paperback Review URL: - https://www.amazon.com/review/create-review?&asin=B0CJL2HD1R

Kindle eBook Review URL: - https://www.amazon.com/review/create-review?&asin=B0CJVSQ6Z6

CCSKv4 900+ Practice Test 2023, Full Explanation

Paperback Review URL: - https://www.amazon.com/review/create-review?&asin=B0CFX2S7D8

Kindle eBook Review URL: - https://www.amazon.com/review/create-review?&asin=B0CFVLS8ZH

CSSLP (2023 New Syllabus) 600+ Practice Test, Set A General Focus

Paperback Review URL: - https://www.amazon.com/review/create-review?&asin=B0CK3VTR9D

Kindle eBook Review URL: - https://www.amazon.com/review/create-review?&asin=PENDING

CSSLP (New Syllabus) 660+ Practice Test B-Trends Focus, SEP 2023

Paperback Review URL: - https://www.amazon.com/review/create-review?&asin=B0CK3XGCBN

Kindle eBook Review URL: - https://www.amazon.com/review/create-review?&asin=PENDING

CISSP-ISSMP 650+ Practice Test, 2023 New syllabus, Set A Core Focused

Paperback Review URL: - https://www.amazon.com/review/create-review?&asin=B0CJLLL4HP

Kindle eBook Review URL: - https://www.amazon.com/review/create-review?&asin=B0CK2Y6XR7

CISSP-ISSMP 650+ Practice Test, 2023 New syllabus, Set B Trends Focused, ISC2	
Paperback Review URL:	- https://www.amazon.com/review/create-review?&asin=B0CJLMV48G
Kindle eBook Review URL:	- https://www.amazon.com/review/create-review?&asin=B0CK2X7CLL

Practice Test for Certified Cloud Security Professional (CCSP): 900+ Practice Test	
Paperback Review URL:	- https://www.amazon.com/review/create-review?&asin=B0CFCLW7HJ
Kindle eBook Review URL:	- https://www.amazon.com/review/create-review?&asin=B0CFKSVKSS

CGRC Practice Test, Set A Data Bank, Learn & Exam, 2023 Update	
Paperback Review URL:	- https://www.amazon.com/review/create-review?&asin=B0CJBC5MX1
Kindle eBook Review URL:	- https://www.amazon.com/review/create-review?&asin=B0CJYQVM22

CGRC Practice Test, Set B Trend Focused, 2023	
Paperback Review URL:	- https://www.amazon.com/review/create-review?&asin=B0CJ43Z8N6
Kindle eBook Review URL:	- https://www.amazon.com/review/create-review?&asin=B0CJ72HWY2

How to give a Review and Rating:

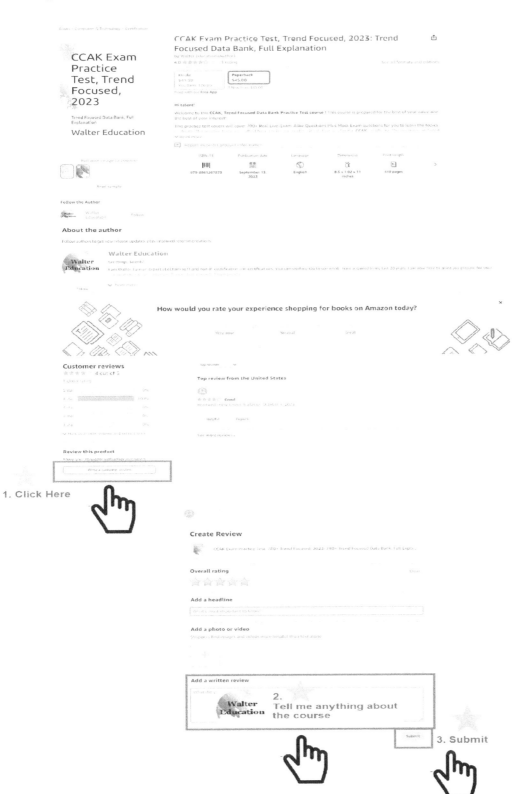

1. Click Here

2. Tell me anything about the course

3. Submit

Contents

Hi talent!

Welcome to this **CGRC, Set B Trend Focused Data Bank Practice Test course** ! This course is prepared for the best of your value and the best of your interest!

This practice test covers will cover 700+ Real-Live-Exam-Alike Questions from topics across the critical domains for the **CGRC** certificate.

The questions included in this course have been thoroughly analyzed with the latest trend in the CGRC exam.

What is covered on the CGRC exam?

GOVERNANCE RISK AND COMPLIANCE

Shows advanced technical skills and knowledge to protect, authorize and maintain information systems within various risk management frameworks.

WHAT TO EXPECT ON THE CGRC EXAM

Domain 1: Information Security Risk Management Program

Domain 2: Scope of the Information System

Domain 3: Selection and Approval of Security and Privacy Controls

Domain 4: Implementation of Security and Privacy Controls

Domain 5: Assessment/Audit of Security and Privacy Controls

Domain 6: Authorization/Approval of Information System

Domain 7: Continuous Monitoring

This practice test has been made with reference to the official guidelines and the exam weight in each domain.

In this CGRC course:

You will go through a journey to acquire 7 critical domains by doing the practice test. I hope you enjoy it and get your **CGRC** exam passed.

Beside doing the practice test, I would suggest you to do as much simulation test / question as you could to get your self well prepared for the exam. More practice test will be released soon. Stay tuned and Good Luck.

Who Earns the CGRC?

The CGRC is ideal for IT, information security and information assurance practitioners who work in Governance, Risk and Compliance (GRC) roles and have a need to understand, apply and/or implement a risk management program for IT systems within an organization, including positions like:

- Cybersecurity Auditor
- Cybersecurity Compliance Officer
- GRC Architect
- GRC Manager
- Cybersecurity Risk & Compliance Project Manager
- Cybersecurity Risk & Controls Analyst
- Cybersecurity Third Party Risk Manager
- Enterprise Risk Manager
- GRC Analyst
- GRC Director
- Information Assurance Manager
-

Are you Ready to get CGRC certification?

About Walter

Greetings, talents!

I am Walter. I am an expert at obtaining IT and non-IT qualification and certifications. You can read my Bio to see what I have acquired in my last 20 years. I am now here to assist you prepare for your exams at the lowest cost and in the shortest amount of time possible.

As I believe that everyone is talented and intelligent. Together, we will discuss the most efficient methods to "**Hack**" the learning process and "**Pass**" your exams without squandering your most valuable assets - **money and time.**

You will find the **best values** through join my course, get the exam **passed**, get the qualification and certifications and be a **Rocket** in achieving the **rocket-high** success in your career path. You will definitely out-perform all of your peers and you will be much more confidence when you talk to your peer and you know **you have achieved something that they didn't!**

You must approach each practice test question as a "Simulation of Real Exam Question" on this voyage. Here, I will provide the precise response to the query. I will also provide you the **FULL** explanation for EACH practice question.

You must investigate why the correct answer is correct and challenge it if you disagree. This is the only method to learn quickly, in-depth, and most importantly, to develop a capacity for self-learning. This WILL be the most valuable weapon in your arsenal for career success.

Believe me, I have *Been there,* and I have *Done that* before.

BIO

Walter Education ("Walter" or "Walter Education Team") is formed by a group of experienced and knowledgeable consultants and auditors. Walter has over 20 years of experience in the industry. Walter has worked as senior management at several major financial institutions in Key Financial Centers across the world.

CISA, CISSP, CRISC, CIA, CAMS, ISO 27001 LA, CEH, Scrum Master, GIAC Security, ITIL, CCIE Routing and Switching, COBIT, CPA and numerous other professional certifications and qualifications are held by Walter.

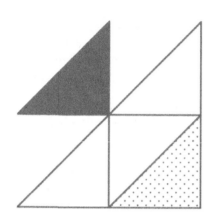

Visit Our Udemy
ONLINE COURSE

Search

Walter Education

www.udemy.com/user/Walter-Education

My Profile in Udemy:

I have a number of **Exam Practice Test Courses** held at Udemy for you to learn and study via a Real-Live-Exam-Alike environment and simulation.

My Homepage: http://waltereducation.com

Udemy: https://www.udemy.com/user/walter-education

Amazon: https://www.amazon.com/author/waltereducation

   udemy.com/user/walter-education/

INSTRUCTOR

Walter Education - Investing in You

- Never Give Up, Never Stop Learning

About me

Greetings, talents!

I am Walter. I am an expert at obtaining IT and non-IT qualification and certifications. You can read my **Bio** to see what I have acquired in my last 20 years. I am now here to assist you prepare for your exams at the lowest cost and in the shortest amount of time possible.

As I believe that everyone is talented and intelligent. Together we will discuss the most efficient methods to "Hack" the learning process and "Pass" your exams without squandering your most valuable assets – money and time.

Show more ⌄

My courses (17)

CSSLP (New Syllabus) Practice Test B-Trends Focus, Oct 2023

Walter Education - Investing in You

626 questions • All Levels

$44.99

New

CSSLP (New Syllabus) Practice Test A-General Focus, Oct 2023

Walter Education - Investing in You

626 questions • All Levels

$39.99

New

Discount Codes for my other Practice Test courses in Udemy:

Please feel free to click the links below to **enjoy discounts:**

ISACA

- CCAK Exam Practice Test, Trend Focused, SEP 2023
  - https://www.udemy.com/course/ccak-exam-practice-test-trend-focused-sep-2023/?referralCode=530219636B779BA4772B
- CISM - ISACA Practice Test A - Core Focus, SEP 2023, New
  - https://www.udemy.com/course/cism-isaca-practice-test-a-core-focus-sep-2023-new/?referralCode=3B6C4E08B23039069E19
- CISM - ISACA Practice Test B - Trends Focus, SEP 2023, New
  - https://www.udemy.com/course/cism-isaca-practice-test-b-trends-focus-sep-2023-new/?referralCode=9E7E1E6527BDA1797922
- **CGEIT 900+ Practice Test, 2023**
  - https://www.udemy.com/course/buy1-get-3-cgeit-900-practice-test-2023-ccsp-ccak/?referralCode=4BF5FF0AAF7B61F47E6D
- **CRISC 1200+ Practice Test, SEP 202**
  - https://www.udemy.com/course/crisc-1200-practice-test-2023-isaca-cisa-cism-cissp-ccak/?referralCode=C913D8A69A91ED9ABB99
- **CDPSE 900+ Practice Test, 2023**
  - https://www.udemy.com/course/cdpse-900-practice-test-2023-full-explanation-cisa-cgeit/?referralCode=F62D674CA2DB5D05CC8C
- **CCAK CCSP CCSKv4 3in1 Practice Test 2023 updated**
  - https://www.udemy.com/course/ccsp-ccskv4-ccak-bundle-3in1-practice-test-2023-updated/?referralCode=ED588D079804F9530244

ISC2

- CISSP-ISSMP Practice Test A - Core Focus, SEP 2023, New
  - https://www.udemy.com/course/cissp-issmp-practice-test-a-core-focus-sep-2023-new/?referralCode=6D5233F6FD3691F9BAD2
- CISSP-ISSMP Practice Test B - Trends Focus, SEP 2023, New
  - https://www.udemy.com/course/cissp-issmp-practice-test-b-trends-focus-sep-2023-new/?referralCode=D374F92DE9D3FCAF27DB
- **CSSLP (New Syllabus) Practice Test, Trend Focus, SEP 2023**
  - **https://www.udemy.com/course/csslp-new-syllabus-practice-test-trend-focus-sep-2023/?referralCode=33AD3DA51E351807C96E**
- **CSSLP (New Syllabus) Practice Test, General Focus, SEP 2023**
  - **https://www.udemy.com/course/csslp-new-syllabus-practice-test-general-focus-sep-2023/?referralCode=C6FC805F549D2580B901CCAK Exam Practice Test, Trend Focused, SEP 2023**
- CSSLP (New Syllabus) Practice Test C- Mock Exams SEP 2023

- https://www.udemy.com/course/csslp-new-syllabus-mock-exams-sep-2023/?referralCode=A4073301648B86362ABD
- **CGRC Practice Test, Set A Data Bank, Learn & Exam, SEP 2023**
  - https://www.udemy.com/course/cgrc-practice-test-set-a-data-bank-learn-exam-sep-2023/?referralCode=E545B726352EFFA1F3D9
- **CGRC Practice Test, Set B Trend Focused, SEP 2023**
  - https://www.udemy.com/course/cgrc-practice-test-set-b-trend-focused-sep-2023/?referralCode=F59A22C25057683C4E04
- **CCSP 900+ Practice Test, 2023**
  - https://www.udemy.com/course/ccsp-certified-cloud-security-professional-practice-test-o/?referralCode=C0C572F978F539E57251

IAPP

- CIPT, Certified Information Privacy Technologists, SEP 2023
  - https://www.udemy.com/course/cipt-certified-information-privacy-technologists-sep-2023/?referralCode=FC0A8099E3A173BDC6AC

CSA

- CCSKv4 900+ Practice Test 2023
  - https://www.udemy.com/course/ccskv4-900-practice-test-2023-full-explanation-ccspccak/?referralCode=E6ADB4B80C52206F55DF

Visit Our Amazon Book Store

WalterEducation.com

Visit Walter's author page:

http://WalterEducation.com

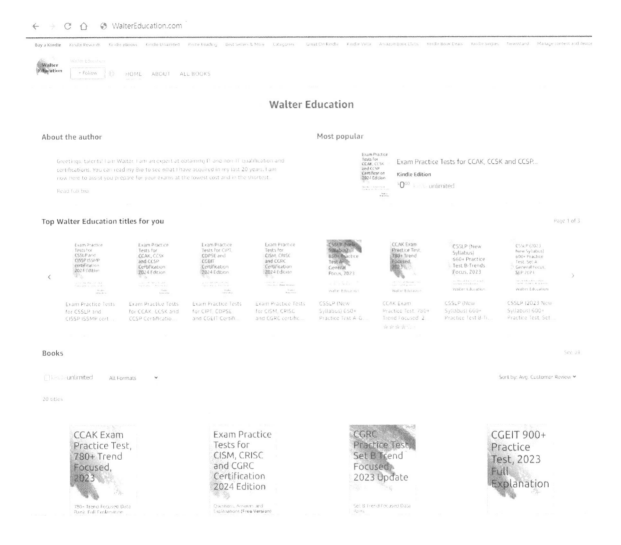

Question Number: 1

Question: Which of the following is a widely recognized information security framework used in risk management?

Option 1: ISO/IEC 27001

Option 2: Six Sigma

Option 3: ITIL (Information Technology Infrastructure Library)

Option 4: COSO (Committee of Sponsoring Organizations of the Treadway Commission)

Correct Response: 1

Explanation: ISO/IEC 27001 is a widely recognized information security framework used in risk management. It provides a systematic approach for establishing, implementing, maintaining, and continually improving an information security management system (ISMS) based on risk management principles and best practices.

Knowledge Area: Domain 1: Information Security Risk Management Program

----

Question Number: 2

Question: Which of the following is an international standard for information security management?

Option 1: ISO/IEC 20000

Option 2: ITIL (Information Technology Infrastructure Library)

Option 3: ISO/IEC 27001

Option 4: COBIT (Control Objectives for Information and Related Technologies)

Correct Response: 3

Explanation: ISO/IEC 27001 is an international standard for information security management. It provides a framework for establishing, implementing, maintaining, and continually improving an information security management system (ISMS) within the context of the organization's overall business risks.

Knowledge Area: Domain 1: Information Security Risk Management Program

----

Question Number: 3

Question: What is the primary goal of information security awareness training in risk management?

Option 1: To ensure employees are aware of potential risks and their responsibilities in protecting information

Option 2: To enhance technical security controls and measures

Option 3: To transfer risks to external parties through contracts

Option 4: To eliminate all risks associated with information security

Correct Response: 1

Explanation: The primary goal of information security awareness training in risk management is to ensure employees are aware of potential risks and their responsibilities in protecting information. By providing training and education, organizations can empower employees to identify and respond to security threats, follow best practices, and contribute to a culture of security awareness and risk mitigation.

Knowledge Area: Domain 1: Information Security Risk Management Program

----

Question Number: 4

Question: What is the purpose of conducting business impact analysis in Business Continuity Management (BCM)?

Option 1: To identify critical business functions and their dependencies

Option 2: To eliminate all risks associated with critical business operations

Option 3: To transfer risks to external parties through contracts

Option 4: To accept risks without taking any proactive measures

Correct Response: 1

Explanation: The purpose of conducting business impact analysis in Business Continuity Management (BCM) is to identify critical business functions and their dependencies. This analysis helps organizations understand the potential impacts of disruptions on these functions, prioritize recovery efforts, and allocate resources effectively to ensure the continuity of essential operations.

Knowledge Area: Domain 1: Information Security Risk Management Program

----

Question Number: 5

Question: What is the primary goal of incorporating data privacy and data protection principles in risk management?

Option 1: To ensure the confidentiality and integrity of sensitive data

Option 2: To eliminate all risks associated with data privacy and protection

Option 3: To transfer risks to external parties through contracts

Option 4: To accept risks without taking any proactive measures

Correct Response: 1

Explanation: The primary goal of incorporating data privacy and data protection principles in risk management is to ensure the confidentiality and integrity of sensitive data. By implementing appropriate controls and practices, organizations can safeguard personal and sensitive information, mitigate the risk of data breaches, and ensure compliance with data protection regulations.

Knowledge Area: Domain 1: Information Security Risk Management Program

----

Question Number: 6

Question: Which of the following is a fundamental principle of data privacy and data protection?

Option 1: Data minimization and purpose limitation

Option 2: Data monetization and commercialization

Option 3: Data obfuscation and manipulation

Option 4: Data deletion and destruction

Correct Response: 1

Explanation: Data minimization and purpose limitation is a fundamental principle of data privacy and data protection. It involves collecting and retaining only the necessary data for a specific purpose and ensuring that the data is not used beyond the intended scope. By applying this principle, organizations can reduce the risk of unauthorized access and misuse of personal information.

Knowledge Area: Domain 1: Information Security Risk Management Program

----

Question Number: 7

Question: How does data privacy and data protection contribute to overall risk management efforts?

Option 1: By mitigating the risk of data breaches and regulatory non-compliance

Option 2: By eliminating all risks associated with data processing

Option 3: By transferring risks to external parties through contracts

Option 4: By accepting risks without taking any proactive measures

Correct Response: 1

Explanation: Data privacy and data protection contribute to overall risk management efforts by mitigating the risk of data breaches and regulatory non-compliance. By implementing appropriate safeguards, organizations can protect sensitive data, reduce the likelihood of security incidents, and ensure compliance with applicable data protection laws and regulations.

Knowledge Area: Domain 1: Information Security Risk Management Program

----

Question Number: 8

Question: Which of the following is a commonly used risk assessment framework in risk management?

Option 1: ISO 31000: Risk Management Principles and Guidelines

Option 2: COSO Enterprise Risk Management Framework

Option 3: NIST SP 800-30: Risk Management Guide for Information Technology Systems

Option 4: All of the above

Correct Response: 1

Explanation: ISO 31000: Risk Management Principles and Guidelines, COSO Enterprise Risk Management Framework, and NIST SP 800-30: Risk Management Guide for Information Technology Systems are all commonly used risk assessment frameworks in risk management. These frameworks provide guidance and best practices for conducting risk assessments and managing risks effectively.

Knowledge Area: Domain 1: Information Security Risk Management Program

----

Question Number: 9

Question: Which of the following risk assessment concepts emphasizes the importance of considering the likelihood and impact of risks?

Option 1: Risk likelihood

Option 2: Risk severity

Option 3: Risk appetite

Option 4: Risk tolerance

Correct Response: 1

Explanation: The concept of risk likelihood emphasizes the importance of considering the likelihood or probability of risks occurring. It helps in understanding the chances or frequency of risks happening and allows organizations to prioritize their risk management efforts accordingly.

Knowledge Area: Domain 1: Information Security Risk Management Program

----

Question Number: 10

Question: Which risk assessment concept refers to the acceptable level of risk that an organization is willing to take?

Option 1: Risk appetite

Option 2: Risk tolerance

Option 3: Risk likelihood

Option 4: Risk severity

Correct Response: 1

Explanation: The risk assessment concept that refers to the acceptable level of risk that an organization is willing to take is called risk appetite. It defines the level of risk that an organization considers acceptable while pursuing its objectives. It helps in guiding risk management decisions and determining the boundaries within which risks can be accepted.

Knowledge Area: Domain 1: Information Security Risk Management Program

----

Question Number: 11

Question: What is COBIT defined as according to ISACA?

Option 1: A framework for information technology governance and management

Option 2: A framework for project management

Option 3: A framework for information security management

Option 4: A framework for risk management

Correct Response: 1

Explanation: COBIT is defined as a framework for information technology governance and management developed by ISACA that provides good practices across five main domains: Evaluate, Direct and Monitor; Align, Plan and Organize; Build, Acquire and Implement; Deliver, Service and Support; and Monitor, Evaluate and Assess.

Knowledge Area: Domain 1: Information Security Risk Management Program

----

Question Number: 12

Question: In the COBIT framework, which of the following is NOT one of the components of the framework?

Option 1: Controls

Option 2: Reference Model

Option 3: Metrics and Measurements

Option 4: Data Controller

Correct Response: 3

Explanation: The five main components of the COBIT framework are Framework, Process, Control, Resource and Enabler. Data Controller is not one of the listed components.

Knowledge Area: Domain 1: Information Security Risk Management Program

----

Question Number: 13

Question: What technique can help evaluate if outcomes of IT projects and initiatives achieve the predefined strategic targets and metrics set by governance bodies?

Option 1: Regular internal risk assessments

Option 2: Annual vendor benchmark comparisons

Option 3: Ongoing balanced scorecard reviews

Option 4: Monthly maturity model evaluations

Correct Response: 3

Explanation: Balanced scorecard reviews help assess if project outcomes meet governance-set strategic targets.

Knowledge Area: Domain 1: Information Security Risk Management Program

----

Question Number: 14

Question: Effective IT governance requires regularly reviewing which elements to ensure technology initiatives adapt appropriately as business strategies and objectives evolve over time?

Option 1: Project budgets and resource allocations

Option 2: Infrastructure capacity and utilization rates

Option 3: Service level agreements and operational metrics

Option 4: All key performance indicators mentioned above

Correct Response: 4

Explanation: Reviewing budgets, capacity, SLAs, metrics helps maintain alignment as business strategies evolve.

Knowledge Area: Domain 1: Information Security Risk Management Program

----

Question Number: 15

Question: Which of the following practices would NOT be recommended for strong performance management of IT and business strategic alignment by governance groups?

Option 1: Soliciting user feedback on new systems

Option 2: Setting goals collaboratively with stakeholders

Option 3: Rigidly tracking lagging indicators alone

Option 4: Routine multi-level reviews of balanced scorecards

Correct Response: 3

Explanation: Only tracking lagging indicators would be ineffective for alignment management.

Knowledge Area: Domain 1: Information Security Risk Management Program

----

Question Number: 16

Question: Scenario: A firm set 3-year targets but projects continually fail to meet goals. What action could improve their governance performance management?

Option 1: Leadership mandating entirely new PM systems

Option 2: Implementing shorter-term targets set collaboratively

Option 3: Increasing external quality assurance audits

Option 4: Conducting user satisfaction surveys on new features

Correct Response: 2

Explanation: Shorter collaborative target setting would enhance this governance performance management.

Knowledge Area: Domain 1: Information Security Risk Management Program

----

Question Number: 17

Question: Which framework can help guide creation of a privacy strategy?

Option 1: COBIT

Option 2: NIST CSF

Option 3: ISO 27001

Option 4: All of the above

Correct Response: 4

Explanation: COBIT, NIST CSF, and ISO 27001 can inform privacy strategy development.

Knowledge Area: Domain 1: Information Security Risk Management Program

----

Question Number: 18

Question: What component of COBIT can support strategic planning?

Option 1: Control objectives

Option 2: Maturity models

Option 3: Key performance indicators

Option 4: Focus areas

Correct Response: 2

Explanation: COBIT maturity models help plan strategic objectives.

Knowledge Area: Domain 1: Information Security Risk Management Program

----

Question Number: 19

Question: How does the NIST CSF assist in strategy formulation?

Option 1: By defining controls

Option 2: By setting maturity targets

Option 3: By conducting risk assessments

Option 4: By prioritizing actions

Correct Response: 3

Explanation: The CSF helps assess risks to address in strategy.

Knowledge Area: Domain 1: Information Security Risk Management Program

----

Question Number: 20

Question: Which ISO 27001 tool enables strategic roadmap creation?

Option 1: Statement of Applicability

Option 2: Controls catalogue

Option 3: Implementation guidance

Option 4: Maturity model

Correct Response: 4

Explanation: The maturity model helps create a strategic roadmap.

Knowledge Area: Domain 1: Information Security Risk Management Program

----

Question Number: 21

Question: What are different risk frameworks used in enterprise risk management?

Option 1: Examples include COSO ERM, ISO 31000, NIST Cybersecurity Framework, and OCTAVE Allegro.

Option 2: Examples include breach notification requirements, Sarbanes-Oxley (SOX), General Data Protection Regulation (GDPR), and Payment Card Industry Data Security Standard (PCI DSS).

Option 3: Examples include physical security measures, data encryption practices, and access controls.

Option 4: Examples include financial performance analysis, auditing of records, and regulatory compliance.

Correct Response: 1

Explanation: Different risk frameworks used in enterprise risk management include COSO ERM (Committee of Sponsoring Organizations of the Treadway Commission Enterprise Risk Management Framework), ISO 31000 (International Organization for Standardization Risk Management Standard), NIST Cybersecurity Framework (National Institute of Standards and Technology), and OCTAVE Allegro (Operationally Critical Threat, Asset, and Vulnerability Evaluation). These frameworks provide structured approaches to identify, assess, and manage risks within organizations.

Knowledge Area: Domain 1: Information Security Risk Management Program

----

Question Number: 22

Question: Which risk framework is widely recognized as a leading framework for enterprise risk management?

Option 1: COSO ERM (Committee of Sponsoring Organizations of the Treadway Commission Enterprise Risk Management Framework)

Option 2: Breach notification requirements

Option 3: Physical security measures

Option 4: Financial performance analysis

Correct Response: 1

Explanation: The risk framework widely recognized as a leading framework for enterprise risk management is COSO ERM (Committee of Sponsoring Organizations of the Treadway Commission Enterprise Risk Management Framework). COSO ERM provides a comprehensive framework for organizations to assess and manage risks, focusing on internal control, risk assessment, and risk response strategies.

Knowledge Area: Domain 1: Information Security Risk Management Program

----

Question Number: 23

Question: Scenario: ABC Company is a technology consulting firm advising clients on risk management. What is a key consideration for ABC Company when recommending a risk framework to clients?

Option 1: Understanding the client's industry, risk management objectives, and specific needs to select an appropriate risk framework.

Option 2: Conducting detailed testing and analysis of financial transactions and records.

Option 3: Reviewing the physical security measures implemented by client organizations.

Option 4: Assessing the data encryption practices in client organizations' cloud environments.

Correct Response: 1

Explanation: A key consideration for ABC Company when recommending a risk framework to clients is understanding the client's industry, risk management objectives, and specific needs. By having a clear understanding of these factors, ABC Company can recommend an appropriate risk framework that aligns with the client's requirements and helps address the unique risks and challenges they face in their industry. This ensures that the client can effectively implement and manage their risk management program.

Knowledge Area: Domain 1: Information Security Risk Management Program

----

Question Number: 24

Question: Which of the following is a commonly used risk assessment framework in risk management?

Option 1: ISO 31000: Risk Management Principles and Guidelines

Option 2: COSO Enterprise Risk Management Framework

Option 3: NIST SP 800-30: Risk Management Guide for Information Technology Systems

Option 4: All of the above

Correct Response: 1

Explanation: ISO 31000: Risk Management Principles and Guidelines, COSO Enterprise Risk Management Framework, and NIST SP 800-30: Risk Management Guide for Information Technology Systems are all commonly used risk assessment frameworks in risk management. These frameworks provide guidance and best practices for conducting risk assessments and managing risks effectively.

Knowledge Area: Domain 1: Information Security Risk Management Program

----

Question Number: 25

Question: Which phase of the System Development Life Cycle (SDLC) is focused on identifying and assessing risks associated with the proposed system?

Option 1: Requirements gathering and analysis

Option 2: Design and development

Option 3: Implementation and testing

Option 4: Maintenance and evaluation

Correct Response: 1

Explanation: The requirements gathering and analysis phase of the SDLC is focused on identifying and assessing risks associated with the proposed system. This phase involves gathering user requirements, analyzing business processes, and identifying potential risks and vulnerabilities that need to be addressed in the system design.

Knowledge Area: Domain 1: Information Security Risk Management Program

----

Question Number: 26

Question: What is the primary goal of integrating risk management into the System Development Life Cycle (SDLC)?

Option 1: To ensure that risks are identified, assessed, and mitigated throughout the development process

Option 2: To eliminate all risks associated with the system development

Option 3: To transfer risks to external parties through insurance or contracts

Option 4: To accept risks without taking any proactive measures

Correct Response: 1

Explanation: The primary goal of integrating risk management into the SDLC is to ensure that risks are identified, assessed, and mitigated throughout the development process. By incorporating risk management practices at each stage of the SDLC, organizations can proactively address potential risks, reduce vulnerabilities, and enhance the overall security and quality of the developed system.

Knowledge Area: Domain 1: Information Security Risk Management Program

----

Question Number: 27

Question: Scenario: A company is evaluating different cloud providers to meet its business needs. One of the company's requirements is to have the flexibility to move its applications and data between different cloud environments. Which of the following options is a characteristic that supports application and data portability in the cloud?

Option 1: Standardized APIs and formats

Option 2: Proprietary APIs and data formats

Option 3: Exclusive vendor partnerships

Option 4: Vendor-managed data encryption

Correct Response: 1

Explanation: Application and data portability in the cloud is supported by standardized APIs and formats. Standardized APIs enable seamless integration and migration between different cloud environments. In contrast, proprietary APIs and data formats can create dependencies and hinder portability. Exclusive vendor partnerships and vendor-managed data encryption do not directly contribute to application and data portability.

Knowledge Area: Domain 1: Information Security Risk Management Program

----

Question Number: 28

Question: What is an internal information security controls system in the context of audit process and methodologies?

Option 1: An organization's framework of controls implemented to protect its information assets and manage information security risks.

Option 2: An assessment of the financial statements to ensure compliance with accounting standards.

Option 3: A review of the physical security measures implemented by an organization.

Option 4: An evaluation of data encryption practices in a cloud environment.

Correct Response: 1

Explanation: An internal information security controls system, in the context of audit process and methodologies, refers to an organization's framework of controls implemented to protect its information assets and manage information security risks. These controls include policies, procedures, and technical measures designed to safeguard information confidentiality, integrity, and availability.

Knowledge Area: Domain 1: Information Security Risk Management Program

----

Question Number: 29

Question: Scenario: ABC Company is a technology consulting firm that provides audit services for organizations in the cloud environment. What is a key consideration for ABC Company when auditing an internal information security controls system?

Option 1: Understanding the organization's unique information security risks and the controls implemented within the system.

Option 2: Conducting detailed testing and analysis of financial transactions and records.

Option 3: Reviewing the physical security measures implemented by client organizations.

Option 4: Assessing the effectiveness of data encryption practices in a cloud environment.

Correct Response: 1

Explanation: A key consideration for ABC Company when auditing an internal information security controls system is understanding the organization's unique information security risks and the controls implemented within the system. This understanding helps ABC Company tailor its audit approach and procedures to address the specific risks and controls associated with the organization's information security controls system. By assessing the organization's controls system, ABC Company can provide valuable insights and recommendations for enhancing the information security posture of client organizations in the cloud environment.

Knowledge Area: Domain 1: Information Security Risk Management Program

----

Question Number: 30

Question: What are access controls for local and remote access in the context of cloud security operations?

Option 1: Security measures and mechanisms implemented to control and manage user access to cloud resources and systems locally and remotely.

Option 2: Encrypting data during transit and at rest in the cloud.

Option 3: Classifying data based on its sensitivity and access requirements.

Option 4: Determining the physical location of data storage in the cloud.

Correct Response: 1

Explanation: Access controls for local and remote access, in the context of cloud security operations, refer to the security measures and mechanisms implemented to control and manage user access to cloud resources and systems both locally and remotely. These controls ensure that only authorized users can access the resources and systems, and they help enforce security policies, authentication, and authorization mechanisms.

Knowledge Area: Domain 1: Information Security Risk Management Program

----

Question Number: 31

Question: What are network security controls in the context of cloud security operations?

Option 1: Security measures and mechanisms implemented to protect network infrastructure and data, such as firewalls, intrusion detection systems (IDS), intrusion prevention systems (IPS), honeypots, vulnerability assessments, network security groups, and bastion hosts.

Option 2: Encrypting data during transit and at rest in the cloud.

Option 3: Classifying data based on its sensitivity and access requirements.

Option 4: Determining the physical location of data storage in the cloud.

Correct Response: 1

Explanation: Network security controls, in the context of cloud security operations, refer to the security measures and mechanisms implemented to protect network infrastructure and data. These controls include technologies such as firewalls, intrusion detection systems (IDS), intrusion prevention systems (IPS), honeypots, vulnerability assessments, network security groups, and bastion hosts. They help detect and prevent unauthorized access, monitor network activity, detect and respond to security incidents, and ensure the integrity and availability of network resources and data.

Knowledge Area: Domain 1: Information Security Risk Management Program

----

Question Number: 32

Question: Why are network security controls important in cloud security operations?

Option 1: Network security controls help protect cloud resources and data from unauthorized access, network-based attacks, and data breaches.

Option 2: Encrypting data during transit and at rest in the cloud.

Option 3: Classifying data based on its sensitivity and access requirements.

Option 4: Determining the physical location of data storage in the cloud.

Correct Response: 1

Explanation: Network security controls are important in cloud security operations as they help protect cloud resources and data from unauthorized access, network-based attacks, and data breaches. These controls enforce security policies, detect and respond to security incidents, and ensure the confidentiality, integrity, and availability of network communications and data within the cloud environment.

Knowledge Area: Domain 1: Information Security Risk Management Program

----

Question Number: 33

Question: Scenario: XYZ Corporation is a company that operates in a cloud environment and wants to enhance their security operations. How can XYZ Corporation benefit from implementing network security controls in their cloud environment?

Option 1: Enhanced protection of cloud resources and data from unauthorized access and network-based attacks.

Option 2: Improved detection and response to security incidents and events.

Option 3: Enforced security policies and compliance with regulatory requirements.

Option 4: All of the above.

Correct Response: 4

Explanation: XYZ Corporation can benefit from implementing network security controls in their cloud environment through enhanced protection of cloud resources and data from unauthorized access and network-based attacks, improved detection and response to security incidents and events, as well as the enforcement of security policies and compliance with regulatory requirements. Implementing network security controls ensures the confidentiality, integrity, and availability of network communications and data, reducing the risk of security breaches and ensuring compliance with security standards.

Knowledge Area: Domain 1: Information Security Risk Management Program

----

Question Number: 34

Question: Scenario: ABC Company is a technology consulting firm that provides cloud security services. They want to design a secure cloud environment. What are the potential challenges or considerations for ABC Company when implementing network security controls in a cloud environment?

Option 1: Ensuring compatibility and interoperability of network security controls with different cloud platforms and services.

Option 2: Addressing performance impacts and scalability considerations of network security controls.

Option 3: Managing and monitoring network security controls to ensure ongoing effectiveness.

Option 4: All of the above.

Correct Response: 4

Explanation: The potential challenges or considerations for ABC Company when implementing network security controls in a cloud environment include ensuring compatibility and interoperability of network security controls with different cloud platforms and services, addressing performance impacts and scalability considerations of network security controls, as well as managing and monitoring network security controls to ensure ongoing effectiveness. Implementing network security controls requires careful planning, consideration of technical requirements, and addressing operational and performance considerations to ensure a seamless and secure network environment within the cloud.

Knowledge Area: Domain 1: Information Security Risk Management Program

----

Question Number: 35

Question: Which of the following is a benefit of intelligent monitoring of security controls in cloud security operations?

Option 1: Enhanced threat detection and response capabilities.

Option 2: Encrypting data during transit and at rest in the cloud.

Option 3: Classifying data based on its sensitivity and access requirements.

Option 4: Determining the physical location of data storage in the cloud.

Correct Response: 1

Explanation: A benefit of intelligent monitoring of security controls in cloud security operations is enhanced threat detection and response capabilities. By leveraging AI and ML techniques, organizations can detect and respond to security threats in real-time, allowing for timely mitigation of risks and minimizing the impact of security incidents.

Knowledge Area: Domain 1: Information Security Risk Management Program

----

Question Number: 36

Question: Scenario: ABC Company is a technology consulting firm that provides cloud security services. They want to implement intelligent monitoring of security controls for their clients. What are the potential challenges or considerations for ABC Company in implementing intelligent monitoring of security controls in cloud security operations?

Option 1: Selecting appropriate AI and ML technologies for security monitoring.

Option 2: Ensuring integration and compatibility with existing security infrastructure and tools.

Option 3: Managing and analyzing large volumes of security data in real-time.

Option 4: All of the above.

Correct Response: 4

Explanation: The potential challenges or considerations for ABC Company in implementing intelligent monitoring of security controls in cloud security operations include selecting appropriate AI and ML technologies for security monitoring, ensuring integration and compatibility with existing security infrastructure and tools, as well as managing and analyzing large volumes of security data in real-time. Implementing intelligent monitoring requires careful planning, consideration of technical requirements, and addressing operational challenges to ensure effective and efficient security monitoring in the cloud environment.

Knowledge Area: Domain 1: Information Security Risk Management Program

----

Question Number: 37

Question: An organization is defining its risk management program. What should be considered FIRST when setting risk priorities?

Option 1: Industry best practices

Option 2: Regulatory obligations

Option 3: Organization's strategy and objectives

Option 4: Risk appetite

Correct Response: 3

Explanation: Strategy and objectives guide risk priorities.

Knowledge Area: Domain 1: Information Security Risk Management Program

----

Question Number: 38

Question: What should a risk manager do when objectives change significantly?

Option 1: Rely on pre-defined risk priorities

Option 2: Wait for new audit findings

Option 3: Conduct refreshed risk assessment

Option 4: Monitor existing dashboards

Correct Response: 3

Explanation: Refreshed risk assessment ensures alignment with new objectives.

Knowledge Area: Domain 1: Information Security Risk Management Program

----

Question Number: 39

Question: A growing company wants to establish a formal risk management program. What is the FIRST step?

Option 1: Hire a dedicated risk manager

Option 2: Implement risk management technology

Option 3: Define risk roles and responsibilities

Option 4: Establish a risk management committee

Correct Response: 3

Explanation: Define risk roles and responsibilities first.

Knowledge Area: Domain 1: Information Security Risk Management Program

----

Question Number: 40

Question: What sources help identify privacy requirements?

Option 1: Internal policies

Option 2: Regulations

Option 3: Contractual obligations

Option 4: All of the above

Correct Response: 4

Explanation: Requirements come from policies, regulations, and contracts.

Knowledge Area: Domain 1: Information Security Risk Management Program

----

Question Number: 41

Question: When should new systems undergo a Privacy Impact Assessment?

Option 1: After implementation

Option 2: During design

Option 3: Before purchase

Option 4: When regulators request it

Correct Response: 2

Explanation: PIAs during design identify requirements proactively.

Knowledge Area: Domain 1: Information Security Risk Management Program

----

Question Number: 42

Question: What technique can map data flows to requirements?

Option 1: Data discovery surveys

Option 2: Data Loss Prevention tools

Option 3: Process flow analysis

Option 4: Annual audits

Correct Response: 3

Explanation: Process flow analysis ties requirements to data flows.

Knowledge Area: Domain 1: Information Security Risk Management Program

----

Question Number: 43

Question: When migrating data to a cloud provider, what action manages privacy risks?

Option 1: Accepting default settings

Option 2: Enabling redundant backups

Option 3: Reviewing access logs frequently

Option 4: Configuring security controls carefully

Correct Response: 4

Explanation: Carefully configuring security controls when migrating to the cloud is crucial for risk management.

Knowledge Area: Domain 1: Information Security Risk Management Program

----

Question Number: 44

Question: Why is evaluating a cloud provider's internal staff screening important?

Option 1: To judge company culture fit

Option 2: To assess staff qualifications

Option 3: To confirm background checks

Option 4: To gauge turnover rates

Correct Response: 3

Explanation: Evaluating staff screening ensures appropriate background checks are conducted.

Knowledge Area: Domain 1: Information Security Risk Management Program

----

Question Number: 45

Question: What ISO 27001 certification indicates?

Option 1: Financial stability

Option 2: Incident response capacity

Option 3: Privacy regulation compliance

Option 4: Security control implementation

Correct Response: 4

Explanation: ISO 27001 certifies implementation of security controls.

Knowledge Area: Domain 1: Information Security Risk Management Program

----

Question Number: 46

Question: Question 2: Which of the following certifications is NOT related to the evaluation and assurance of security features in IT products and systems?

Option 1: HIPAA

Option 2: FIPS 140-2

Option 3: Common Criteria (C

Option 4: ISO/IEC 27001

Correct Response: 1

Explanation: HIPAA is not directly related to the evaluation and assurance of security features in IT products and systems. HIPAA (Health Insurance Portability and Accountability Act) is a regulation that focuses on the privacy and security of protected health information (PHI) in the healthcare industry. FIPS 140-2, Common Criteria (CC), and ISO/IEC 27001 are certifications and standards specifically related to security features and assurance in IT products and systems.

Knowledge Area: Domain 1: Information Security Risk Management Program

----

Question Number: 47

Question: An organization is implementing the Risk Management Framework (RMF) to comply with FISMA. What should be the FIRST step when starting the RMF process?

Option 1: Conduct system implementation

Option 2: Establish information security continuous monitoring

Option 3: Select security controls

Option 4: Categorize the system and information

Correct Response: 4

Explanation: Categorizing systems and data is the first step in implementing the RMF per FISMA.

Knowledge Area: Domain 1: Information Security Risk Management Program

----

Question Number: 48

Question: An organization wants to reduce the effort required for annual FISMA reporting. Which of the following would BEST accomplish this?

Option 1: Conduct audits annually instead of monthly

Option 2: Automate collection of security control data

Option 3: Eliminate tracking of POAMs

Option 4: Only report on critical systems

Correct Response: 2

Explanation: Automating security control data collection reduces manual FISMA reporting efforts.

Knowledge Area: Domain 1: Information Security Risk Management Program

----

Question Number: 49

Question: You are the CISO for an organization that must comply with FISMA requirements. Several new cloud services have been implemented that process sensitive data. What should you ensure is done FIRST for these new services?

Option 1: Request authority to operate (ATO)

Option 2: Conduct pilot testing

Option 3: Update system inventory

Option 4: Perform security categorization

Correct Response: 3

Explanation: Updating the system inventory is the first step to ensure new services comply with FISMA requirements

Knowledge Area: Domain 1: Information Security Risk Management Program

----

Question Number: 50

Question: An organization wants to use a new SaaS application that stores customer PII. What should be validated FIRST per FedRAMP requirements?

Option 1: Encryption implementation

Option 2: Access control policies

Option 3: Vendor financial stability

Option 4: FedRAMP authorization status

Correct Response: 4

Explanation: FedRAMP first requires validating the cloud service has a FedRAMP authorization.

Knowledge Area: Domain 1: Information Security Risk Management Program

----

Question Number: 51

Question: A cloud service provider achieved a FedRAMP authorization 6 months ago. What must be done annually to maintain FedRAMP compliance?

Option 1: 3PAO assessment

Option 2: Penetration testing

Option 3: Data center audit

Option 4: Security control assessment

Correct Response: 4

Explanation: Annual assessments validate continued security control effectiveness.

Knowledge Area: Domain 1: Information Security Risk Management Program

----

Question Number: 52

Question: An organization is adopting a new IaaS cloud provider storing sensitive data. What artifact will the provider produce to detail their implementation of required security controls?

Option 1: Interconnection security agreement

Option 2: FedRAMP SSP

Option 3: Service level agreement

Option 4: Bill of materials

Correct Response: 2

Explanation: The FedRAMP SSP documents the cloud provider's security controls.

Knowledge Area: Domain 1: Information Security Risk Management Program

----

Question Number: 53

Question: What contractual item helps ensure GDPR obligations are met with vendors?

Option 1: Indemnification terms

Option 2: Data processing agreements

Option 3: Insurance requirements

Option 4: Limitation of liability

Correct Response: 2

Explanation: Data processing agreements outline GDPR duties.

Knowledge Area: Domain 1: Information Security Risk Management Program

----

Question Number: 54

Question: To manage GDPR responsibilities, what assessments are crucial?

Option 1: Company culture evaluations

Option 2: Onsite audits

Option 3: Business continuity testing

Option 4: Background checks

Correct Response: 2

Explanation: Onsite audits help manage GDPR obligations.

Knowledge Area: Domain 1: Information Security Risk Management Program

----

Question Number: 55

Question: The privacy operations team is creating new procedures for managing data subject access requests (DSARs). What key steps should be included?

Option 1: Verifying the identity of the requestor, locating relevant data, reviewing data for exceptions, providing required info in a timely manner

Option 2: Deleting all data after fulfilling request, generating monthly metrics reports, training staff annually, presenting findings to executives

Option 3: Outsourcing DSAR processing to vendors, charging requestors for access, strictly limiting data provided, denying requests by default

Option 4: Ignoring requests mentioning 'GDPR', waiting for formal legal requests before investigating, redacting all sensitive info, delaying response by allowable timeframe

Correct Response: 1

Explanation: Key DSAR steps include identification, data gathering, review for exceptions, and timely provision of access.

Knowledge Area: Domain 1: Information Security Risk Management Program

----

Question Number: 56

Question: What is the PRIMARY purpose of the Privacy Rule under the Health Insurance Portability and Accountability Act (HIPAA)?

Option 1: Ensure the security of electronic health information

Option 2: Protect the privacy of individually identifiable health information

Option 3: Establish standards for electronic transactions and code sets

Option 4: Safeguard the integrity of healthcare data

Correct Response: 2

Explanation: The PRIMARY purpose of the Privacy Rule under HIPAA is to protect the privacy of individually identifiable health information. The Privacy Rule sets standards for the use and disclosure of protected health information (PHI) and gives individuals control over their health information by establishing their rights to access and control how their PHI is used and shared.

Knowledge Area: Domain 1: Information Security Risk Management Program

----

Question Number: 57

Question: Which of the following is the MOST important consideration when handling electronic protected health information (ePHI) under the Health Insurance Portability and Accountability Act (HIPAA)?

Option 1: Implementing technical safeguards for ePHI

Option 2: Conducting regular audits and assessments

Option 3: Obtaining written consent for ePHI disclosure

Option 4: Encrypting ePHI during transmission and storage

Correct Response: 1

Explanation: The MOST important consideration when handling ePHI under HIPAA is implementing technical safeguards for ePHI. Technical safeguards, such as encryption, access controls, and audit controls, help protect the confidentiality, integrity, and availability of ePHI. By implementing these safeguards, organizations can reduce the risk of unauthorized access, disclosure, or alteration of ePHI, ensuring compliance with HIPAA requirements.

Knowledge Area: Domain 1: Information Security Risk Management Program

----

Question Number: 58

Question: Scenario: A healthcare organization is planning to implement a new electronic health records (EHR) system. Which of the following actions is the MOST important to ensure compliance with the Health Insurance Portability and Accountability Act (HIPAA)?

Option 1: Conduct a privacy impact assessment for the EHR system

Option 2: Train employees on the proper use and handling of EHRs

Option 3: Implement technical controls to secure the EHR system

Option 4: Develop policies and procedures for EHR data management and access controls

Correct Response: 1

Explanation: Conducting a privacy impact assessment for the EHR system is the MOST important action to ensure compliance with HIPAA. A privacy impact assessment evaluates the potential privacy risks associated with the implementation of the EHR system, identifies mitigating measures, and ensures that privacy requirements are incorporated into the system design and operations. This helps protect the privacy of individually identifiable health information and ensures compliance with HIPAA regulations.

Knowledge Area: Domain 1: Information Security Risk Management Program

----

Question Number: 59

Question: Internal reviewers focus on improving risk management while external reviewers provide independent assurance of effectiveness to meet compliance mandates.

Option 1: Tools and techniques

Option 2: Risk identification

Option 3: Risk monitoring

Option 4: Objectives

Correct Response: 3

Explanation: Internal vs. external reviewers have different focuses.

Knowledge Area: Domain 1: Information Security Risk Management Program

----

Question Number: 60

Question: The primary objective of a risk awareness program is nurturing a culture focused on managing risks in alignment with organizational goals through consistent messaging from leadership.

Option 1: Reduce human errors

Option 2: Meet training mandates

Option 3: Lessen skill gaps

Option 4: Enable faster reporting

Correct Response: 2

Explanation: Awareness aligns behaviors to goals.

Knowledge Area: Domain 1: Information Security Risk Management Program

----

Question Number: 61

Question: Documenting control performance provides quantified metrics and trends demonstrating effectiveness to drive improvements in risk management over time.

Option 1: Meet compliance mandates

Option 2: Clarify business impact

Option 3: Enable quarterly reporting

Option 4: Identify audit priorities

Correct Response: 3

Explanation: Performance documentation provides risk insights.

Knowledge Area: Domain 1: Information Security Risk Management Program

----

Question Number: 62

Question: You are kicking off a new project to implement a customer relationship management (CRM) system. What should be done FIRST to determine the scope?

Option 1: Document business requirements

Option 2: Evaluate potential vendors

Option 3: Interview end users

Option 4: Define project objectives

Correct Response: 4

Explanation: Defining objectives and goals sets the scope.

Knowledge Area: Domain 2: Scope of the Information System

Question Number: 63

Question: A key criteria when determining the scope of a new system is:

Option 1: Project budget

Option 2: Implementation timeline

Option 3: Ongoing support model

Option 4: Business needs being met

Correct Response: 4

Explanation: The scope should foremost address business needs.

Knowledge Area: Domain 2: Scope of the Information System

Question Number: 64

Question: When determining the scope of a system change, the MOST important element to consider is:

Option 1: Technical requirements

Option 2: Cost and schedule

Option 3: Testing approach

Option 4: Impact on business objectives

Correct Response: 4

Explanation: The impact on business objectives drives scope decisions.

Knowledge Area: Domain 2: Scope of the Information System

Question Number: 65

Question: You are implementing a new cloud-based supply chain management system. Defining which of the following would establish the appropriate scope?

Option 1: Data interfaces needed

Option 2: Number of system users

Option 3: Required uptime and performance

Option 4: Key supply chain processes to improve

Correct Response: 4

Explanation: The processes to improve should determine the scope.

Knowledge Area: Domain 2: Scope of the Information System

Question Number: 66

Question: Which of the following is the PRIMARY consideration when designing the data flow within an information system architecture?

Option 1: Ensuring efficient data processing

Option 2: Minimizing data storage requirements

Option 3: Maximizing data security and privacy

Option 4: Streamlining data input methods

Correct Response: 3

Explanation: The PRIMARY consideration when designing the data flow within an information system architecture is maximizing data security and privacy. While efficient data processing, minimizing storage requirements, and streamlining input methods are important, data security and privacy are critical aspects that should be prioritized to protect sensitive information from unauthorized access or disclosure.

Knowledge Area: Domain 2: Scope of the Information System

Question Number: 67

Question: You are implementing a new cloud-based payroll system. Which of the following BEST describes the system's purpose?

Option 1: Number of expected users

Option 2: Technical specifications

Option 3: Internal payroll processes improved

Option 4: Vendor selection criteria

Correct Response: 3

Explanation: The processes improved describe the purpose.

Knowledge Area: Domain 2: Scope of the Information System

Question Number: 68

Question: How are data classification levels typically set?

Option 1: By executives

Option 2: Via audits

Option 3: Following regulations

Option 4: Through data analysis

Correct Response: 4

Explanation: Analysis of data itself guides classification.

Knowledge Area: Domain 2: Scope of the Information System

Question Number: 69

Question: Why classify tangible assets like devices?

Option 1: To gauge depreciation

Option 2: To enable insurance

Option 3: To highlight security risks

Option 4: To set maintenance cycles

Correct Response: 3

Explanation: Device classification also highlights security risks.

Knowledge Area: Domain 2: Scope of the Information System

Question Number: 70

Question: Why must asset inventories be regularly updated?

Option 1: Regulations require it.

Option 2: Markets evolve quickly.

Option 3: New assets are acquired.

Option 4: All of the above.

Correct Response: 4

Explanation: Regulations, markets, acquisitions prompt updates.

Knowledge Area: Domain 2: Scope of the Information System

Question Number: 71

Question: How are data classification levels typically set?

Option 1: By executives

Option 2: Via audits

Option 3: Following regulations

Option 4: Through data analysis

Correct Response: 4

Explanation: Analysis of data itself guides classification.

Knowledge Area: Domain 2: Scope of the Information System

Question Number: 72

Question: Why classify tangible assets like devices?

Option 1: To gauge depreciation

Option 2: To enable insurance

Option 3: To highlight security risks

Option 4: To set maintenance cycles

Correct Response: 3

Explanation: Device classification also highlights security risks.

Knowledge Area: Domain 2: Scope of the Information System

Question Number: 73

Question: What methods help estimate potential losses from incidents?

Option 1: Annualized loss expectancy

Option 2: Security budgets

Option 3: Historic comparisons

Option 4: Threat analysis

Correct Response: 1

Explanation: Annualized loss expectancy quantifies potential impact.

Knowledge Area: Domain 2: Scope of the Information System

Question Number: 74

Question: Why value intangible assets like reputation?

Option 1: For insurance purposes

Option 2: To enable cost analysis

Option 3: To inform risk analysis

Option 4: To meet accounting standards

Correct Response: 3

Explanation: Valuing reputation informs risk analysis.

Knowledge Area: Domain 2: Scope of the Information System

Question Number: 75

Question: Which of the following data types would likely require a LOW confidentiality categorization per ISO 27002 guidelines?

Option 1: Trade secrets

Option 2: Customer PII

Option 3: Executive communications

Option 4: Internal memos

Correct Response: 4

Explanation: Internal memos have low confidentiality needs.

Knowledge Area: Domain 2: Scope of the Information System

Question Number: 76

Question: Scenario: An organization holds customer financial data, employee payroll information, and marketing campaign strategies. Which of the following information types would have the HIGHEST impact level on confidentiality if compromised?

Option 1: Customer financial data

Option 2: Employee payroll information

Option 3: Marketing campaign strategies

Option 4: All information types have equal impact on confidentiality

Correct Response: 1

Explanation: Customer financial data would have the HIGHEST impact level on confidentiality if compromised. Financial data typically contains sensitive and confidential information such as account numbers, transaction details, and personal identification. Unauthorized disclosure or access to such data can have severe consequences, including financial loss, identity theft, and reputational damage.

Knowledge Area: Domain 2: Scope of the Information System

Question Number: 77

Question: Scenario: An organization holds customer personal information, financial data, and proprietary business processes. Which of the following information types would have the GREATEST impact level on confidentiality, integrity, and availability if compromised?

Option 1: Customer personal information

Option 2: Financial data

Option 3: Proprietary business processes

Option 4: All information types have equal impact on confidentiality, integrity, and availability

Correct Response: 4

Explanation: All information types—customer personal information, financial data, and proprietary business processes—would have an equal impact level on confidentiality, integrity, and availability if compromised. Each information type carries its own set of risks and potential consequences. The compromise of customer personal information can lead to privacy breaches, financial data compromise can result in fraud or financial loss, and unauthorized access to proprietary business processes can impact competitiveness and operational efficiency. Protecting all information types is essential for maintaining the organization's overall security and operational continuity.

Knowledge Area: Domain 2: Scope of the Information System

Question Number: 78

Question: What makes external hackers a challenging and evolving threat to privacy?

Option 1: Continuously adapting attack techniques and strategies

Option 2: Exploiting new vulnerabilities arising from technology changes

Option 3: High sophistication and persistence of state-sponsored attackers

Option 4: All of the above

Correct Response: 4

Explanation: Hackers dynamically adapt attacks, exploit new tech risks, and sophisticated state actors.

Knowledge Area: Domain 2: Scope of the Information System

Question Number: 79

Question: How can service providers and vendors pose threats to an organization's data privacy?

Option 1: By misusing entrusted data for their own secondary purposes

Option 2: By failing to adequately secure and protect data in their systems

Option 3: By improperly retaining data beyond service engagements

Option 4: All of the above

Correct Response: 4

Explanation: Vendors may misuse, insufficiently protect, or over retain data.

Knowledge Area: Domain 2: Scope of the Information System

Question Number: 80

Question: Why must organizations look beyond current threats when assessing privacy risks?

Option 1: Evolving technologies introduce new vulnerabilities

Option 2: Bad actors continuously adapt and innovate attacks

Option 3: New competitors and adversaries arise over time

Option 4: All of the above

Correct Response: 4

Explanation: Evolving tech, adaptive adversaries, and new players drive evolving threats.

Knowledge Area: Domain 2: Scope of the Information System

Question Number: 81

Question: What is a benefit of data anonymization and pseudonymization?

Option 1: Removed direct identifiers reduce the privacy impact of exposure

Option 2: Aggregated data avoids highlighting individuals in analysis results

Option 3: Retaining pseudonym links enables re-identification if necessary

Option 4: All of the above

Correct Response: 4

Explanation: Anonymization limits individual exposure, enables aggregation, and retains re-ID options.

Knowledge Area: Domain 2: Scope of the Information System

Question Number: 82

Question: What is a gap analysis in the context of audit process and methodologies?

Option 1: A methodical assessment that identifies the differences between current controls and desired control objectives or industry best practices.

Option 2: An evaluation of the financial statements to ensure compliance with accounting standards.

Option 3: A review of the physical security measures implemented by an organization.

Option 4: An assessment of the cloud service provider's data encryption practices.

Correct Response: 1

Explanation: A gap analysis, in the context of audit process and methodologies, is a methodical assessment that identifies the differences between current controls and desired control objectives or industry best practices. It helps organizations understand the gaps or deficiencies in their control environment, allowing them to develop action plans to address those gaps and improve their overall control posture.

Knowledge Area: Domain 3: Selection and Approval of Security and Privacy Controls

----

Question Number: 83

Question: An organization handles sensitive customer financial information. Which control enhancement would be MOST helpful to implement?

Option 1: Annual cybersecurity training

Option 2: Daily vulnerability scanning

Option 3: Multi-factor authentication

Option 4: Monthly log reviews

Correct Response: 3

Explanation: MFA enhances controls for sensitive financial data.

Knowledge Area: Domain 3: Selection and Approval of Security and Privacy Controls

----

Question Number: 84

Question: A healthcare organization is enhancing controls to safeguard patient medical records. Which of the following would offer the GREATEST protection?

Option 1: Classify data into sensitivity tiers

Option 2: Implement end-user training

Option 3: Perform regular penetration tests

Option 4: Encrypt stored and transmitted data

Correct Response: 4

Explanation: Encryption is a key control enhancement for PHI.

Knowledge Area: Domain 3: Selection and Approval of Security and Privacy Controls

----

Question Number: 85

Question: What technical control overlay would BEST enhance security for an industrial control system?

Option 1: COBIT 2019

Option 2: PCI DSS

Option 3: NERC CIP

Option 4: NIST CSF

Correct Response: 3

Explanation: NERC CIP overlays counter ICS risks.

Knowledge Area: Domain 3: Selection and Approval of Security and Privacy Controls

----

Question Number: 86

Question: A web application displays sensitive customer financial data. Which control enhancement would offer the MOST protection?

Option 1: OWASP Top 10

Option 2: ISO 27001

Option 3: COBIT 2019

Option 4: CIS Controls

Correct Response: 1

Explanation: OWASP counters web application risks.

Knowledge Area: Domain 3: Selection and Approval of Security and Privacy Controls

----

Question Number: 87

Question: You are implementing a continuous monitoring program. Which of the following should be established FIRST?

Option 1: Tool selection

Option 2: Control baseline

Option 3: Staffing plan

Option 4: Monitoring strategy and requirements

Correct Response: 4

Explanation: The strategy and requirements drive subsequent continuous monitoring program development.

Knowledge Area: Domain 3: Selection and Approval of Security and Privacy Controls

----

Question Number: 88

Question: Which of the following would provide the BEST metric for continuous monitoring of access control effectiveness?

Option 1: Unauthorized access attempts

Option 2: Access policy updates

Option 3: Access provisioning volume

Option 4: Audit log review results

Correct Response: 1

Explanation: Monitoring unauthorized access attempts evaluates access control efficacy.

Knowledge Area: Domain 3: Selection and Approval of Security and Privacy Controls

----

Question Number: 89

Question: An organization is implementing continuous monitoring for a new system. What is MOST important when establishing the timeline?

Option 1: Technical feasibility

Option 2: Compliance deadlines

Option 3: Staffing resources

Option 4: Meeting business needs

Correct Response: 4

Explanation: The timeline must align to business requirements.

Knowledge Area: Domain 3: Selection and Approval of Security and Privacy Controls

----

Question Number: 90

Question: During a continuous monitoring program assessment, several gaps were found in log analysis processes. What should occur NEXT?

Option 1: Purchase additional tools

Option 2: Reassess the control baseline

Option 3: Conduct training

Option 4: Update the strategy

Correct Response: 1

Explanation: Gaps mean updating the continuous monitoring strategy.

Knowledge Area: Domain 3: Selection and Approval of Security and Privacy Controls

----

Question Number: 91

Question: An organization is implementing a new continuous monitoring program. Which of the following should be established FIRST?

Option 1: Metrics and requirements

Option 2: Control baseline

Option 3: Staff training

Option 4: Tool implementation

Correct Response: 1

Explanation: Requirements drive subsequent program development.

Knowledge Area: Domain 3: Selection and Approval of Security and Privacy Controls

----

Question Number: 92

Question: A continuous monitoring program is being developed for a new system. What timeline consideration is MOST important?

Option 1: Technical constraints

Option 2: Compliance deadlines

Option 3: Implementation costs

Option 4: Impact on business processes

Correct Response: 4

Explanation: The timeline must align with business needs.

Knowledge Area: Domain 3: Selection and Approval of Security and Privacy Controls

----

Question Number: 93

Question: When developing a continuous monitoring strategy, which of the following is LEAST important to consider?

Option 1: Types of controls to monitor

Option 2: Frequency of assessments

Option 3: Locations of monitoring tools

Option 4: Format of reports

Correct Response: 4

Explanation: Tool locations do not significantly impact the strategy.

Knowledge Area: Domain 3: Selection and Approval of Security and Privacy Controls

----

Question Number: 94

Question: Which of the following would provide the BEST evidence of continuous monitoring program effectiveness?

Option 1: Number of alerts triggered

Option 2: Time to generate reports

Option 3: Trends in key risk metrics

Option 4: Adherence to assessment schedule

Correct Response: 3

Explanation: Risk metric trends indicate program efficacy.

Knowledge Area: Domain 3: Selection and Approval of Security and Privacy Controls

----

Question Number: 95

Question: Scenario: An organization has developed a comprehensive security plan as part of its ISMS. What is the BEST next step for ensuring the plan's effectiveness?

Option 1: Obtain approval from senior management

Option 2: Conduct a risk assessment

Option 3: Implement security controls immediately

Option 4: Communicate the plan to all employees

Correct Response: 1

Explanation: The BEST next step for ensuring the effectiveness of the security plan is to obtain approval from senior management. Management support and approval demonstrate a commitment to implementing the plan and provide the necessary authority and resources for its successful implementation.

Knowledge Area: Domain 3: Selection and Approval of Security and Privacy Controls

----

Question Number: 96

Question: When reviewing and approving a security plan/ISMS, what is the PRIMARY objective?

Option 1: Ensure compliance with industry standards

Option 2: Identify potential security vulnerabilities

Option 3: Establish a baseline for security controls

Option 4: Align the plan with organizational objectives

Correct Response: 4

Explanation: The PRIMARY objective when reviewing and approving a security plan/ISMS is to align the plan with organizational objectives. The security plan should be designed to address the specific risks and requirements of the organization and support its strategic goals. Approval ensures that the plan is consistent with the organization's mission, vision, and objectives, ensuring effective alignment between security measures and organizational priorities.

Knowledge Area: Domain 3: Selection and Approval of Security and Privacy Controls

----

Question Number: 97

Question: An organization must implement configuration standards for servers per the TSSIT. Which of the following would be a mandatory setting?

Option 1: BIOS password protection

Option 2: Application whitelisting

Option 3: Daily vulnerability scanning

Option 4: Server build standard

Correct Response: 4

Explanation: TSSIT specifies mandatory server build standards.

Knowledge Area: Domain 4: Implementation of Security and Privacy Controls

----

Question Number: 98

Question: You are verifying configuration compliance to the CIS Controls. Which of the following would be a mandatory setting?

Option 1: Log retention period

Option 2: Firewall rules

Option 3: Password length

Option 4: VPN protocol

Correct Response: 2

Explanation: The CIS Controls define required firewall rules.

Knowledge Area: Domain 4: Implementation of Security and Privacy Controls

----

Question Number: 99

Question: When reviewing system configurations against ISO 27001 standards, which of the following would be LEAST likely to be a mandated setting?

Option 1: Log retention period

Option 2: Password complexity

Option 3: Data encryption

Option 4: Firewall rules

Correct Response: 1

Explanation: Log retention is unlikely to be required in ISO 27001.

Knowledge Area: Domain 4: Implementation of Security and Privacy Controls

----

Question Number: 100

Question: Scenario: An organization wants to ensure its systems comply with current industry standards for security. What is the BEST first step to determine mandatory configuration settings?

Option 1: Conduct a vulnerability assessment

Option 2: Review technical guidelines and standards

Option 3: Implement baseline security controls

Option 4: Engage a third-party auditor

Correct Response: 2

Explanation: The BEST first step to determine mandatory configuration settings is to review technical guidelines and standards. Technical guidelines provide specific recommendations and requirements for security configurations based on industry best practices. By reviewing these guidelines, organizations can identify the mandatory configuration settings necessary to align their systems with industry standards.

Knowledge Area: Domain 4: Implementation of Security and Privacy Controls

----

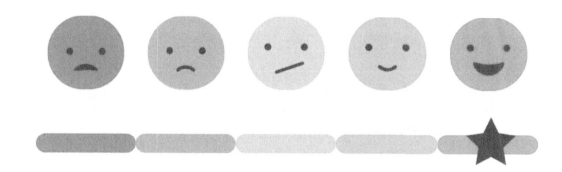

HELP US IMPROVE!

WE WANT YOUR FEEDBACK

Amazing!

You have been studying very hard to this stage.

How is your exam preparation so far? Can the practice test meet your needs and expectation? I desperately desire your voice.

Please kindly consider

1. Visiting my exam practice test books and consider purchasing them to assist you to pass your target exam, though the direct links provided at the beginning of this book
2. Visiting my exam practice test courses held at Udemy though the direct links provided at the beginning of this book
3. Leaving a positive review and feedback to me though the direct book review links provided at the next page.

Keep going! See you at the end of the book.

Warm regards,

Walter

Direct URLs to visit all Walter's Practice Tests at Amazon

Visit Walter's author page:

http://WalterEducation.com

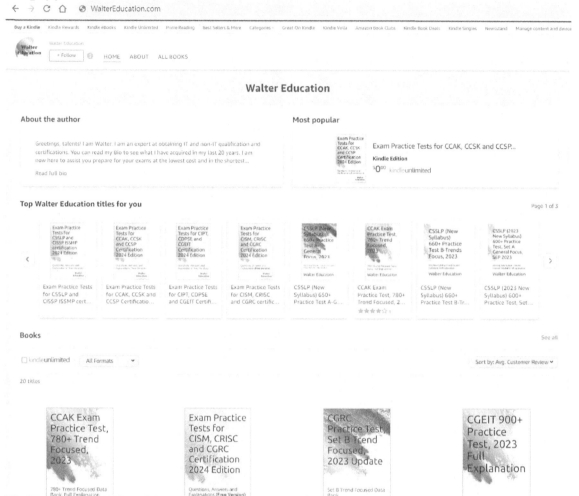

Or the **Links at Amazon Book Store:**

CCAK Exam Practice Test, 780+ Trend Focused, 2023	
Paperback Review URL:	- https://www.amazon.com/review/create-review?&asin=B0CJSXPYM7
Kindle eBook Review URL:	- https://www.amazon.com/review/create-review?&asin=B0CK9QQ44B

CERTIFIED DATA PRIVACY SOLUTIONS ENGINEER (CDPSE) 900+ PRACTICE TEST, 2023, FULL EXPLANATION	
Paperback Review URL:	- https://www.amazon.com/review/create-review?&asin=B0CGL3S5BH
Kindle eBook Review URL:	- https://www.amazon.com/review/create-review?&asin=B0CGL91NQ9

CGEIT 900+ Practice Test, 2023

| Paperback Review URL: | - https://www.amazon.com/review/create-review?&asin=B0CGW1Y1X9 |
| Kindle eBook Review URL: | - https://www.amazon.com/review/create-review?&asin=B0CJ8388ZB |

CIPT, Certified Information Privacy Technologists, Practice Test

| Paperback Review URL: | - https://www.amazon.com/review/create-review?&asin=B0CJ4DLHG2 |
| Kindle eBook Review URL: | - https://www.amazon.com/review/create-review?&asin=B0CJ72MR4M |

CRISC 1200+ Practice Test, 2023 (Exam Simulation and Core & Advanced Knowledge)

| Paperback Review URL: | - https://www.amazon.com/review/create-review?&asin=B0CJ43R78T |
| Kindle eBook Review URL: | - https://www.amazon.com/review/create-review?&asin=B0CJ72JJLY |

CISM 1050+ Practice Test,2023 Updated, Set B - Trends Focused, ISACA

| Paperback Review URL: | - https://www.amazon.com/review/create-review?&asin=B0CJSNR5Z2 |
| Kindle eBook Review URL: | - https://www.amazon.com/review/create-review?&asin=B0CJVWHJHW |

CISM 1050+ Practice Test A - Core Focus, ISACA

| Paperback Review URL: | - https://www.amazon.com/review/create-review?&asin=B0CJL2HD1R |
| Kindle eBook Review URL: | - https://www.amazon.com/review/create-review?&asin=B0CJVSQ6Z6 |

CCSKv4 900+ Practice Test 2023, Full Explanation

| Paperback Review URL: | - https://www.amazon.com/review/create-review?&asin=B0CFX2S7D8 |
| Kindle eBook Review URL: | - https://www.amazon.com/review/create-review?&asin=B0CFVLS8ZH |

CSSLP (2023 New Syllabus) 600+ Practice Test, Set A General Focus

| Paperback Review URL: | - https://www.amazon.com/review/create-review?&asin=B0CK3VTR9D |
| Kindle eBook Review URL: | - https://www.amazon.com/review/create-review?&asin=PENDING |

CSSLP (New Syllabus) 660+ Practice Test B-Trends Focus, SEP 2023

| Paperback Review URL: | - https://www.amazon.com/review/create-review?&asin=B0CK3XGCBN |
| Kindle eBook Review URL: | - https://www.amazon.com/review/create-review?&asin=PENDING |

CISSP-ISSMP 650+ Practice Test, 2023 New syllabus, Set A Core Focused

| Paperback Review URL: | - https://www.amazon.com/review/create-review?&asin=B0CJLLL4HP |
| Kindle eBook Review URL: | - https://www.amazon.com/review/create-review?&asin=B0CK2Y6XR7 |

CISSP-ISSMP 650+ Practice Test, 2023 New syllabus, Set B Trends Focused, ISC2

Paperback Review URL:	- https://www.amazon.com/review/create-review?&asin=B0CJLMV48G
Kindle eBook Review URL:	- https://www.amazon.com/review/create-review?&asin=B0CK2X7CLL

Practice Test for Certified Cloud Security Professional (CCSP): 900+ Practice Test

Paperback Review URL:	- https://www.amazon.com/review/create-review?&asin=B0CFCLW7HJ
Kindle eBook Review URL:	- https://www.amazon.com/review/create-review?&asin=B0CFKSVKSS

CGRC Practice Test, Set A Data Bank, Learn & Exam, 2023 Update

Paperback Review URL:	- https://www.amazon.com/review/create-review?&asin=B0CJBC5MX1
Kindle eBook Review URL:	- https://www.amazon.com/review/create-review?&asin=B0CJYQVM22

CGRC Practice Test, Set B Trend Focused, 2023

Paperback Review URL:	- https://www.amazon.com/review/create-review?&asin=B0CJ43Z8N6
Kindle eBook Review URL:	- https://www.amazon.com/review/create-review?&asin=B0CJ72HWY2

How to give a Review and Rating:

1. Click Here

2. Tell me anything about the course

3. Submit

Question Number: 101

Question: When verifying the implementation of mandatory configuration settings, what is the PRIMARY objective?

Option 1: Ensure compliance with regulatory requirements

Option 2: Identify any deviations from industry standards

Option 3: Minimize the risk of security breaches

Option 4: Optimize system performance

Correct Response: 1

Explanation: The PRIMARY objective when verifying the implementation of mandatory configuration settings is to ensure compliance with regulatory requirements. Regulatory requirements often mandate specific security configurations to protect sensitive data, ensure privacy, and mitigate risks. Verifying implementation ensures that the organization adheres to these requirements and reduces the potential for non-compliance penalties and security breaches.

Knowledge Area: Domain 4: Implementation of Security and Privacy Controls

----

Question Number: 102

Question: What is the MOST important consideration when determining mandatory configuration settings?

Option 1: Industry-specific regulations and guidelines

Option 2: Compatibility with existing systems and infrastructure

Option 3: Ease of implementation and maintenance

Option 4: Cost-effectiveness and resource allocation

Correct Response: 1

Explanation: The MOST important consideration when determining mandatory configuration settings is industry-specific regulations and guidelines. These regulations outline the minimum security measures and configurations required for specific industries or sectors. Adhering to these regulations ensures compliance and helps protect sensitive information, maintain customer trust, and mitigate risks associated with the industry.

Knowledge Area: Domain 4: Implementation of Security and Privacy Controls

----

Question Number: 103

Question: You need to apply USGCB standards to web servers. Which of the following settings would be mandated?

Option 1: SSL certificate

Option 2: Log retention period

Option 3: File permissions

Option 4: Password complexity

Correct Response: 4

Explanation: The USGCB defines required password complexity.

Knowledge Area: Domain 4: Implementation of Security and Privacy Controls

----

Question Number: 104

Question: Scenario: An organization wants to implement the NIST Cybersecurity Framework. What is the BEST first step to begin implementation?

Option 1: Identify and prioritize critical assets

Option 2: Conduct a comprehensive risk assessment

Option 3: Develop incident response procedures

Option 4: Establish employee security awareness training program

Correct Response: 1

Explanation: The BEST first step to begin implementing the NIST Cybersecurity Framework is to identify and prioritize critical assets. This step helps organizations understand their most valuable and sensitive assets, allowing them to allocate appropriate resources and prioritize security measures to protect those assets.

Knowledge Area: Domain 4: Implementation of Security and Privacy Controls

----

Question Number: 105

Question: An organization must implement database STIG standards. Which of the following would be a mandatory configuration?

Option 1: Connection timeout

Option 2: TLS version

Option 3: File permissions

Option 4: User account lockout

Correct Response: 2

Explanation: DB STIGs define required TLS versions.

Knowledge Area: Domain 4: Implementation of Security and Privacy Controls

----

Question Number: 106

Question: You are assessing systems against STIG benchmarks. Which of the following would indicate non-compliance with Apache STIGs?

Option 1: Outdated SSL certificate

Option 2: Excessive file permissions

Option 3: Lack of input validation

Option 4: Enabled directory listing

Correct Response: 2

Explanation: Excessive permissions violate Apache STIGs.

Knowledge Area: Domain 4: Implementation of Security and Privacy Controls

----

Question Number: 107

Question: Which of the following represents a mandatory web server STIG configuration setting?

Option 1: HTTP redirect to HTTPS

Option 2: Disable unused services

Option 3: Log retention period

Option 4: File permission auditing

Correct Response: 2

Explanation: STIGs require disabling unneeded services

Knowledge Area: Domain 4: Implementation of Security and Privacy Controls

----

Question Number: 108

Question: An organization is implementing CIS benchmarks. Which of the following represents a CIS Linux mandate?

Option 1: SSH key-based authentication

Option 2: Unused service removal

Option 3: Real-time log monitoring

Option 4: Firewall configuration

Correct Response: 2

Explanation: CIS Linux requires disabling unused services.

Knowledge Area: Domain 4: Implementation of Security and Privacy Controls

----

Question Number: 109

Question: An auditor is reviewing your CIS benchmark evidence. Which of the following would be mandatory for Linux servers?

Option 1: Package update frequency

Option 2: SSH cipher algorithms

Option 3: Password expiration period

Option 4: Firewall rule auditing

Correct Response: 2

Explanation: CIS Linux specifies required SSH ciphers.

Knowledge Area: Domain 4: Implementation of Security and Privacy Controls

----

Question Number: 110

Question: To comply with CIS Solaris benchmarks, which of the following MUST be implemented?

Option 1: Packet filtering firewall

Option 2: Privileged user auditing

Option 3: Third-party security extensions

Option 4: Password complexity requirements

Correct Response: 4

Explanation: CIS Solaris mandates password complexity.

Knowledge Area: Domain 4: Implementation of Security and Privacy Controls

----

Question Number: 111

Question: An auditor is reviewing your GDPR controls. Which of the following would be mandatory documentation?

Option 1: System user guide

Option 2: Access control policy

Option 3: Data Protection Impact Assessment

Option 4: Change management procedures

Correct Response: 3

Explanation: GDPR requires a Data Protection Impact Assessment.

Knowledge Area: Domain 4: Implementation of Security and Privacy Controls

----

Question Number: 112

Question: To comply with GDPR, which of the following MUST be implemented when collecting customer personal information?

Option 1: Consent forms

Option 2: Encryption

Option 3: Anonymization

Option 4: Activity monitoring

Correct Response: 1

Explanation: GDPR requires consent for collecting personal data.

Knowledge Area: Domain 4: Implementation of Security and Privacy Controls

----

Question Number: 113

Question: Scenario: An organization is implementing new security controls as part of its security and privacy architecture. What is the BEST first step to ensure the implementation is consistent with the organizational architecture?

Option 1: Conduct a gap analysis between the existing architecture and the new controls

Option 2: Consult with stakeholders to gather input on the implementation approach

Option 3: Update the organizational architecture to align with the new controls

Option 4: Develop a comprehensive implementation plan for the new controls

Correct Response: 1

Explanation: The BEST first step to ensure the consistent implementation of controls with the organizational architecture is to conduct a gap analysis between the existing architecture and the new controls. This analysis helps identify any misalignments or gaps between the controls and the organizational architecture, providing insights into the necessary adjustments or modifications required for a consistent implementation.

Knowledge Area: Domain 4: Implementation of Security and Privacy Controls

----

Question Number: 114

Question: Scenario: An organization has implemented new security controls in accordance with its security and privacy architecture. What is the correct approach to ensure the controls are consistently implemented with the organizational architecture?

Option 1: Conduct regular audits to verify control implementation

Option 2: Update the security and privacy architecture to reflect the new controls

Option 3: Perform periodic risk assessments to validate control effectiveness

Option 4: Conduct a review to compare the controls against the organizational architecture

Correct Response: 4

Explanation: The correct approach to ensure the consistent implementation of controls with the organizational architecture is to conduct a review to compare the controls against the organizational architecture. This review helps identify any discrepancies or misalignments between the controls and the architecture, ensuring that the controls are implemented consistently and in accordance with the organization's security and privacy objectives.

Knowledge Area: Domain 4: Implementation of Security and Privacy Controls

----

Question Number: 115

Question: Your organization is using a SaaS provider's application that processes customer data. What should you obtain from the provider to validate inherited controls?

Option 1: System availability reports

Option 2: Breach notification policies

Option 3: SOC2 audit report

Option 4: Vulnerability scan results

Correct Response: 3

Explanation: A SOC2 report documents the SaaS provider's controls.

Knowledge Area: Domain 4: Implementation of Security and Privacy Controls

----

Question Number: 116

Question: You are auditing a system that connects to a partner network. Which of the following provides the BEST evidence of inherited control implementation?

Option 1: Interconnection security agreement

Option 2: UL/KPMG certification

Option 3: Penetration test results

Option 4: Vulnerability assessment report

Correct Response: 1

Explanation: An ISA details the partner's inherited controls.

Knowledge Area: Domain 4: Implementation of Security and Privacy Controls

----

Question Number: 117

Question: A control gap was identified during an assessment. Which of the following would be the BEST compensating control?

Option 1: Increased logging

Option 2: Additional firewall rules

Option 3: Stronger encryption

Option 4: Multifactor authentication

Correct Response: 1

Explanation: Increased logging helps compensate for control gaps.

Knowledge Area: Domain 4: Implementation of Security and Privacy Controls

----

Question Number: 118

Question: Your organization cannot implement a required firewall due to legacy systems. Which of the following would be a viable alternate control?

Option 1: Intrusion detection system

Option 2: Access control lists

Option 3: Log auditing

Option 4: Vulnerability scanning

Correct Response: 2

Explanation: ACLs can provide alternate segmentation.

Knowledge Area: Domain 4: Implementation of Security and Privacy Controls

----

Question Number: 119

Question: You cannot implement a required password complexity standard due to user complaints. Which control could BEST compensate?

Option 1: Key rotation frequency

Option 2: Multifactor authentication

Option 3: Access revocation

Option 4: Background checks

Correct Response: 2

Explanation: MFA compensates for weak passwords.

Knowledge Area: Domain 4: Implementation of Security and Privacy Controls

----

Question Number: 120

Question: Scenario: An organization is documenting inputs to planned controls for a new information security program. What is the PRIMARY reason for documenting the inputs?

Option 1: To ensure compliance with regulatory requirements

Option 2: To identify potential deviations or risks

Option 3: To establish a baseline for control behavior

Option 4: To communicate the expected control outcomes

Correct Response: 4

Explanation: The PRIMARY reason for documenting the inputs to planned controls is to communicate the expected control outcomes. Documenting inputs helps establish a clear understanding of what inputs are required for the controls to function effectively. It ensures that all stakeholders have a common understanding of the expected behavior and outcomes of the controls.

Knowledge Area: Domain 4: Implementation of Security and Privacy Controls

----

Question Number: 121

Question: When documenting the expected behavior of controls, what is the MOST important consideration?

Option 1: Alignment with industry standards and best practices

Option 2: Compatibility with existing systems and infrastructure

Option 3: Adherence to regulatory requirements and guidelines

Option 4: Optimization of resource allocation and cost-effectiveness

Correct Response: 1

Explanation: The MOST important consideration when documenting the expected behavior of controls is alignment with industry standards and best practices. Industry standards and best practices provide guidance on the expected behavior of controls based on proven methodologies. Aligning with these standards helps ensure that the controls are designed to meet industry expectations and achieve desired outcomes.

Knowledge Area: Domain 4: Implementation of Security and Privacy Controls

----

Question Number: 122

Question: What is the NEXT ACTION after documenting the expected outputs or deviations of controls?

Option 1: Implement the controls and monitor their performance

Option 2: Test the controls against various scenarios and use cases

Option 3: Review the controls' expected behavior with stakeholders

Option 4: Update the organization's security policies and procedures

Correct Response: 1

Explanation: The NEXT ACTION after documenting the expected outputs or deviations of controls is to implement the controls and monitor their performance. Implementation involves putting the controls into action according to their documented expected behavior and outcomes. Monitoring their performance ensures that the controls are functioning as intended and achieving the desired results.

Knowledge Area: Domain 4: Implementation of Security and Privacy Controls

----

Question Number: 123

Question: You are implementing a new cloud-based payroll system handling sensitive employee salary data. Which of the following controls would BEST match the system's risk profile?

Option 1: Log reviews

Option 2: Firewall rules

Option 3: Multifactor authentication

Option 4: Intrusion detection

Correct Response: 3

Explanation: MFA helps mitigate risks related to sensitive payroll data.

Knowledge Area: Domain 4: Implementation of Security and Privacy Controls

----

Question Number: 124

Question: You are selecting controls for a new email system containing unclassified internal communications. Which control would provide the LEAST value given the purpose?

Option 1: SPAM filtering

Option 2: DKIM/DMARC

Option 3: Data loss prevention

Option 4: Access controls

Correct Response: 3

Explanation: DLP provides little benefit for low-risk email.

Knowledge Area: Domain 4: Implementation of Security and Privacy Controls

----

Question Number: 125

Question: Scenario: An organization is implementing a new physical security measure as part of its security program. What is the BEST first step to obtain and document implementation details?

Option 1: Consult with physical security experts and stakeholders

Option 2: Conduct a risk assessment for the physical security measure

Option 3: Review industry best practices for physical security implementation

Option 4: Develop a comprehensive implementation plan for the physical security measure

Correct Response: 1

Explanation: The BEST first step to obtain and document implementation details for a new physical security measure is to consult with physical security experts and stakeholders. Their expertise and insights will provide valuable information about the implementation requirements, considerations, and best practices specific to the organization's context.

Knowledge Area: Domain 4: Implementation of Security and Privacy Controls

----

Question Number: 126

Question: When documenting the expected behavior of a physical security measure, what is the PRIMARY consideration?

Option 1: Alignment with industry standards and regulations

Option 2: Compatibility with existing physical security infrastructure

Option 3: Adherence to organizational security policies and guidelines

Option 4: Optimization of resource allocation and cost-effectiveness

Correct Response: 3

Explanation: The PRIMARY consideration when documenting the expected behavior of a physical security measure is adherence to organizational security policies and guidelines. The documentation should reflect the specific requirements and expectations of the organization, ensuring that the physical security measure aligns with the expected outcomes and adheres to the established security policies and guidelines.

Knowledge Area: Domain 4: Implementation of Security and Privacy Controls

----

Question Number: 127

Question: You are documenting a new system's security controls. Which role would be BEST to consult on physical security implementation?

Option 1: System administrator

Option 2: Network engineer

Option 3: Facilities manager

Option 4: Security manager

Correct Response: 3

Explanation: Facilities managers implement physical controls.

Knowledge Area: Domain 4: Implementation of Security and Privacy Controls

----

Question Number: 128

Question: An organization is deploying a new cloud-based payroll system. Who should provide documentation on inherited cloud security controls?

Option 1: Cloud architect

Option 2: Security manager

Option 3: Payroll manager

Option 4: Cloud service provider

Correct Response: 4

Explanation: The provider gives documentation on inherited controls.

Knowledge Area: Domain 4: Implementation of Security and Privacy Controls

----

Question Number: 129

Question: Scenario: An organization is implementing a new privacy program. What is the BEST first step to obtain and document implementation details?

Option 1: Consult with legal and compliance teams

Option 2: Review privacy regulations and industry standards

Option 3: Conduct a privacy impact assessment

Option 4: Develop privacy policies and procedures

Correct Response: 1

Explanation: The BEST first step to obtain and document implementation details for a new privacy program is to consult with legal and compliance teams. These teams possess the expertise and understanding of privacy regulations and requirements, enabling them to provide guidance on the implementation details that need to be documented.

Knowledge Area: Domain 4: Implementation of Security and Privacy Controls

----

Question Number: 130

Question: When documenting the expected behavior of privacy controls, what is the PRIMARY consideration?

Option 1: Alignment with privacy regulations and industry standards

Option 2: Compatibility with existing privacy infrastructure

Option 3: Adherence to organizational privacy policies and guidelines

Option 4: Optimization of resource allocation and cost-effectiveness

Correct Response: 1

Explanation: The PRIMARY consideration when documenting the expected behavior of privacy controls is alignment with privacy regulations and industry standards. Privacy controls should adhere to the requirements outlined in privacy regulations and industry standards to ensure compliance and protect individuals' privacy rights.

Knowledge Area: Domain 4: Implementation of Security and Privacy Controls

----

Question Number: 131

Question: Scenario: An organization is implementing a new privacy program. During the implementation, unexpected deviations are identified. What is the correct course of action?

Option 1: Modify the privacy controls to address the deviations

Option 2: Ignore the deviations if they are deemed low-risk

Option 3: Review the implementation plan to identify the cause of the deviations

Option 4: Consult with privacy experts to assess the impact of the deviations

Correct Response: 1

Explanation: The correct course of action when unexpected deviations are identified during the implementation of a privacy program is to modify the privacy controls to address the deviations. Deviations may indicate potential vulnerabilities or gaps that need to be addressed to ensure the effectiveness and integrity of the privacy program. Modifying the controls helps mitigate risks and ensures that the program aligns with the expected outputs and objectives.

Knowledge Area: Domain 4: Implementation of Security and Privacy Controls

----

Question Number: 132

Question: Scenario: An organization is planning to conduct an assessment of its security and privacy controls. What is the BEST first step to determine the requirements for assessors/auditors?

Option 1: Identify the scope and objectives of the assessment

Option 2: Review industry standards and regulatory requirements

Option 3: Define the qualifications and expertise needed for the assessment

Option 4: Develop a detailed assessment plan

Correct Response: 1

Explanation: The BEST first step to determine the requirements for assessors/auditors is to identify the scope and objectives of the assessment. Understanding the scope and objectives helps in determining the specific knowledge, skills, and expertise required from the assessors/auditors to effectively evaluate the security and privacy controls within the defined context.

Knowledge Area: Domain 5: Assessment/Audit of Security and Privacy Controls

----

Question Number: 133

Question: When determining assessor/auditor requirements for security and privacy controls, what is the PRIMARY consideration?

Option 1: Knowledge of industry standards and best practices

Option 2: Familiarity with relevant regulatory requirements

Option 3: Technical expertise in security and privacy domains

Option 4: Experience in conducting assessments or audits

Correct Response: 3

Explanation: The PRIMARY consideration when determining assessor/auditor requirements for security and privacy controls is technical expertise in security and privacy domains. Assessors/auditors need to possess the necessary knowledge and skills in security and privacy practices, frameworks, and technologies to effectively evaluate the controls. This expertise ensures that the assessment is thorough, accurate, and aligned with industry best practices and standards.

Knowledge Area: Domain 5: Assessment/Audit of Security and Privacy Controls

----

Question Number: 134

Question: You are planning an assessment of security controls for a new cloud-based ERP system. Which of the following should be defined FIRST?

Option 1: Control selection

Option 2: Assessment budget

Option 3: Assessment scope

Option 4: Staffing requirements

Correct Response: 3

Explanation: The scope informs subsequent planning decisions.

Knowledge Area: Domain 5: Assessment/Audit of Security and Privacy Controls

----

Question Number: 135

Question: You need to scope a penetration test for a new patient health portal. Which of the following would BEST align to the system's key risks?

Option 1: Network infrastructure

Option 2: Web application

Option 3: Mobile app back-end

Option 4: Admin workstations

Correct Response: 2

Explanation: Web app testing aligns to online health risks.

Knowledge Area: Domain 5: Assessment/Audit of Security and Privacy Controls

----

Question Number: 136

Question: You are selecting the assessment method for a new system handling sensitive customer data. Which approach would provide the MOST assurance?

Option 1: Policy review

Option 2: Control questionnaire

Option 3: Vulnerability scan

Option 4: Penetration testing

Correct Response: 4

Explanation: Pen testing provides more assurance than less hands-on methods.

Knowledge Area: Domain 5: Assessment/Audit of Security and Privacy Controls

----

Question Number: 137

Question: A auditor is determining the level of effort for an upcoming audit. Which of the following would warrant the MOST audit scrutiny?

Option 1: Minor system changes

Option 2: New sensitive system

Option 3: Compliance concerns

Option 4: Past audit findings

Correct Response: 3

Explanation: Major compliance issues mean more audit effort.

Knowledge Area: Domain 5: Assessment/Audit of Security and Privacy Controls

----

Question Number: 138

Question: Scenario: An organization is planning to implement a new IT project. What is the BEST first step to determine the necessary resources and logistics?

Option 1: Identify project deliverables and milestones

Option 2: Assess the project budget and funding requirements

Option 3: Define the project scope and objectives

Option 4: Conduct a resource availability assessment

Correct Response: 1

Explanation: The BEST first step to determine the necessary resources and logistics for a new IT project is to identify the project deliverables and milestones. This step helps in understanding the specific outcomes and objectives of the project, which are essential for identifying the resources and logistics required to achieve those deliverables and milestones.

Knowledge Area: Domain 5: Assessment/Audit of Security and Privacy Controls

----

Question Number: 139

Question: When determining necessary resources and logistics, what is the PRIMARY consideration?

Option 1: Availability of budget and funding

Option 2: Technical expertise and skills

Option 3: Project timeline and deadlines

Option 4: Stakeholder requirements and expectations

Correct Response: 2

Explanation: The PRIMARY consideration when determining necessary resources and logistics is the technical expertise and skills required for the project. The availability of skilled resources is crucial for successful project implementation. It ensures that the required knowledge and capabilities are in place to handle the technical aspects and challenges of the project.

Knowledge Area: Domain 5: Assessment/Audit of Security and Privacy Controls

----

Question Number: 140

Question: Which of the following artifacts should be reviewed FIRST when planning an audit?

Option 1: Prior assessment results

Option 2: Compliance requirements

Option 3: System design documents

Option 4: Control implementation details

Correct Response: 1

Explanation: Prior audits indicate scope and gaps.

Knowledge Area: Domain 5: Assessment/Audit of Security and Privacy Controls

----

Question Number: 141

Question: You are reviewing artifacts to begin a security controls assessment. Which of the following would provide the MOST important information?

Option 1: Data flow diagrams

Option 2: Network vulnerability scans

Option 3: Threat modeling

Option 4: System architecture

Correct Response: 3

Explanation: Threat modeling provides control priorities.

Knowledge Area: Domain 5: Assessment/Audit of Security and Privacy Controls

----

Question Number: 142

Question: You are gathering documentation to begin a controls assessment. Which artifact provides the MOST value?

Option 1: DLP reports

Option 2: IDS logs

Option 3: Data classifications

Option 4: System architecture

Correct Response: 3

Explanation: Data classification helps determine scope.

Knowledge Area: Domain 5: Assessment/Audit of Security and Privacy Controls

----

Question Number: 143

Question: You are preparing for a PCI-DSS assessment. Which documentation is MOST important to review first?

Option 1: Prior audits

Option 2: Compliance roadmap

Option 3: Data flow diagrams

Option 4: Threat model

Correct Response: 2

Explanation: The compliance roadmap helps determine scope.

Knowledge Area: Domain 5: Assessment/Audit of Security and Privacy Controls

----

Question Number: 144

Question: An internal audit is being planned. Which policy review would provide the LEAST value?

Option 1: Encryption policy

Option 2: Third-party management policy

Option 3: Incident response policy

Option 4: Access control policy

Correct Response: 3

Explanation: Incident response policies offer little for scoping.

Question Number: 145

Question: You are completing an assessment plan for a new mobile app. Which of the following should be documented to finalize the effort estimation?

Option 1: App permissions

Option 2: Types of vulnerabilities

Option 3: Interfaces and data flows

Option 4: Recovery capabilities

Correct Response: 3

Explanation: Interfaces and data inform level of effort.

Knowledge Area: Domain 5: Assessment/Audit of Security and Privacy Controls

----

Question Number: 146

Question: When collecting assessment/audit evidence, what is the PRIMARY consideration?

Option 1: Completeness and accuracy of the evidence

Option 2: Alignment with industry standards and best practices

Option 3: Availability and reliability of the evidence

Option 4: Adherence to regulatory requirements and guidelines

Correct Response: 3

Explanation: The PRIMARY consideration when collecting assessment/audit evidence is the availability and reliability of the evidence. It is important to ensure that the evidence collected is accessible, trustworthy, and can be relied upon to support the assessment/audit findings and conclusions.

Knowledge Area: Domain 5: Assessment/Audit of Security and Privacy Controls

----

Question Number: 147

Question: A PCI DSS audit is being conducted. Which method provides the BEST validation of proper cardholder data storage?

Option 1: Examine database schema

Option 2: Interview DBAs

Option 3: Review policies

Option 4: Scan file servers

Correct Response: 1

Explanation: Reviewing the schema validates PCI compliance.

Knowledge Area: Domain 5: Assessment/Audit of Security and Privacy Controls

----

Question Number: 148

Question: An assessor is validating encryption controls on laptops. Which method provides the HIGHEST assurance?

Option 1: Review key management

Option 2: Examine policies

Option 3: Interview users

Option 4: Inspect encrypted drives

Correct Response: 4

Explanation: Inspecting encrypted drives provides empirical evidence.

Knowledge Area: Domain 5: Assessment/Audit of Security and Privacy Controls

----

Question Number: 149

Question: You are auditing access control settings for a critical system. Which method would provide the MOST assurance?

Option 1: Review IAM policies

Option 2: Interview system admins

Option 3: Examine entitlement reports

Option 4: Inspect user permissions

Correct Response: 4

Explanation: Directly verifying permissions provides the highest fidelity.

Knowledge Area: Domain 5: Assessment/Audit of Security and Privacy Controls

----

Question Number: 150

Question: An assessor is validating multi-factor authentication on VPN servers. Which method provides the HIGHEST assurance?

Option 1: Examine RADIUS configs

Option 2: Review Auth logs

Option 3: Interview helpdesk staff

Option 4: Perform authentication testing

Correct Response: 4

Explanation: Testing the VPN login provides empirical evidence.

Knowledge Area: Domain 5: Assessment/Audit of Security and Privacy Controls

----

Question Number: 151

Question: You are assessing patching processes by examining system updates. Which provides the MOST meaningful evidence?

Option 1: Review patch audits

Option 2: Verify update tools

Option 3: Confirm reporting

Option 4: Inspect installed patches

Correct Response: 4

Explanation: Examining installed patches demonstrates implementation.

Knowledge Area: Domain 5: Assessment/Audit of Security and Privacy Controls

----

Question Number: 152

Question: An assessor is validating logging includes all required event types. Which method is BEST?

Option 1: Review log policy

Option 2: Examine log audits

Option 3: Interview SOC staff

Option 4: Inspect log contents

Correct Response: 4

Explanation: Inspecting actual logs provides the best fidelity.

Knowledge Area: Domain 5: Assessment/Audit of Security and Privacy Controls

----

Question Number: 153

Question: What is the MOST important factor to consider when identifying vulnerabilities from assessment/audit results?

Option 1: Technical expertise and knowledge of security controls

Option 2: Adherence to industry standards and regulations

Option 3: Availability of resources to address the vulnerabilities

Option 4: Relevance and alignment with organizational objectives

Correct Response: 1

Explanation: The MOST important factor to consider when identifying vulnerabilities from assessment/audit results is technical expertise and knowledge of security controls. This expertise ensures that vulnerabilities are accurately identified and evaluated, considering their potential impact on the organization's security and the effectiveness of existing control measures.

Knowledge Area: Domain 5: Assessment/Audit of Security and Privacy Controls

----

Question Number: 154

Question: Scenario: An organization has completed an assessment of its information security controls and identified several vulnerabilities. What is the BEST first step in proposing remediation actions?

Option 1: Prioritize vulnerabilities based on their severity and potential impact

Option 2: Consult with stakeholders to gather input on remediation priorities

Option 3: Develop an action plan for addressing the identified vulnerabilities

Option 4: Conduct a cost-benefit analysis for each potential remediation action

Correct Response: 1

Explanation: The BEST first step in proposing remediation actions is to prioritize vulnerabilities based on their severity and potential impact. This enables the organization to allocate resources effectively and address the most critical vulnerabilities first, reducing the overall risk to the organization.

Knowledge Area: Domain 5: Assessment/Audit of Security and Privacy Controls

----

Question Number: 155

Question: Scenario: An organization has conducted an assessment of its information security controls and identified several vulnerabilities. What is the correct approach to proposing remediation actions?

Option 1: Conduct a cost-benefit analysis for each potential remediation action

Option 2: Prioritize vulnerabilities based on their severity and potential impact

Option 3: Engage external experts to recommend remediation actions

Option 4: Develop an action plan for remediation based on stakeholder opinions and feedback

Correct Response: 2

Explanation: The correct approach to proposing remediation actions for identified vulnerabilities is to prioritize vulnerabilities based on their severity and potential impact. This ensures that resources are focused on addressing the most critical vulnerabilities first, reducing the overall risk to the organization. Prioritization allows for efficient allocation of resources and effective mitigation of the identified vulnerabilities.

Knowledge Area: Domain 5: Assessment/Audit of Security and Privacy Controls

----

Question Number: 156

Question: What is the MOST important factor to consider when selecting a risk response?

Option 1: Feasibility of implementing the response measures

Option 2: Compliance with legal and regulatory requirements

Option 3: Availability of resources to support the response measures

Option 4: Alignment with the organization's risk tolerance and objectives

Correct Response: 4

Explanation: The MOST important factor to consider when selecting a risk response is the alignment with the organization's risk tolerance and objectives. The response should be in line with the organization's overall risk management strategy and its specific risk tolerance levels. This ensures that the response is appropriate and consistent with the organization's goals and objectives.

Knowledge Area: Domain 5: Assessment/Audit of Security and Privacy Controls

----

Question Number: 157

Question: Scenario: An organization has identified a significant operational risk. What is the correct risk response in this situation?

Option 1: Accept the risk and continue operations as usual

Option 2: Transfer the risk through insurance or contractual agreements

Option 3: Mitigate the risk by implementing control measures

Option 4: Avoid the risk by ceasing the operation or process

Correct Response: 3

Explanation: The correct risk response in the situation of a significant operational risk is to mitigate the risk by implementing control measures. Mitigation involves taking specific actions to reduce the likelihood or impact of the identified risk. By implementing control measures, the organization can effectively manage the risk and ensure the continuity and resilience of its operations.

Knowledge Area: Domain 5: Assessment/Audit of Security and Privacy Controls

----

Question Number: 158

Question: Scenario: An organization has identified a security vulnerability in its network infrastructure. What is the BEST first step in applying remediations?

Option 1: Assess the potential impact of the vulnerability

Option 2: Develop an action plan for remediation

Option 3: Test and validate the proposed remediations

Option 4: Implement temporary mitigations to reduce the risk

Correct Response: 2

Explanation: The BEST first step in applying remediations for a security vulnerability is to develop an action plan for remediation. This step involves outlining the specific steps and measures needed to address the vulnerability effectively. By having a clear and comprehensive plan, the organization can ensure that the remediations are implemented in a systematic and coordinated manner.

Knowledge Area: Domain 5: Assessment/Audit of Security and Privacy Controls

----

Question Number: 159

Question: What is the MOST important factor to consider when selecting remediation measures?

Option 1: Severity of the vulnerability and potential impact

Option 2: Compatibility with existing infrastructure and systems

Option 3: Technical feasibility of implementing the measures

Option 4: Approval and support from stakeholders

Correct Response: 1

Explanation: The MOST important factor to consider when selecting remediation measures is the severity of the vulnerability and its potential impact. Remediation measures should prioritize addressing vulnerabilities that pose the greatest risk to the organization's security and have the potential for significant impact. By focusing on these high-risk vulnerabilities, the organization can allocate resources effectively and reduce the overall risk.

Knowledge Area: Domain 5: Assessment/Audit of Security and Privacy Controls

----

Question Number: 160

Question: Scenario: An organization has identified a critical software vulnerability in its IT systems. What is the correct approach to apply remediations?

Option 1: Patch the software vulnerability immediately and monitor for any issues

Option 2: Conduct thorough testing before applying any remediations

Option 3: Develop a detailed plan for applying remediations in a controlled manner

Option 4: Disable affected systems until a permanent fix is available

Correct Response: 3

Explanation: The correct approach to apply remediations for a critical software vulnerability is to develop a detailed plan for applying remediations in a controlled manner. This approach ensures that the remediations are implemented following best practices and guidelines, minimizing the risk of potential disruptions or unintended consequences. By applying remediations in a controlled manner, the organization can effectively address the vulnerability while minimizing any negative impact on operations.

Knowledge Area: Domain 5: Assessment/Audit of Security and Privacy Controls

----

Question Number: 161

Question: Scenario: An organization has implemented remediations for identified security vulnerabilities. What is the BEST first step in reassessing and validating the effectiveness of the remediated controls?

Option 1: Conduct a comprehensive vulnerability scan and penetration test

Option 2: Engage an external auditor to review the remediated controls

Option 3: Review the updated security policies and procedures

Option 4: Assess the implementation of the remediations against the initial risk assessment

Correct Response: 1

Explanation: The BEST first step in reassessing and validating the effectiveness of the remediated controls is to conduct a comprehensive vulnerability scan and penetration test. This step helps in identifying any residual vulnerabilities or potential weaknesses in the remediated controls. By conducting thorough testing, the organization can ensure that the remediations have effectively addressed the identified vulnerabilities and mitigated the associated risks.

Knowledge Area: Domain 5: Assessment/Audit of Security and Privacy Controls

----

Question Number: 162

Question: When reassessing and validating the remediated controls, what is the PRIMARY consideration?

Option 1: Alignment with industry standards and regulatory requirements

Option 2: Effectiveness in mitigating the identified vulnerabilities

Option 3: Compatibility with existing infrastructure and systems

Option 4: Cost-effectiveness of the implemented remediations

Correct Response: 2

Explanation: The PRIMARY consideration when reassessing and validating the remediated controls is their effectiveness in mitigating the identified vulnerabilities. The focus should be on evaluating how well the remediated controls address the specific vulnerabilities and whether they effectively reduce or eliminate the associated risks. This assessment ensures that the organization's security posture has improved and that the vulnerabilities have been adequately addressed.

Knowledge Area: Domain 5: Assessment/Audit of Security and Privacy Controls

----

Question Number: 163

Question: Scenario: After completing an assessment of an organization's information security controls, what is the BEST first step in developing the final assessment report?

Option 1: Review and analyze the assessment findings and evidence

Option 2: Compile a summary of the identified vulnerabilities and risks

Option 3: Structure the report based on the organization's reporting template

Option 4: Seek input and feedback from key stakeholders

Correct Response: 1

Explanation: The BEST first step in developing the final assessment report is to review and analyze the assessment findings and evidence. This step involves thoroughly examining the assessment results, identifying key findings, and analyzing the evidence collected during the assessment. This analysis provides the foundation for an accurate and comprehensive final assessment report.

Knowledge Area: Domain 5: Assessment/Audit of Security and Privacy Controls

----

Question Number: 164

Question: When developing a final assessment report, what is the PRIMARY consideration?

Option 1: Adherence to the organization's reporting guidelines and templates

Option 2: Clarity and readability of the report for the intended audience

Option 3: Accuracy and completeness of the assessment findings and recommendations

Option 4: Alignment with industry standards and best practices

Correct Response: 3

Explanation: The PRIMARY consideration when developing a final assessment report is the accuracy and completeness of the assessment findings and recommendations. The report should accurately reflect the assessment results, including the identified vulnerabilities, risks, and recommended remediation actions. By ensuring accuracy and completeness, the report provides a reliable resource for decision-making and remediation efforts.

Knowledge Area: Domain 5: Assessment/Audit of Security and Privacy Controls

----

Question Number: 165

Question: Scenario: After conducting a security assessment, an organization has identified residual vulnerabilities. What is the BEST first step in analyzing these vulnerabilities?

Option 1: Determine the potential impact and likelihood of exploitation

Option 2: Evaluate the effectiveness of existing controls in mitigating the vulnerabilities

Option 3: Prioritize the vulnerabilities based on their severity and potential impact

Option 4: Engage external experts to conduct a detailed vulnerability assessment

Correct Response: 3

Explanation: The BEST first step in analyzing residual vulnerabilities is to prioritize them based on their severity and potential impact. By prioritizing the vulnerabilities, the organization can ensure that resources are allocated effectively to address the most critical risks first, reducing the overall risk to the organization.

Knowledge Area: Domain 5: Assessment/Audit of Security and Privacy Controls

----

Question Number: 166

Question: When analyzing identified residual vulnerabilities, what is the PRIMARY consideration?

Option 1: Alignment with industry standards and best practices

Option 2: Potential impact on the organization's operations and assets

Option 3: Availability of resources to mitigate the vulnerabilities

Option 4: Compatibility with existing security infrastructure

Correct Response: 1

Explanation: The PRIMARY consideration when analyzing identified residual vulnerabilities is alignment with industry standards and best practices. Ensuring that the vulnerabilities are addressed in accordance with recognized standards and best practices helps to ensure that the organization's security posture is in line with industry norms and that effective measures are in place to mitigate the risks.

Knowledge Area: Domain 5: Assessment/Audit of Security and Privacy Controls

----

Question Number: 167

Question: What is the MOST important factor to consider when prioritizing residual vulnerabilities?

Option 1: Severity of the vulnerabilities and their potential impact

Option 2: Complexity of mitigating the vulnerabilities

Option 3: Availability of resources to address the vulnerabilities

Option 4: Compliance with regulatory requirements

Correct Response: 1

Explanation: The MOST important factor to consider when prioritizing residual vulnerabilities is the severity of the vulnerabilities and their potential impact. Prioritizing based on severity ensures that the most critical risks are addressed first, reducing the overall potential impact on the organization. By focusing on the most severe vulnerabilities, resources can be allocated effectively to mitigate the highest-risk areas.

Knowledge Area: Domain 5: Assessment/Audit of Security and Privacy Controls

----

Question Number: 168

Question: Scenario: An organization has identified multiple risks from a recent risk assessment. What is the BEST first step in prioritizing the responses to these risks?

Option 1: Assess the potential impact and likelihood of each risk

Option 2: Consult with stakeholders to gather input on risk priorities

Option 3: Review industry standards and best practices for risk mitigation

Option 4: Develop an action plan to address all identified risks

Correct Response: 1

Explanation: The BEST first step in prioritizing the responses to multiple risks is to assess the potential impact and likelihood of each risk. This step involves analyzing the severity of each risk and its likelihood of occurrence. By assessing the risks, the organization can determine their relative importance and prioritize the responses accordingly.

Knowledge Area: Domain 5: Assessment/Audit of Security and Privacy Controls

----

Question Number: 169

Question: Scenario: An organization has completed a security assessment and identified several residual vulnerabilities. What is the correct approach to analyze and address these vulnerabilities?

Option 1: Conduct a detailed root cause analysis for each vulnerability

Option 2: Seek external assistance to validate the identified vulnerabilities

Option 3: Prioritize the vulnerabilities based on their severity and potential impact

Option 4: Develop an action plan to address all identified vulnerabilities

Correct Response: 3

Explanation: The correct approach to analyze and address residual vulnerabilities is to prioritize them based on their severity and potential impact. By prioritizing, the organization can focus on addressing the vulnerabilities that pose the greatest risk first. Developing an action plan based on this prioritization ensures that resources are allocated effectively, mitigating the identified vulnerabilities in a systematic manner.

Knowledge Area: Domain 5: Assessment/Audit of Security and Privacy Controls

----

Question Number: 170

Question: Penetration testing revealed default credentials on remote access points. What resources are needed for remediation?

Option 1: Budget approval

Option 2: Technical staff

Option 3: Policy update

Option 4: Training program

Correct Response: 2

Explanation: Technical staff resources are needed to update default credentials.

Knowledge Area: Domain 5: Assessment/Audit of Security and Privacy Controls

----

Question Number: 171

Question: An external auditor has completed their evaluation of security controls. What should they provide for the authorization package?

Option 1: Audit findings report

Option 2: Attestation of compliance

Option 3: Security roadmap

Option 4: Issue remediations

Correct Response: 1

Explanation: The findings report informs the authorization decision.

Knowledge Area: Domain 6: Authorization/Approval of Information System

----

Question Number: 172

Question: A system is undergoing its periodic authorization review next month. Which documentation is MOST critical?

Option 1: Accreditation statement

Option 2: Interconnection agreements

Option 3: Control test results

Option 4: Incident response plan

Correct Response: 3

Explanation: Control test results demonstrate security posture.

Knowledge Area: Domain 6: Authorization/Approval of Information System

----

Question Number: 173

Question: You need to compile documentation for an internal system's upcoming reauthorization. What provides the LEAST value?

Option 1: Risk assessment

Option 2: Previous authorization letter

Option 3: Control gap analysis

Option 4: Penetration test report

Correct Response: 2

Explanation: Previous auth. decisions have limited current value.

Knowledge Area: Domain 6: Authorization/Approval of Information System

----

Question Number: 174

Question: An internal audit is assessing risks related to ICS systems. Which factor represents the BIGGEST risk indicator?

Option 1: Patching cadence

Option 2: Physical access controls

Option 3: Age of equipment

Option 4: Malware protection

Correct Response: 2

Explanation: Poor physical access controls are a major ICS risk.

Knowledge Area: Domain 6: Authorization/Approval of Information System

----

Question Number: 175

Question: A threat assessment revealed vulnerabilities in internet-facing web applications containing sensitive customer data. Which risk treatment option would provide the GREATEST security enhancement?

Option 1: Purchase cyber insurance

Option 2: Classify data

Option 3: Harden web servers

Option 4: Implement WAF

Correct Response: 4

Explanation: A WAF provides the greatest benefit against web app vulnerabilities with sensitive data.

Knowledge Area: Domain 6: Authorization/Approval of Information System

----

Question Number: 176

Question: A risk assessment identified vulnerable wireless access points. Which risk treatment would MOST reduce the associated risks?

Option 1: Accept the risk

Option 2: Disable wireless

Option 3: Encrypt transmissions

Option 4: Limit access locations

Correct Response: 2

Explanation: Disabling wireless functionality avoids related vulnerabilities.

Knowledge Area: Domain 6: Authorization/Approval of Information System

----

Question Number: 177

Question: Unnecessary server services with known vulnerabilities were found on Internet-facing systems. Which risk treatment is MOST effective?

Option 1: Apply patches

Option 2: Disable services

Option 3: Harden configurations

Option 4: Increase monitoring

Correct Response: 2

Explanation: Disabling unnecessary services avoids their inherent risks.

Knowledge Area: Domain 6: Authorization/Approval of Information System

----

Question Number: 178

Question: risk assessment identified potential costs from breaches of sensitive customer data. Which risk treatment would transfer those costs?

Option 1: Encrypt data

Option 2: Purchase insurance

Option 3: Harden systems

Option 4: Train personnel

Correct Response: 2

Explanation: Cyber insurance transfers financial risk of a breach.

Knowledge Area: Domain 6: Authorization/Approval of Information System

----

Question Number: 179

Question: Threat modeling revealed data exfiltration risks for an outsourced CRM system. Which treatment would BEST transfer that risk?

Option 1: Enforce data policies

Option 2: Renegotiate contracts

Option 3: Encrypt data transmissions

Option 4: Accept the risk

Correct Response: 2

Explanation: Updated vendor SLAs transfer responsibility for data exfiltration risks.

Knowledge Area: Domain 6: Authorization/Approval of Information System

----

Question Number: 180

Question: The internal audit revealed excessive user permissions. Which option would BEST mitigate associated risks?

Option 1: Increase audits

Option 2: Access certification

Option 3: Privilege escalation controls

Option 4: Accept the risk

Correct Response: 2

Explanation: Access certification mitigates risks from excessive entitlements.

Knowledge Area: Domain 6: Authorization/Approval of Information System

----

Question Number: 181

Question: Threat modeling identified account hijacking risks on a cloud-based HR system. Which option BEST shares identity management risks?

Option 1: MFA requirements

Option 2: Password policies

Option 3: Federated login

Option 4: Access certifications

Correct Response: 3

Explanation: Federated login shares identity risks with the cloud provider.

Knowledge Area: Domain 6: Authorization/Approval of Information System

----

Question Number: 182

Question: A merger has introduced new backup systems. Which option BEST shares availability risks?

Option 1: Redundant infrastructure

Option 2: Business continuity plan

Option 3: Scheduled restorations

Option 4: Backup reporting

Correct Response: 2

Explanation: The BCP defines shared recovery responsibilities.

Knowledge Area: Domain 6: Authorization/Approval of Information System

----

Question Number: 183

Question: Unpatched open source libraries were found in proprietary software. Which option BEST shares remediation risks?

Option 1: SLA enforcement

Option 2: Vulnerability scanning

Option 3: Library replacements

Option 4: Developer training

Correct Response: 1

Explanation: The SLA defines patching responsibilities.

Knowledge Area: Domain 6: Authorization/Approval of Information System

----

Question Number: 184

Question: A firewall was implemented to address external attack risks on a payment system. Penetration testing indicates the firewall mitigates 60% of identified risks. What is the residual risk level?

Option 1: Low

Option 2: Moderate

Option 3: High

Option 4: Very high

Correct Response: 2

Explanation: Moderate residual risk remains after partial risk treatment.

Knowledge Area: Domain 6: Authorization/Approval of Information System

----

Question Number: 185

Question: A legacy operating system was upgraded to address vulnerabilities. Scanning reveals the new OS mitigates 90% of known risks. What is the residual risk level?

Option 1: Low

Option 2: Moderate

Option 3: High

Option 4: Very high

Correct Response: 1

Explanation: Low residual risk remains after extensive risk treatment.

Knowledge Area: Domain 6: Authorization/Approval of Information System

----

Question Number: 186

Question: Scenario: An organization is planning to implement significant changes to its information system and environment. What is the BEST first step to determine the potential threat and impact to the operation of the information system and environment?

Option 1: Conduct a risk assessment to identify potential threats and impacts

Option 2: Review industry best practices for implementing changes

Option 3: Consult with stakeholders to gather their input on potential threats and impacts

Option 4: Develop an action plan to address all identified risks

Correct Response: 1

Explanation: The BEST first step to determine the potential threat and impact to the operation of the information system and environment is to conduct a risk assessment. This step helps identify and evaluate potential threats and impacts associated with the changes. By conducting a comprehensive risk assessment, the organization can understand the potential risks, prioritize responses, and develop effective mitigation strategies.

Knowledge Area: Domain 7: Continuous Monitoring

Question Number: 187

Question: When determining the potential threat and impact to the operation of the information system and environment, what is the PRIMARY consideration?

Option 1: Compliance with industry regulations and standards

Option 2: Alignment with the organization's objectives and goals

Option 3: Potential for disruption to critical business processes

Option 4: Availability of resources for implementing the changes

Correct Response: 3

Explanation: The PRIMARY consideration when determining the potential threat and impact to the operation of the information system and environment is the potential for disruption to critical business processes. Understanding the impact on the organization's core operations helps assess the severity of potential threats and their implications for the overall performance and continuity of the business.

Knowledge Area: Domain 7: Continuous Monitoring

Question Number: 188

Question: A new external network connection is proposed for a sensitive system. This exceeds the organization's normal risk tolerance. What is recommended?

Option 1: Additional safeguards

Option 2: Limit data access

Option 3: Reduce connection speed

Option 4: Deny the request

Correct Response: 4

Explanation: Changes exceeding risk tolerance should be denied.

Knowledge Area: Domain 7: Continuous Monitoring

Question Number: 189

Question: What is the MOST important factor to consider when evaluating the impact and risks of a proposed change?

Option 1: Potential benefits and opportunities associated with the change

Option 2: Complexity and technical feasibility of implementing the change

Option 3: Potential adverse effects and disruptions to existing systems or processes

Option 4: Availability of resources and support for implementing the change

Correct Response: 3

Explanation: The MOST important factor to consider when evaluating the impact and risks of a proposed change is the potential adverse effects and disruptions to existing systems or processes. It is crucial to assess the potential risks and unintended consequences that the change may introduce to ensure minimal disruptions to the organization's operations. Understanding the potential risks helps in implementing appropriate mitigation measures.

Knowledge Area: Domain 7: Continuous Monitoring

Question Number: 190

Question: Scenario: An organization has received a proposed change request for an enterprise-wide software upgrade. What is the correct approach to approve and document the proposed change?

Option 1: Conduct a technical review to assess the feasibility of the software upgrade

Option 2: Present the proposed change to the technical review board for evaluation

Option 3: Assign an appropriate change owner to coordinate and oversee the software upgrade

Option 4: Document the proposed change, including its impact and approval details

Correct Response: 4

Explanation: The correct approach to approve and document the proposed change for an enterprise-wide software upgrade is to document the proposed change, including its impact and approval details. This ensures that there is a formal record of the decision-making process, capturing the impact assessment and approval details. By documenting the proposed change, the organization maintains transparency and accountability in the change management process.

Knowledge Area: Domain 7: Continuous Monitoring

Question Number: 191

Question: Software-defined networking is being implemented. What should occur prior to cutover?

Option 1: Load testing

Option 2: Security policy updates

Option 3: Backout plan development

Option 4: Additional redundancy

Correct Response: 3

Explanation: Having a backout plan is critical before major changes like SDN cutover.

Knowledge Area: Domain 7: Continuous Monitoring

Question Number: 192

Question: What is the MOST important factor to consider when performing testing and verification of implemented changes?

Option 1: Completeness and accuracy of the test cases and scenarios

Option 2: Availability of resources for conducting the testing and verification

Option 3: Relevance and alignment of the changes with the system requirements

Option 4: Involvement of key stakeholders in the testing and verification process

Correct Response: 1

Explanation: The MOST important factor to consider when performing testing and verification of implemented changes is the completeness and accuracy of the test cases and scenarios. Thorough testing ensures that the changes have been implemented correctly and are functioning as intended. By using comprehensive and well-designed test cases and scenarios, the organization can identify any issues, defects, or gaps in the implementation, allowing for appropriate remediation.

Knowledge Area: Domain 7: Continuous Monitoring

Question Number: 193

Question: A new cloud email service is being rolled out across the organization. What change management task is critical?

Option 1: User acceptance testing

Option 2: Security controls review

Option 3: Data migration

Option 4: Training program development

Correct Response: 2

Explanation: Reviewing planned security controls is vital for cloud changes.

Knowledge Area: Domain 7: Continuous Monitoring

Question Number: 194

Question: The helpdesk system is being upgraded to the latest version. Which change task should occur first?

Option 1: Backout plan testing

Option 2: Role-based access review

Option 3: Business process validation

Option 4: Security patching schedule

Correct Response: 1

Explanation: Validating the backout plan takes priority for major IT system upgrades.

Knowledge Area: Domain 7: Continuous Monitoring

Question Number: 195

Question: Multi-factor authentication is being implemented for remote access. What change task is most important?

Option 1: Pilot program

Option 2: Training videos

Option 3: Implementation schedule

Option 4: Security policy update

Correct Response: 3

Explanation: An implementation schedule ensures systematic MFA roll-out.

Knowledge Area: Domain 7: Continuous Monitoring

Question Number: 196

Question: What is the MOST important factor to consider when monitoring network, physical, and personnel activities to detect unauthorized assets, personnel, and related activities?

Option 1: Availability of robust monitoring tools and technologies

Option 2: Timeliness and accuracy of incident detection and response

Option 3: Collaboration between different departments and teams

Option 4: Regular training and awareness programs for employees

Correct Response: 2

Explanation: The MOST important factor to consider when monitoring network, physical, and personnel activities to detect unauthorized assets, personnel, and related activities is the timeliness and accuracy of incident detection and response. Detecting unauthorized activities promptly and responding effectively helps mitigate potential risks and minimize the impact of unauthorized actions. Timely incident detection and response are crucial to mitigating the potential consequences of unauthorized activities.

Knowledge Area: Domain 7: Continuous Monitoring

Question Number: 197

Question: Scenario: An organization wants to enhance its ongoing assessments/audits to detect unauthorized assets, personnel, and related activities. What is the correct approach to achieve this goal?

Option 1: Implement security monitoring tools and technologies

Option 2: Conduct regular vulnerability assessments and penetration tests

Option 3: Establish incident response procedures and incident management teams

Option 4: Develop comprehensive security policies and procedures

Correct Response: 4

Explanation: The correct approach to enhance ongoing assessments/audits to detect unauthorized assets, personnel, and related activities is to develop comprehensive security policies and procedures. Well-defined policies and procedures establish clear guidelines for monitoring, auditing, and responding to unauthorized activities. They provide a framework for consistent and effective assessments/audits, ensuring that unauthorized entities are detected and addressed promptly.

Knowledge Area: Domain 7: Continuous Monitoring

Question Number: 198

Question: Which approach helps ensure vulnerability scanning has minimal impact on production systems?

Option 1: Schedule scans during maintenance windows

Option 2: Throttle scan rate

Option 3: Isolate scanned systems

Option 4: Use credentialed scanning

Correct Response: 2

Explanation: Throttling scan rate helps minimize scanning system impact.

Knowledge Area: Domain 7: Continuous Monitoring

Question Number: 199

Question: When reviewing automated logs and alerts for anomalies, what is the PRIMARY consideration?

Option 1: Availability of skilled analysts to analyze the logs and alerts

Option 2: Accuracy and reliability of the automated logging and alerting systems

Option 3: Relevance and significance of the identified anomalies

Option 4: Compliance with industry regulations and standards

Correct Response: 3

Explanation: The PRIMARY consideration when reviewing automated logs and alerts for anomalies is the relevance and significance of the identified anomalies. It is essential to prioritize the analysis of anomalies based on their potential impact and likelihood. By focusing on the most relevant and significant anomalies, organizations can allocate resources effectively and address the most critical security issues promptly.

Knowledge Area: Domain 7: Continuous Monitoring

Question Number: 200

Question: What data source is BEST for gaining awareness of counterfeit hardware risks?

Option 1: SANS Security Alerts

Option 2: CISA Alerts

Option 3: Device firmware analysis

Option 4: Social media monitoring

Correct Response: 2

Explanation: CISA alerts often contain notices of counterfeit hardware risks.

Knowledge Area: Domain 7: Continuous Monitoring

Amazing!

You have been studying very hard to this stage.

How is your exam preparation so far? Can the practice test meet your needs and expectation? I desperately desire your voice.

Please kindly consider

1. Visiting my exam practice test books and consider purchasing them to assist you to pass your target exam, though the direct links provided at the beginning of this book
2. Visiting my exam practice test courses held at Udemy though the direct links provided at the beginning of this book
3. Leaving a positive review and feedback to me though the direct book review links provided at the next page.

Keep going! See you at the end of the book.

Warm regards,

Walter

Direct URLs to visit all Walter's Practice Tests at Amazon

Visit Walter's author page:

http://WalterEducation.com

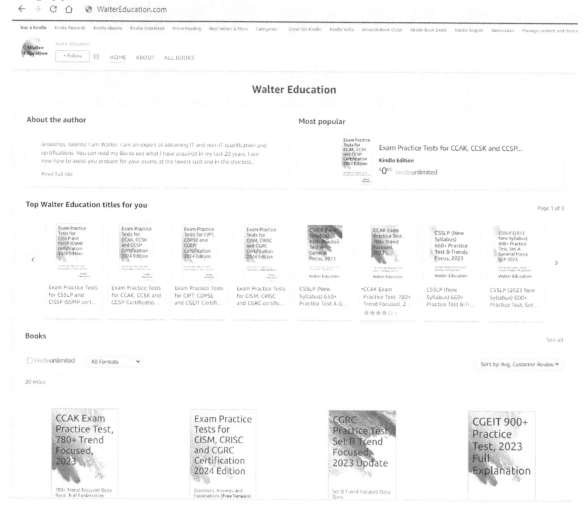

Or the **Links at Amazon Book Store:**

CCAK Exam Practice Test, 780+ Trend Focused, 2023	
Paperback Review URL:	- https://www.amazon.com/review/create-review?&asin=B0CJSXPYM7
Kindle eBook Review URL:	- https://www.amazon.com/review/create-review?&asin=B0CK9QQ44B

CERTIFIED DATA PRIVACY SOLUTIONS ENGINEER (CDPSE) 900+ PRACTICE TEST, 2023, FULL EXPLANATION	
Paperback Review URL:	- https://www.amazon.com/review/create-review?&asin=B0CGL3S5BH
Kindle eBook Review URL:	- https://www.amazon.com/review/create-review?&asin=B0CGL91NQ9

CGEIT 900+ Practice Test, 2023	
Paperback Review URL:	- https://www.amazon.com/review/create-review?&asin=B0CGW1Y1X9
Kindle eBook Review URL:	- https://www.amazon.com/review/create-review?&asin=B0CJ8388ZB

CIPT, Certified Information Privacy Technologists, Practice Test	
Paperback Review URL:	- https://www.amazon.com/review/create-review?&asin=B0CJ4DLHG2
Kindle eBook Review URL:	- https://www.amazon.com/review/create-review?&asin=B0CJ72MR4M

CRISC 1200+ Practice Test, 2023 (Exam Simulation and Core & Advanced Knowledge)	
Paperback Review URL:	- https://www.amazon.com/review/create-review?&asin=B0CJ43R78T
Kindle eBook Review URL:	- https://www.amazon.com/review/create-review?&asin=B0CJ72JJLY

CISM 1050+ Practice Test,2023 Updated, Set B - Trends Focused, ISACA	
Paperback Review URL:	- https://www.amazon.com/review/create-review?&asin=B0CJSNR5Z2
Kindle eBook Review URL:	- https://www.amazon.com/review/create-review?&asin=B0CJVWHJHW

CISM 1050+ Practice Test A - Core Focus, ISACA	
Paperback Review URL:	- https://www.amazon.com/review/create-review?&asin=B0CJL2HD1R
Kindle eBook Review URL:	- https://www.amazon.com/review/create-review?&asin=B0CJVSQ6Z6

CCSKv4 900+ Practice Test 2023, Full Explanation	
Paperback Review URL:	- https://www.amazon.com/review/create-review?&asin=B0CFX2S7D8
Kindle eBook Review URL:	- https://www.amazon.com/review/create-review?&asin=B0CFVLS8ZH

CSSLP (2023 New Syllabus) 600+ Practice Test, Set A General Focus	
Paperback Review URL:	- https://www.amazon.com/review/create-review?&asin=B0CK3VTR9D
Kindle eBook Review URL:	- https://www.amazon.com/review/create-review?&asin=PENDING

CSSLP (New Syllabus) 660+ Practice Test B-Trends Focus, SEP 2023	
Paperback Review URL:	- https://www.amazon.com/review/create-review?&asin=B0CK3XGCBN
Kindle eBook Review URL:	- https://www.amazon.com/review/create-review?&asin=PENDING

CISSP-ISSMP 650+ Practice Test, 2023 New syllabus, Set A Core Focused	
Paperback Review URL:	- https://www.amazon.com/review/create-review?&asin=B0CJLLL4HP
Kindle eBook Review URL:	- https://www.amazon.com/review/create-review?&asin=B0CK2Y6XR7

CISSP-ISSMP 650+ Practice Test, 2023 New syllabus, Set B Trends Focused, ISC2	
Paperback Review URL:	- https://www.amazon.com/review/create-review?&asin=B0CJLMV48G
Kindle eBook Review URL:	- https://www.amazon.com/review/create-review?&asin=B0CK2X7CLL

Practice Test for Certified Cloud Security Professional (CCSP): 900+ Practice Test	
Paperback Review URL:	- https://www.amazon.com/review/create-review?&asin=B0CFCLW7HJ
Kindle eBook Review URL:	- https://www.amazon.com/review/create-review?&asin=B0CFKSVKSS

CGRC Practice Test, Set A Data Bank, Learn & Exam, 2023 Update	
Paperback Review URL:	- https://www.amazon.com/review/create-review?&asin=B0CJBC5MX1
Kindle eBook Review URL:	- https://www.amazon.com/review/create-review?&asin=B0CJYQVM22

CGRC Practice Test, Set B Trend Focused, 2023	
Paperback Review URL:	- https://www.amazon.com/review/create-review?&asin=B0CJ43Z8N6
Kindle eBook Review URL:	- https://www.amazon.com/review/create-review?&asin=B0CJ72HWY2

How to give a Review and Rating:

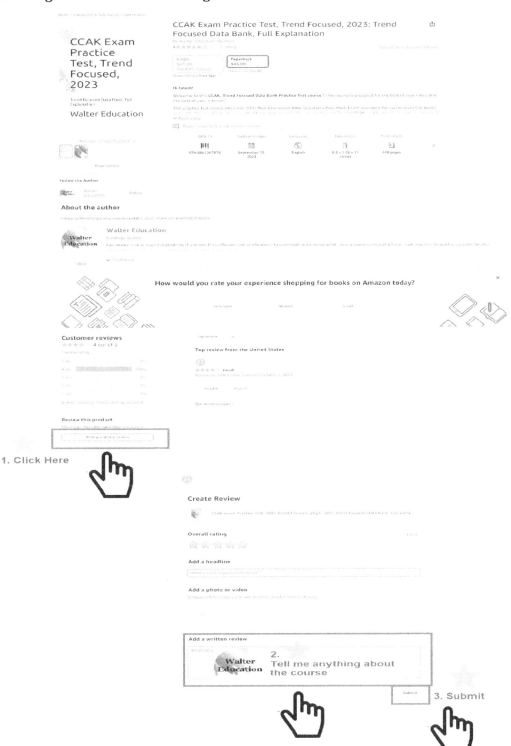

1. Click Here

2. Tell me anything about the course

3. Submit

Question Number: 201

Question: Scenario: An organization is actively participating in response planning for a potential cyber event. What is the correct approach to ensure response activities are coordinated with internal and external stakeholders?

Option 1: Develop a communication plan to establish channels for information sharing

Option 2: Conduct regular coordination meetings with key stakeholders

Option 3: Assign roles and responsibilities to internal and external stakeholders

Option 4: Share incident response plans and procedures with external partners

Correct Response: 3

Explanation: The correct approach to ensure response activities are coordinated with internal and external stakeholders is to assign roles and responsibilities to internal and external stakeholders. By clearly defining and communicating the roles and responsibilities, the organization can ensure a coordinated response effort among all stakeholders. This approach helps establish accountability, streamline communication, and enhance the effectiveness of the response activities.

Knowledge Area: Domain 7: Continuous Monitoring

Question Number: 202

Question: Scenario: An organization has experienced a cyber event and is actively participating in response planning. What is the BEST first step in updating documentation, strategies, and tactics incorporating lessons learned?

Option 1: Conduct a thorough analysis of the incident and identify key lessons learned

Option 2: Review existing documentation and identify areas for improvement based on lessons learned

Option 3: Update incident response plans and procedures to reflect the lessons learned

Option 4: Communicate the lessons learned to relevant stakeholders and update response strategies

Correct Response: 1

Explanation: The BEST first step in updating documentation, strategies, and tactics incorporating lessons learned is to conduct a thorough analysis of the incident and identify key lessons learned. This step involves reviewing the incident, understanding the root causes and impacts, and extracting valuable insights to improve future response efforts. By conducting a comprehensive analysis, the organization can identify specific areas for improvement and ensure that the documentation, strategies, and tactics are updated accordingly.

Knowledge Area: Domain 7: Continuous Monitoring

Question Number: 203

Question: Scenario: An organization has experienced a significant cyber event and wants to update its incident response documentation and strategies based on lessons learned. What is the correct approach to update the documentation and strategies?

Option 1: Conduct a comprehensive review of the incident, identify key insights, and update the documentation and strategies accordingly

Option 2: Engage external consultants to provide recommendations for updating the documentation and strategies

Option 3: Conduct employee training sessions to disseminate the lessons learned and update the documentation and strategies

Option 4: Establish a cross-functional team to review and update the documentation and strategies based on lessons learned

Correct Response: 1

Explanation: The correct approach to update the incident response documentation and strategies based on lessons learned is to conduct a comprehensive review of the incident, identify key insights, and update the documentation and strategies accordingly. This ensures that the updates are based on a thorough understanding of the incident and the specific lessons learned. By conducting a comprehensive review, the organization can incorporate valuable insights and improve its response capabilities for future cyber events.

Knowledge Area: Domain 7: Continuous Monitoring

Question Number: 204

Question: New regulations require monitoring of PII data exposure via cloud services. What should be implemented?

Option 1: DLP scanning of cloud storage

Option 2: Agent-based cloud workload scanning

Option 3: Cloud access proxy and logging

Option 4: Annual cloud vendor security audits

Correct Response: 1

Explanation: DLP scanning is needed to monitor PII in cloud storage.

Knowledge Area: Domain 7: Continuous Monitoring

Question Number: 205

Question: New criteria for the Cybersecurity Maturity Model Certification impacts monitoring scope. What helps ensure maintain compliance?

Option 1: Engage external audit assistance

Option 2: Develop gap assessment plan

Option 3: Purchase integrated GRC platform

Option 4: Increase vulnerability scanning frequency

Correct Response: 2

Explanation: A CMMC gap plan will identify monitoring needs.

Knowledge Area: Domain 7: Continuous Monitoring

Question Number: 206

Question: A new cloud email system is being implemented across the organization. What is the BEST metric for the CISO to include in monthly updates to maintain ATO?

Option 1: Employee training completion

Option 2: Planned security control gap analysis

Option 3: Security incident response trends

Option 4: System vulnerability scanning results

Correct Response: 2

Explanation: Gaps in planned cloud controls are most relevant for ATO.

Knowledge Area: Domain 7: Continuous Monitoring

Question Number: 207

Question: The CXO has requested a weekly phishing campaign update to stay informed on user security awareness. What is the BEST metric for the CISO to report?

Option 1: Simulated phishing emails sent

Option 2: Phishing click-through rate

Option 3: Training module completion percentage

Option 4: User password resets requested

Correct Response: 2

Explanation: Click-through rates convey the effectiveness of phishing simulations.

Knowledge Area: Domain 7: Continuous Monitoring

Question Number: 208

Question: A new financial application is being deployed containing sensitive customer data. What is the FIRST step to update the risk register?

Option 1: Classify data sensitivity

Option 2: Develop security test plan

Option 3: Update system inventory list

Option 4: Assign risk ranking

Correct Response: 4

Explanation: The risk ranking must be assigned first.

Knowledge Area: Domain 7: Continuous Monitoring

Question Number: 209

Question: The help desk system is being upgraded. What requires an update in the risk register after implementation?

Option 1: Asset inventory list

Option 2: Data classification

Option 3: Breach impact estimates

Option 4: Control test results

Correct Response: 4

Explanation: Updated control testing results validate security.

Knowledge Area: Domain 7: Continuous Monitoring

Question Number: 210

Question: Regulations expanded to require retention of communications data for 7 years. What should the risk treatment plan address?

Option 1: Increase email storage quotas

Option 2: Implement archiving solution

Option 3: Restrict internal messaging apps

Option 4: Notify employees of new retention rules

Correct Response: 2

Explanation: An archiving system is needed to meet expanded retention requirements.

Knowledge Area: Domain 7: Continuous Monitoring

Question Number: 211

Question: Cloud migration was completed for several business applications. What risk treatment priority needs updating?

Option 1: Cloud access management

Option 2: Vendor management program

Option 3: Data classification procedures

Option 4: Internal network segregation

Correct Response: 1

Explanation: Updating cloud access controls is now a priority.

Knowledge Area: Domain 7: Continuous Monitoring

Question Number: 212

Question: Improperly configured AWS S3 buckets exposed files. What helps prevent this in the future?

Option 1: Conduct remediation training

Option 2: Remove public access options

Option 3: Increase IAM role auditing

Option 4: Review bucket policies more frequently

Correct Response: 2

Explanation: Removing public access is key to remediate misconfigurations.

Knowledge Area: Domain 7: Continuous Monitoring

Question Number: 213

Question: Mergers and acquisitions integration is kicking off. What should the remediation plan update FIRST?

Option 1: Security policy consolidation

Option 2: Staff training program development

Option 3: Asset inventory integration

Option 4: Compliance certification roadmap

Correct Response: 1

Explanation: Policy remediation drives integration efforts.

Knowledge Area: Domain 7: Continuous Monitoring

Question Number: 214

Question: Scenario: An organization is planning to decommission an information system. What is the BEST first step in determining the decommissioning requirements?

Option 1: Assess the system's current functionality and usage

Option 2: Identify the system's dependencies and interconnections

Option 3: Evaluate regulatory and compliance requirements

Option 4: Engage stakeholders to gather input on decommissioning requirements

Correct Response: 1

Explanation: The BEST first step in determining the decommissioning requirements is to assess the system's current functionality and usage. This step involves understanding the purpose and scope of the system, as well as evaluating its current state and relevance to the organization. By assessing the system's functionality and usage, the organization can determine the extent of decommissioning required and gather essential information for further planning.

Knowledge Area: Domain 7: Continuous Monitoring

Question Number: 215

Question: When determining information system decommissioning requirements, what is the PRIMARY consideration?

Option 1: Compliance with regulatory and legal obligations

Option 2: Environmental impact and sustainability considerations

Option 3: Preservation of data integrity and security

Option 4: Cost-effectiveness of the decommissioning process

Correct Response: 4

Explanation: The PRIMARY consideration when determining information system decommissioning requirements is the cost-effectiveness of the decommissioning process. Organizations need to assess the financial implications of decommissioning, including associated costs such as data migration, hardware disposal, and potential impacts on related systems. Evaluating cost-effectiveness ensures that resources are allocated efficiently and that the decommissioning process aligns with the organization's budget and priorities.

Knowledge Area: Domain 7: Continuous Monitoring

Question Number: 216

Question: What is the MOST important factor to consider when identifying dependencies and interconnections during information system decommissioning?

Option 1: Impact on other systems and processes

Option 2: Compatibility with legacy infrastructure and technologies

Option 3: Potential disruption to business operations

Option 4: Availability of resources for the decommissioning process

Correct Response: 1

Explanation: The MOST important factor to consider when identifying dependencies and interconnections during information system decommissioning is the impact on other systems and processes. Understanding how the system being decommissioned interacts with other systems and processes is crucial to minimize potential disruptions and ensure a smooth transition. By identifying dependencies and interconnections, the organization can mitigate risks and plan for any necessary adjustments or replacements.

Knowledge Area: Domain 7: Continuous Monitoring

Question Number: 217

Question: When communicating the decommissioning of an information system, what is the PRIMARY consideration?

Option 1: Accuracy and clarity of the information being communicated

Option 2: Sensitivity to potential concerns and impacts on stakeholders

Option 3: Compliance with legal and regulatory requirements for notification

Option 4: Timeliness and effectiveness of the communication process

Correct Response: 2

Explanation: The PRIMARY consideration when communicating the decommissioning of an information system is sensitivity to potential concerns and impacts on stakeholders. It is important to consider how the decommissioning may affect stakeholders, such as employees, customers, and partners, and to address their concerns proactively. By being sensitive to their needs and providing clear information, the organization can mitigate potential negative impacts and maintain stakeholder trust.

Knowledge Area: Domain 7: Continuous Monitoring

Question Number: 218

Question: Scenario: An organization is planning to decommission a critical information system. What is the correct approach to communicate the decommissioning to stakeholders?

Option 1: Develop a formal communication plan, including key messages and target audience

Option 2: Send a mass email to all employees and stakeholders announcing the decommissioning

Option 3: Schedule a series of town hall meetings to discuss the decommissioning

Option 4: Engage a public relations firm to manage the communication process

Correct Response: 1

Explanation: The correct approach to communicate the decommissioning of a critical information system to stakeholders is to develop a formal communication plan, including key messages and a target audience. A communication plan ensures that the organization communicates the decommissioning in a planned, consistent, and effective manner. By identifying key messages and the appropriate target audience, the organization can tailor the communication to meet the specific needs and concerns of stakeholders, ensuring that they are well-informed and engaged throughout the decommissioning process.

Knowledge Area: Domain 7: Continuous Monitoring

Question Number: 219

Question: Scenario: An organization is planning to remove an information system from operations. What is the BEST first step in the removal process?

Option 1: Conduct a thorough inventory of the system's hardware and software components

Option 2: Identify dependencies and interconnections with other systems and processes

Option 3: Develop a detailed removal plan outlining necessary steps and timelines

Option 4: Communicate the removal plan and its implications to relevant stakeholders

Correct Response: 1

Explanation: The BEST first step in the removal process of an information system is to conduct a thorough inventory of its hardware and software components. This step ensures that all components are identified and accounted for, enabling proper planning and coordination for the removal. By conducting an inventory, the organization can assess the scope of the removal process and identify any potential challenges or dependencies.

Knowledge Area: Domain 7: Continuous Monitoring

Question Number: 220

Question: When removing an information system from operations, what is the PRIMARY consideration?

Option 1: Preservation of data integrity and security

Option 2: Compliance with legal and regulatory requirements

Option 3: Minimization of operational disruptions

Option 4: Proper disposal or repurposing of system components

Correct Response: 1

Explanation: The PRIMARY consideration when removing an information system from operations is the preservation of data integrity and security. It is crucial to ensure that sensitive data is properly handled and protected throughout the removal process to prevent unauthorized access or data breaches. By prioritizing data integrity and security, the organization can mitigate risks and maintain the confidentiality, integrity, and availability of its information assets.

Knowledge Area: Domain 7: Continuous Monitoring

Question Number: 221

Question: What is the MOST important factor to consider when identifying dependencies and interconnections during the removal of an information system?

Option 1: Potential impact on other systems and processes

Option 2: Compatibility with legacy infrastructure and technologies

Option 3: Complexity and technical feasibility of the removal process

Option 4: Availability of resources for the removal process

Correct Response: 1

Explanation: The MOST important factor to consider when identifying dependencies and interconnections during the removal of an information system is the potential impact on other systems and processes. It is essential to understand how the system being removed interacts with other systems and processes to minimize potential disruptions and ensure a smooth transition. By identifying dependencies and interconnections, the organization can mitigate risks and plan for any necessary adjustments or replacements.

Knowledge Area: Domain 7: Continuous Monitoring

Amazing!

You have worked very hard to this stage.

How is your exam preparation so far? Can the practice test meet your needs and expectation? I desperately desire your voice.

Please kindly consider leaving a review and feedback to me and I have prepared a free gift as a token of gratitude. For details, please refer to the first Three pages at the beginning of this book.

Keep going! See you at the end of the book.

Warm regards,

Walter

Question Number: 222

Question: The CIO has requested a review of user access controls across critical systems to reduce risk. Which of the following is the BEST approach for the risk practitioner?

Option 1: Review entitlements against policy

Option 2: Conduct access certification

Option 3: Implement MFA globally

Option 4: Rescind excessive privileges

Correct Response: 2

Explanation: Access certification involves reviewing and confirming user access is appropriate, which helps reduce risk.

Knowledge Area: Real_Life_Exam_Sim

Question Number: 223

Question: Which process involves communicating risk-related info between stakeholders to support strategy and objectives?

Option 1: Risk identification

Option 2: Risk monitoring

Option 3: Risk governance

Option 4: Risk communication

Correct Response: 4

Explanation: Risk communication facilitates sharing risk insights between stakeholders to align on priorities.

Knowledge Area: Real_Life_Exam_Sim

Question Number: 224

Question: Which process involves determining risk likelihood and potential impacts to help prioritize responses?

Option 1: Risk analysis

Option 2: Risk framing

Option 3: Risk treatment

Option 4: Risk assessment

Correct Response: 4

Explanation: Risk assessment evaluates probability and impact to help rank risks.

Knowledge Area: Real_Life_Exam_Sim

Question Number: 225

Question: Jill is performing qualitative risk analysis for a project using risk urgency assessment. Which artifact will NOT help with this activity?

Option 1: Risk register

Option 2: Scope baseline

Option 3: Stakeholder analysis

Option 4: Progress reports

Correct Response: 4

Explanation: Progress reports track status but don't help assess risk impacts.

Knowledge Area: Real_Life_Exam_Sim

Question Number: 226

Question: A project manager wants to reduce potential financial losses from supply chain disruptions. What is the most effective risk mitigation?

Option 1: Dual source critical components

Option 2: Improve inventory forecasting

Option 3: Increase safety stock levels

Option 4: Negotiate supplier discounts

Correct Response: 1

Explanation: Dual sourcing critical items mitigates supply chain risk.

Knowledge Area: Real_Life_Exam_Sim

Question Number: 227

Question: What provides the most valuable input when assessing disaster recovery capabilities?

Option 1: More systems meeting RTOs

Option 2: Fewer systems needing plans

Option 3: More tested systems

Option 4: Less systems with long RTOs

Correct Response: 2

Explanation: The number of systems with long RTOs highlights gaps.

Knowledge Area: Real_Life_Exam_Sim

Question Number: 228

Question: An organization is adopting a new cloud infrastructure platform. What activity will provide the most risk insights before migrating applications?

Option 1: Review vendor security policy compliance

Option 2: Conduct due diligence on provider security controls

Option 3: Update internal security and architecture standards

Option 4: Train staff on new administration procedures

Correct Response: 2

Explanation: Conducting thorough due diligence on the cloud provider's security controls and architecture before adopting the platform will provide valuable risk insights.

Knowledge Area: Real_Life_Exam_Sim

Question Number: 229

Question: To optimize resources for risk management, what input should guide the focus areas?

Option 1: Industry benchmarking results

Option 2: Risk register totals

Option 3: Senior management concerns

Option 4: Assessment of risk appetite and tolerance

Correct Response: 4

Explanation: Aligning risk management focus with organizational risk appetite and tolerance designated by senior leaders will help optimize resource allocation.

Knowledge Area: Real_Life_Exam_Sim

Question Number: 230

Question: A supply chain manager wants to reduce financial risks from potential component shortages. What option would be most effective?

Option 1: Increase inventory at distribution centers

Option 2: Improve demand forecasting accuracy

Option 3: Dual source critical materials and parts

Option 4: Negotiate volume discounts with suppliers

Correct Response: 3

Explanation: Dual sourcing key components through alternate suppliers reduces supply chain disruption risks.

Knowledge Area: Real_Life_Exam_Sim

Question Number: 231

Question: What data provides the most valuable input when evaluating disaster recovery capabilities?

Option 1: Higher percentage of systems meeting RTOs

Option 2: Fewer systems requiring disaster recovery plans

Option 3: More systems undergoing testing

Option 4: Lower percentage of systems with lengthy RTOs

Correct Response: 4

Explanation: A lower percentage of systems with lengthy recovery time objectives indicates gaps in disaster recovery capabilities.

Knowledge Area: Real_Life_Exam_Sim

Question Number: 232

Question: When implementing encryption, what is critical for assessing residual risk?

Option 1: Data retention rules

Option 2: Cloud architecture

Option 3: Destruction procedures

Option 4: Key management

Correct Response: 4

Explanation: Effective key management is crucial for managing encryption residual risk.

Knowledge Area: Real_Life_Exam_Sim

Question Number: 233

Question: How can risk management help justify additional investment in network resilience?

Option 1: Present related risk trends

Option 2: Compare to benchmarks

Option 3: Highlight ROI

Option 4: Show reduced risk exposure

Correct Response: 4

Explanation: Quantifying risk reduction demonstrates value gained.

Knowledge Area: Real_Life_Exam_Sim

Question Number: 234

Question: After internal audit finds IAM control gaps, what should the risk practitioner focus on?

Option 1: Replacing the system

Option 2: Training IAM staff

Option 3: Verifying risk owner awareness

Option 4: Performing added assessment

Correct Response: 3

Explanation: Ensuring risk owners understand the implications is critical.

Knowledge Area: Real_Life_Exam_Sim

Question Number: 235

Question: A business unit wants to accept the risk of weak password controls in a software application. What should be the response?

Option 1: Obtain an exception

Option 2: Proceed as planned

Option 3: Develop stronger passwords

Option 4: Select a more secure application

Correct Response: 4

Explanation: An alternative with stronger controls should be selected.

Knowledge Area: Real_Life_Exam_Sim

Question Number: 236

Question: What metric evaluates and compares the efficiency of different IT investments?

Option 1: Total cost of ownership

Option 2: Redundancy level

Option 3: Return on investment

Option 4: Recovery time objective

Correct Response: 3

Explanation: ROI evaluates and compares the efficiency of investments.

Knowledge Area: Real_Life_Exam_Sim

Question Number: 237

Question: Who should a data loss risk at a cloud provider be assigned to?

Option 1: CRO

Option 2: Vendor manager

Option 3: Data owner

Option 4: Senior management

Correct Response: 3

Explanation: The data owner should be the risk owner.

Knowledge Area: Real_Life_Exam_Sim

Question Number: 238

Question: After an audit finds major control gaps at a cloud provider, what should happen next?

Option 1: Verify with a follow-up audit

Option 2: Review contract for penalties

Option 3: Analyze business impact

Option 4: Migrate data to new provider

Correct Response: 3

Explanation: The impact to the business should be analyzed first.

Knowledge Area: Real_Life_Exam_Sim

Question Number: 239

Question: Getting the right information to the right people when needed aligns with which risk?

Option 1: Integrity risk

Option 2: Availability risk

Option 3: Relevance risk

Option 4: Access risk

Correct Response: 3

Explanation: Ensuring information relevance addresses relevance risk.

Knowledge Area: Real_Life_Exam_Sim

Question Number: 240

Question: What term refers to the type of loss when unauthorized changes are made to a website?

Option 1: Loss of confidentiality

Option 2: Loss of integrity

Option 3: Loss of availability

Option 4: Loss of revenue

Correct Response: 2

Explanation: Loss of integrity refers to the type of loss that occurs when unauthorized changes are made to a website. It compromises the accuracy, completeness, or reliability of the information contained on the website.

Knowledge Area: Real_Life_Exam_Sim

Question Number: 241

Question: What control best limits access to sensitive data?

Option 1: Logon attempt monitoring

Option 2: Forced password changes

Option 3: Challenge response system

Option 4: Need-to-know access

Correct Response: 4

Explanation: Need-to-know access limits exposure.

Knowledge Area: Real_Life_Exam_Sim

Question Number: 242

Question: If risk mitigation differs from the approved plan, what should happen first?

Option 1: Revert the mitigation

Option 2: Validate mitigation adequacy

Option 3: Notify the CRO

Option 4: Update the risk register

Correct Response: 2

Explanation: The mitigation should be validated.

Knowledge Area: Real_Life_Exam_Sim

Question Number: 243

Question: If risk is now below appetite, what should be recommended?

Option 1: Reduce scenarios

Option 2: Optimize controls

Option 3: Realign appetite

Option 4: Cut risk budget

Correct Response: 2

Explanation: The control environment should be optimized.

Knowledge Area: Real_Life_Exam_Sim

Question Number: 244

Question: For outsourced IT security, who should own the controls?

Option 1: Organization's risk function

Option 2: Provider's audit function

Option 3: Organization's IT management

Option 4: Provider's security team

Correct Response: 1

Explanation: The organization retains responsibility.

Knowledge Area: Real_Life_Exam_Sim

Question Number: 245

Question: After a process change reduces risk, what should happen first?

Option 1: Reallocate resources

Option 2: Review KRIs

Option 3: Conduct analysis

Option 4: Update register

Correct Response: 3

Explanation: Analysis should validate reduced risk.

Knowledge Area: Real_Life_Exam_Sim

Question Number: 246

Question: An organization is permitting access to data from personal mobile devices. What is the most important factor when evaluating this risk?

Option 1: Amount of data accessed

Option 2: Device management capabilities

Option 3: Data classification level

Option 4: Type of personal device

Correct Response: 3

Explanation: The classification level of the data being accessed from personal devices is the most important factor when assessing the risk.

Knowledge Area: Real_Life_Exam_Sim

Question Number: 247

Question: In a mature risk management program, what best indicates the IT risk profile is current?

Option 1: Compliance manual

Option 2: Management assertion

Option 3: Risk questionnaire

Option 4: Risk register

Correct Response: 2

Explanation: Regular updates to the risk register provide the best evidence that the IT risk profile reflects the current state.

Knowledge Area: Real_Life_Exam_Sim

Question Number: 248

Question: How should training effectiveness be assessed after required security awareness training?

Option 1: Audit training materials

Option 2: Perform vulnerability testing

Option 3: Conduct social engineering

Option 4: Administer a training quiz

Correct Response: 3

Explanation: Social engineering testing best assesses real-world effectiveness of security awareness training.

Knowledge Area: Real_Life_Exam_Sim

Question Number: 249

Question: If the risk register has not been updated in a year, what should happen first?

Option 1: Redesign risk management

Option 2: Outsource risk updates

Option 3: Initiate risk reviews

Option 4: Replace old register

Correct Response: 3

Explanation: Key risk factors should be reviewed to identify necessary updates.

Knowledge Area: Real_Life_Exam_Sim

Question Number: 250

Question: Who should own the risk of a problematic technology?

Option 1: Business process owner

Option 2: CFO

Option 3: CRO

Option 4: IT system owner

Correct Response: 4

Explanation: The system owner should own technology risks.

Knowledge Area: Real_Life_Exam_Sim

Question Number: 251

Question: What is the most important risk management training topic for leadership?

Option 1: Strategic initiatives

Option 2: Resource allocation

Option 3: Risk appetite and tolerance

Option 4: Responsibilities

Correct Response: 3

Explanation: Understanding risk appetite is critical.

Knowledge Area: Real_Life_Exam_Sim

Question Number: 252

Question: Which is NOT an indicator of risk priority during qualitative analysis?

Option 1: Symptoms

Option 2: Warning signs

Option 3: Risk rating

Option 4: Project cost

Correct Response: 4

Explanation: Project cost does not indicate inherent risk priority.

Knowledge Area: Real_Life_Exam_Sim

Question Number: 253

Question: What control ensures users have appropriate but minimal access rights?

Option 1: Access control

Option 2: ID and authentication

Option 3: Audit and accountability

Option 4: System and comms protection

Correct Response: 1

Explanation: Access controls provide need-to-know access.

Knowledge Area: Real_Life_Exam_Sim

Question Number: 254

Question: What best indicates an improved risk-aware culture after security training?

Option 1: Fewer access resets

Option 2: More reported incidents

Option 3: Fewer help desk calls

Option 4: More identified system flaws

Correct Response: 2

Explanation: More willingness to report shows awareness.

Knowledge Area: Real_Life_Exam_Sim

Question Number: 255

Question: How can risk management best address cyber risks?

Option 1: Conduct executive training

Option 2: Follow industry practices

Option 3: Use risk framework

Option 4: Define responsibilities

Correct Response: 3

Explanation: The risk framework optimally governs cyber risk.

Knowledge Area: Real_Life_Exam_Sim

Question Number: 256

Question: The primary concern with production data in a test environment is:

Option 1: Test environment security

Option 2: Data availability

Option 3: Data readability

Option 4: Data sensitivity

Correct Response: 4

Explanation: Data sensitivity is the main concern.

Knowledge Area: Real_Life_Exam_Sim

Question Number: 257

Question: Which monitoring tool aspect ensures scalability?

Option 1: Customizability

Option 2: Sustainability

Option 3: Impact on performance

Option 4: Scalability

Correct Response: 4

Explanation: Scalability allows growth alignment.

Knowledge Area: Real_Life_Exam_Sim

Question Number: 258

Question: To minimize analytics risk from bad data, what helps most?

Option 1: Benchmark practices

Option 2: Review IP agreements

Option 3: Assess data sources

Option 4: Evaluate strategies

Correct Response: 3

Explanation: Reviewing data sources is critical.

Knowledge Area: Real_Life_Exam_Sim

Question Number: 259

Question: If code rework tickets exceed thresholds, what should be recommended?

Option 1: Implement training

Option 2: Do code reviews

Option 3: Perform root cause analysis

Option 4: Use version control

Correct Response: 3

Explanation: A root cause analysis will reveal reasons.

Knowledge Area: Real_Life_Exam_Sim

Question Number: 260

Question: What is most important to include in a risk report to management?

Option 1: Decreased key controls

Option 2: Changes in design

Option 3: Increased residual risk

Option 4: Changes in ownership

Correct Response: 3

Explanation: Increases in residual risk are critical.

Knowledge Area: Real_Life_Exam_Sim

Question Number: 261

Question: What best indicates approaching unacceptable risk levels?

Option 1: ROI

Option 2: Risk register

Option 3: Cause/effect diagram

Option 4: Risk indicator

Correct Response: 3

Explanation: Risk indicators provide early warnings.

Knowledge Area: Real_Life_Exam_Sim

Question Number: 262

Question: What is most important to provide internal audit during planning?

Option 1: Closed actions

Option 2: Risk assessments

Option 3: Vulnerability report

Option 4: Generic scenarios

Correct Response: 2

Explanation: Current risk assessment results inform audits.

Knowledge Area: Real_Life_Exam_Sim

Question Number: 263

Question: Who is ultimately accountable for outsourced IT security operations?

Option 1: The organization's management

Option 2: Third party management

Option 3: Vendor management office

Option 4: Control operators

Correct Response: 2

Explanation: The organization retains accountability.

Question Number: 264

Question: What is the most important outsourced data center SLA metric?

Option 1: Systems hosted

Option 2: Response time

Option 3: Availability

Option 4: Recovery inclusion

Correct Response: 3

Explanation: Availability percentage is critical.

Knowledge Area: Real_Life_Exam_Sim

Question Number: 265

Question: If an organization is non-compliant, the best action is to:

Option 1: Modify assurance activities

Option 2: Conduct a gap analysis

Option 3: Collaborate to meet compliance

Option 4: Identify needed controls

Correct Response: 2

Explanation: A gap analysis defines required actions.

Knowledge Area: Real_Life_Exam_Sim

Question Number: 266

Question: After finding terminated employees with account access, the first step should be to:

Option 1: Develop access policies

Option 2: Disable user access

Option 3: Perform risk assessment

Option 4: Do root cause analysis

Correct Response: 2

Explanation: Disabling access immediately reduces risk exposure.

Knowledge Area: Real_Life_Exam_Sim

Question Number: 267

Question: What is most helpful to understand a new system's risk impact?

Option 1: Review mitigations

Option 2: Hire consultants

Option 3: Conduct gap analysis

Option 4: Perform risk assessment

Correct Response: 4

Explanation: An assessment reveals how it affects the profile.

Knowledge Area: Real_Life_Exam_Sim

Question Number: 268

Question: With ineffective security controls, the first action should be to:

Option 1: Request risk acceptance

Option 2: Report in next audit

Option 3: Deploy compensating controls

Option 4: Assess impact

Correct Response: 4

Explanation: Understanding the impact guides next steps.

Knowledge Area: Real_Life_Exam_Sim

Question Number: 269

Question: What gives executives the best data for risk decisions from an assessment?

Option 1: Maturity assessment

Option 2: Qualitative results

Option 3: Quantitative results

Option 4: Desired state comparison

Correct Response: 3

Explanation: Quantitative data provides the most insight.

Knowledge Area: Real_Life_Exam_Sim

Question Number: 270

Question: What risk refers to lower than expected investment returns?

Option 1: Project ownership risk

Option 2: Integrity risk

Option 3: Expense risk

Option 4: Relevance risk

Correct Response: 4

Explanation: Relevance risk reflects return shortfalls.

Knowledge Area: Real_Life_Exam_Sim

Question Number: 271

Question: What is the best KPI for incident response maturity?

Option 1: Resolved incidents

Option 2: Escalated incidents

Option 3: Identified incidents

Option 4: Recurring incidents

Correct Response: 4

Explanation: Recurrences indicate process gaps.

Knowledge Area: Real_Life_Exam_Sim

Question Number: 272

Question: After finding a control design gap, what should happen next?

Option 1: Re-evaluate KRIs

Option 2: Invoke response plan

Option 3: Document in register

Option 4: Modify control design

Correct Response: 4

Explanation: The control design should be remediated.

Knowledge Area: Real_Life_Exam_Sim

Question Number: 273

Question: What is most important in regulatory and risk updates?

Option 1: Recommended KRIs

Option 2: Change costs

Option 3: Noncompliance risk

Option 4: Remediation timeframe

Correct Response: 3

Explanation: The risk of noncompliance is critical.

Knowledge Area: Real_Life_Exam_Sim

Question Number: 274

Question: How should compliance impact on objectives be evaluated?

Option 1: Map to policies

Option 2: Impact analysis

Option 3: Gap analysis

Option 4: Stakeholder communication

Correct Response: 2

Explanation: An impact analysis quantifies effects.

Knowledge Area: Real_Life_Exam_Sim

Question Number: 275

Question: When control costs exceed ALE, it indicates the:

Option 1: Risk is inefficiently controlled

Option 2: Control is ineffective

Option 3: Risk is efficiently controlled

Option 4: Control is weak

Correct Response: 3

Explanation: Costs exceeding ALE show efficient control.

Knowledge Area: Real_Life_Exam_Sim

Question Number: 276

Question: When reporting risks to management, what is most important?

Option 1: Assets with highest risk

Option 2: Action plans and owners

Option 3: Losses compared to treatment

Option 4: Recent assessment results

Correct Response: 2

Explanation: Loss vs treatment cost enables decisions.

Knowledge Area: Real_Life_Exam_Sim

Question Number: 277

Question: What serves as the starting point for the IT continuity strategy?

Option 1: Index of Disaster Information

Option 2: Availability Testing Schedule

Option 3: Business Continuity Strategy

Option 4: Disaster Guideline

Correct Response: 3

Explanation: The business strategy guides IT continuity.

Knowledge Area: Real_Life_Exam_Sim

Question Number: 278

Question: How can control implementation be validated?

Option 1: Implement KRIs

Option 2: Test control design

Option 3: Test environment

Option 4: Implement KPIs

Correct Response: 2

Explanation: Testing the design verifies effectiveness.

Knowledge Area: Real_Life_Exam_Sim

Question Number: 279

Question: Who helps understand IT impact on objectives?

Option 1: IT management

Option 2: Senior management

Option 3: Internal audit

Option 4: Process owners

Correct Response: 4

Explanation: Process owners know operational impacts.

Knowledge Area: Real_Life_Exam_Sim

Question Number: 280

Question: What demonstrates evaluation of risk alternatives?

Option 1: Trend analysis

Option 2: Control chart

Option 3: Decision tree

Option 4: Sensitivity analysis

Correct Response: 3

Explanation: A decision tree maps out options.

Knowledge Area: Real_Life_Exam_Sim

Question Number: 281

Question: After identifying high data loss probability, the next step should be to:

Option 1: Enhance awareness

Option 2: Increase reporting

Option 3: Buy insurance

Option 4: Do control assessment

Correct Response: 4

Explanation: Assessing controls will reveal response options.

Knowledge Area: Real_Life_Exam_Sim

Question Number: 282

Question: What is the best justification for a GRC solution?

Option 1: Ensure compliance

Option 2: Close audit findings

Option 3: Demonstrate commitment

Option 4: Enable risk decisions

Correct Response: 4

Explanation: It facilitates risk-aware choices.

Knowledge Area: Real_Life_Exam_Sim

Question Number: 283

Question: With many vulnerabilities found, what should happen next?

Option 1: Handle as risks

Option 2: Prioritize by impact

Option 3: Analyze controls

Option 4: Evaluate threats, impacts, costs

Correct Response: 4

Explanation: A risk approach considers multiple facets.

Knowledge Area: Real_Life_Exam_Sim

Question Number: 284

Question: At what maturity are appetite and tolerance episodic?

Option 1: Level 1

Option 2: Level 2

Option 3: Level 3

Option 4: Level 4

Correct Response: 1

Explanation: Level 1 has ad hoc appetite application.

Knowledge Area: Real_Life_Exam_Sim

Question Number: 285

Question: After identifying high data loss probability, the next step should be to:

Option 1: Enhance awareness

Option 2: Increase reporting

Option 3: Buy insurance

Option 4: Do control assessment

Correct Response: 4

Explanation: Assessing controls will reveal response options.

Knowledge Area: Real_Life_Exam_Sim

Question Number: 286

Question: What is the best justification for a GRC solution?

Option 1: Ensure compliance

Option 2: Close audit findings

Option 3: Demonstrate commitment

Option 4: Enable risk decisions

Correct Response: 4

Explanation: It facilitates risk-aware choices.

Knowledge Area: Real_Life_Exam_Sim

Question Number: 287

Question: What component examines risks in change requests?

Option 1: Risk monitoring

Option 2: Configuration management

Option 3: Integrated change control

Option 4: Scope change control

Correct Response: 3

Explanation: Integrated change control governs all changes.

Knowledge Area: Real_Life_Exam_Sim

Question Number: 288

Question: At what maturity are appetite and tolerance episodic?

Option 1: Level 1

Option 2: Level 2

Option 3: Level 3

Option 4: Level 4

Correct Response: 1

Explanation: Level 1 has ad hoc appetite application.

Knowledge Area: Real_Life_Exam_Sim

Question Number: 289

Question: What best addresses piggybacking risk?

Option 1: Security training

Option 2: Biometric locks

Option 3: Two-factor authentication

Option 4: ID badges

Correct Response: 4

Explanation: ID badges enable access validation.

Knowledge Area: Real_Life_Exam_Sim

Question Number: 290

Question: Why use qualitative residual risk measures for new threats?

Option 1: Regulatory alignment

Option 2: Expert judgment

Option 3: Easier updating

Option 4: Less monitoring

Correct Response: 3

Explanation: Qualitative incorporates judgment better.

Knowledge Area: Real_Life_Exam_Sim

Question Number: 291

Question: With offshore cloud data storage, the primary concern is:

Option 1: Data validation

Option 2: Data aggregation

Option 3: Data quality

Option 4: Data privacy

Correct Response: 2

Explanation: Offshore increases privacy risks.

Knowledge Area: Real_Life_Exam_Sim

Question Number: 292

Question: After more emergency changes, the best action is to:

Option 1: Reconfigure infrastructure

Option 2: Conduct root cause analysis

Option 3: Evaluate control impact

Option 4: Validate processes

Correct Response: 2

Explanation: Analysis reveals reasons for the changes.

Knowledge Area: Real_Life_Exam_Sim

Question Number: 293

Question: With multiple risk owners, what is most important?

Option 1: Treatment plan updates

Option 2: Consistent assessments

Option 3: Escalation procedures

Option 4: Risk/control alignment

Correct Response: 2

Explanation: Consistent assessments ensure coherence.

Knowledge Area: Real_Life_Exam_Sim

Question Number: 294

Question: What helps ensure mitigated risk stays acceptable?

Option 1: Risk owner reviews

Option 2: Profile updates

Option 3: Control testing participation

Option 4: Effectiveness monitoring

Correct Response: 4

Explanation: Ongoing monitoring maintains awareness.

Knowledge Area: Real_Life_Exam_Sim

Question Number: 295

Question: What best informs risk decisions in control reporting?

Option 1: Audit plan

Option 2: Implementation spend

Option 3: Deployment status

Option 4: Testing deficiencies

Correct Response: 4

Explanation: Deficiencies highlight issues.

Knowledge Area: Real_Life_Exam_Sim

Question Number: 296

Question: What improves risk indicator buy-in?

Option 1: Lag indicator

Option 2: Root cause

Option 3: Lead indicator

Option 4: Stakeholder

Correct Response: 4

Explanation: Stakeholder input enables engagement.

Knowledge Area: Real_Life_Exam_Sim

Question Number: 297

Question: A reciprocal DR agreement applies what treatment?

Option 1: Avoidance

Option 2: Mitigation

Option 3: Acceptance

Option 4: Transfer

Correct Response: 4

Explanation: It transfers risk through sharing.

Knowledge Area: Real_Life_Exam_Sim

Question Number: 298

Question: What best prevents unauthorized data retrieval?

Option 1: Single sign-on

Option 2: Digital signatures

Option 3: Access policy enforcement

Option 4: Segregation of duties

Correct Response: 3

Explanation: An access policy restricts visibility.

Knowledge Area: Real_Life_Exam_Sim

Question Number: 299

Question: When evaluating control adequacy, the PRIMARY focus should be:

Option 1: Residual risk level

Option 2: Risk appetite

Option 3: Cost-benefit analysis

Option 4: Sensitivity analysis

Correct Response: 3

Explanation: Cost-benefit analysis determines efficient mitigation.

Knowledge Area: Real_Life_Exam_Sim

Question Number: 300

Question: Regarding KRI monitoring, the GREATEST concern is:

Option 1: Excessive log retention

Option 2: Encrypted log transmission

Option 3: Pre-analysis log modification

Option 4: Limited data sources

Correct Response: 3

Explanation: Modified logs undermine analysis.

Knowledge Area: Real_Life_Exam_Sim

HELP US IMPROVE!

WE WANT YOUR FEEDBACK

WalterEducation.com

Amazing!

You have been studying very hard to this stage.

How is your exam preparation so far? Can the practice test meet your needs and expectation? I desperately desire your voice.

Please kindly consider

1. Visiting my exam practice test books and consider purchasing them to assist you to pass your target exam, though the direct links provided at the beginning of this book
2. Visiting my exam practice test courses held at Udemy though the direct links provided at the beginning of this book
3. Leaving a positive review and feedback to me though the direct book review links provided at the next page.

Keep going! See you at the end of the book.

Warm regards,

Walter

Direct URLs to visit all Walter's Practice Tests at Amazon

Visit Walter's author page:
http://WalterEducation.com

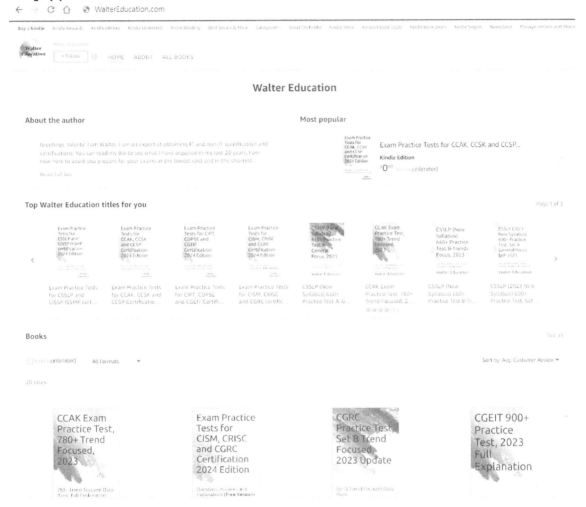

Or the **Links at Amazon Book Store:**

CCAK Exam Practice Test, 780+ Trend Focused, 2023	
Paperback Review URL:	- https://www.amazon.com/review/create-review?&asin=B0CJSXPYM7
Kindle eBook Review URL:	- https://www.amazon.com/review/create-review?&asin=B0CK9QQ44B

CERTIFIED DATA PRIVACY SOLUTIONS ENGINEER (CDPSE) 900+ PRACTICE TEST, 2023, FULL EXPLANATION	
Paperback Review URL:	- https://www.amazon.com/review/create-review?&asin=B0CGL3S5BH
Kindle eBook Review URL:	- https://www.amazon.com/review/create-review?&asin=B0CGL91NQ9

CGEIT 900+ Practice Test, 2023

Paperback Review URL:	- https://www.amazon.com/review/create-review?&asin=B0CGW1Y1X9
Kindle eBook Review URL:	- https://www.amazon.com/review/create-review?&asin=B0CJ8388ZB

CIPT, Certified Information Privacy Technologists, Practice Test

Paperback Review URL:	- https://www.amazon.com/review/create-review?&asin=B0CJ4DLHG2
Kindle eBook Review URL:	- https://www.amazon.com/review/create-review?&asin=B0CJ72MR4M

CRISC 1200+ Practice Test, 2023 (Exam Simulation and Core & Advanced Knowledge)

Paperback Review URL:	- https://www.amazon.com/review/create-review?&asin=B0CJ43R78T
Kindle eBook Review URL:	- https://www.amazon.com/review/create-review?&asin=B0CJ72JJLY

CISM 1050+ Practice Test,2023 Updated, Set B - Trends Focused, ISACA

Paperback Review URL:	- https://www.amazon.com/review/create-review?&asin=B0CJSNR5Z2
Kindle eBook Review URL:	- https://www.amazon.com/review/create-review?&asin=B0CJVWHJHW

CISM 1050+ Practice Test A - Core Focus, ISACA

Paperback Review URL:	- https://www.amazon.com/review/create-review?&asin=B0CJL2HD1R
Kindle eBook Review URL:	- https://www.amazon.com/review/create-review?&asin=B0CJVSQ6Z6

CCSKv4 900+ Practice Test 2023, Full Explanation

Paperback Review URL:	- https://www.amazon.com/review/create-review?&asin=B0CFX2S7D8
Kindle eBook Review URL:	- https://www.amazon.com/review/create-review?&asin=B0CFVLS8ZH

CSSLP (2023 New Syllabus) 600+ Practice Test, Set A General Focus

Paperback Review URL:	- https://www.amazon.com/review/create-review?&asin=B0CK3VTR9D
Kindle eBook Review URL:	- https://www.amazon.com/review/create-review?&asin=PENDING

CSSLP (New Syllabus) 660+ Practice Test B-Trends Focus, SEP 2023

Paperback Review URL:	- https://www.amazon.com/review/create-review?&asin=B0CK3XGCBN
Kindle eBook Review URL:	- https://www.amazon.com/review/create-review?&asin=PENDING

CISSP-ISSMP 650+ Practice Test, 2023 New syllabus, Set A Core Focused

Paperback Review URL:	- https://www.amazon.com/review/create-review?&asin=B0CJLLL4HP
Kindle eBook Review URL:	- https://www.amazon.com/review/create-review?&asin=B0CK2Y6XR7

CISSP-ISSMP 650+ Practice Test, 2023 New syllabus, Set B Trends Focused, ISC2	
Paperback Review URL:	- https://www.amazon.com/review/create-review?&asin=B0CJLMV48G
Kindle eBook Review URL:	- https://www.amazon.com/review/create-review?&asin=B0CK2X7CLL

Practice Test for Certified Cloud Security Professional (CCSP): 900+ Practice Test	
Paperback Review URL:	- https://www.amazon.com/review/create-review?&asin=B0CFCLW7HJ
Kindle eBook Review URL:	- https://www.amazon.com/review/create-review?&asin=B0CFKSVKSS

CGRC Practice Test, Set A Data Bank, Learn & Exam, 2023 Update	
Paperback Review URL:	- https://www.amazon.com/review/create-review?&asin=B0CJBC5MX1
Kindle eBook Review URL:	- https://www.amazon.com/review/create-review?&asin=B0CJYQVM22

CGRC Practice Test, Set B Trend Focused, 2023	
Paperback Review URL:	- https://www.amazon.com/review/create-review?&asin=B0CJ43Z8N6
Kindle eBook Review URL:	- https://www.amazon.com/review/create-review?&asin=B0CJ72HWY2

How to give a Review and Rating:

1. Click Here

2. Tell me anything about the course

3. Submit

Question Number: 301

Question: A key project success factor is:

Option 1: Motivation

Option 2: Political/cultural awareness

Option 3: Communication

Option 4: Influencing

Correct Response: 3

Explanation: Effective communication enables collaboration.

Knowledge Area: Real_Life_Exam_Sim

Question Number: 302

Question: Expert judgment for risks provides:

Option 1: Contingent strategies

Option 2: Risk transfer

Option 3: External guidance

Option 4: Risk acceptance

Correct Response: 3

Explanation: Experts give informed recommendations.

Knowledge Area: Real_Life_Exam_Sim

Question Number: 303

Question: The GREATEST generic risk concern is:

Option 1: Higher costs

Option 2: Irrelevant factors

Option 3: Lack of inherent risk

Option 4: No quantification

Correct Response: 3

Explanation: Irrelevant factors undermine analysis.

Knowledge Area: Real_Life_Exam_Sim

Question Number: 304

Question: Numerically analyzing risk impact is:

Option 1: Monitoring risks

Option 2: Qualitative assessment

Option 3: Identifying risks

Option 4: Quantitative assessment

Correct Response: 4

Explanation: This defines the quantitative process.

Knowledge Area: Real_Life_Exam_Sim

Question Number: 305

Question: To effectively monitor KRIs, the most critical element is:

Option 1: Escalation procedures

Option 2: Automated data feeds

Option 3: Threshold definitions

Option 4: Controls monitoring

Correct Response: 2

Explanation: Automated data enables real-time tracking.

Knowledge Area: Real_Life_Exam_Sim

Question Number: 306

Question: Recurring security exceptions likely indicate:

Option 1: Decreased threats

Option 2: Ineffective governance

Option 3: Lack of mitigation

Option 4: Poor service delivery

Correct Response: 2

Explanation: Governance should ensure policy compliance.

Knowledge Area: Real_Life_Exam_Sim

Question Number: 307

Question: The most useful IAM efficiency KPI is:

Option 1: Password resets

Option 2: Tickets created

Option 3: Provisioning time

Option 4: Account lockout time

Correct Response: 3

Explanation: Provisioning time impacts productivity.

Knowledge Area: Real_Life_Exam_Sim

Question Number: 308

Question: Risk analysis results should be quantitative or qualitative based on:

Option 1: Organizational tolerance

Option 2: Management needs

Option 3: Framework used

Option 4: Assessment results

Correct Response: 4

Explanation: Actual results guide ideal presentation.

Knowledge Area: Real_Life_Exam_Sim

Question Number: 309

Question: Process awareness enables a risk practitioner to:

Option 1: Establish guidelines

Option 2: Identify risk sources

Option 3: Understand control design

Option 4: Perform BIAs

Correct Response: 4

Explanation: It reveals potential risk origins.

Knowledge Area: Real_Life_Exam_Sim

Question Number: 310

Question: ERM oversight of IT risk is most valuable for:

Option 1: Focusing on risk impact

Option 2: Aligning IT to strategy

Option 3: Enabling risk resources

Option 4: Prioritizing customers

Correct Response: 2

Explanation: It aligns technology risk management.

Knowledge Area: Real_Life_Exam_Sim

Question Number: 311

Question: Anti-virus effectiveness is best measured by:

Option 1: Update frequency

Option 2: Alert quantity

Option 3: Definition currency

Option 4: False positives

Correct Response: 3

Explanation: Current definitions ensure protection.

Question Number: 312

Question: When developing a risk register, focus on:

Option 1: Risk management strategy

Option 2: Risk identification

Option 3: Risk monitoring

Option 4: Response planning

Correct Response: 2

Explanation: The register captures identified risks.

Knowledge Area: Real_Life_Exam_Sim

Question Number: 313

Question: Backup effectiveness is best measured by:

Option 1: Recovery requests

Option 2: Monitoring reports

Option 3: Allocation of resources

Option 4: Recurring failures

Correct Response: 4

Explanation: Failures indicate issues.

Knowledge Area: Real_Life_Exam_Sim

Question Number: 314

Question: A policy forbidding personal email use is an:

Option 1: Anti-harassment policy

Option 2: Intellectual property policy

Option 3: Acceptable use policy

Option 4: Privacy policy

Correct Response: 3

Explanation: An AUP covers appropriate usage

Knowledge Area: Real_Life_Exam_Sim

Question Number: 315

Question: What type of assessment would help determine vulnerabilities in an organization's critical assets?

Option 1: Threat assessment

Option 2: Vulnerability assessment

Option 3: Risk assessment

Option 4: Penetration testing

Correct Response: 2

Explanation: A vulnerability assessment specifically looks for weaknesses in critical assets that could be exploited by threats, making it the best choice to identify vulnerabilities.

Knowledge Area: Real_Life_Exam_Sim

Question Number: 316

Question: Which of the following is the BEST way to promote a risk-aware culture?

Option 1: Mandating risk training

Option 2: Establishing risk tolerances

Option 3: Implementing financial controls

Option 4: Hiring a risk officer

Correct Response: 2

Explanation: Setting risk tolerances helps define acceptable levels of risk for staff, promoting awareness of how much risk can be taken.

Knowledge Area: Real_Life_Exam_Sim

Question Number: 317

Question: Which risk analysis method uses scenarios to estimate potential losses from threats?

Option 1: HERA

Option 2: Failure modes and effects analysis

Option 3: Annualized loss expectancy

Option 4: Three lines of defense

Correct Response: 3

Explanation: ALE analysis looks at potential loss scenarios to quantify possible losses from threats manifesting.

Knowledge Area: Real_Life_Exam_Sim

Question Number: 318

Question: What is a PRIMARY benefit of qualitative risk analysis?

Option 1: It is easy to automate

Option 2: It provides quantifiable results

Option 3: It gives contextual insights

Option 4: It requires minimal resources

Correct Response: 3

Explanation: Qualitative analysis provides subjective but important context around risks that quantitative data lacks.

Knowledge Area: Real_Life_Exam_Sim

Question Number: 319

Question: What should be done AFTER implementing a risk response?

Option 1: Conduct a cost-benefit analysis

Option 2: Identify the risk owner

Option 3: Monitor the risk

Option 4: Calculate residual risk

Correct Response: 3

Explanation: Post-implementation monitoring verifies if the response is working as intended.

Knowledge Area: Real_Life_Exam_Sim

Question Number: 320

Question: After undertaking a risk assessment of a production system, the MOST appropriate action is for the risk manager to:

Option 1: Develop a risk treatment plan

Option 2: Document the risk assessment findings

Option 3: Implement risk mitigation measures

Option 4: Review and update risk assessment periodically

Correct Response: 1

Explanation: The most appropriate action for the risk manager after undertaking a risk assessment of a production system is to develop a risk treatment plan. Based on the assessment findings, the risk manager can prioritize and plan for risk mitigation measures, allocate resources, and establish timelines for implementation. The risk treatment plan helps in addressing identified risks effectively and reducing their potential impact.

Knowledge Area: Real_Life_Exam_Sim

Question Number: 321

Question: Which of the following is the FIRST step in managing the risk associated with the leakage of confidential data?

Option 1: Conduct a data classification assessment

Option 2: Implement access controls and encryption measures

Option 3: Develop and enforce data handling policies

Option 4: Identify the sources and potential causes of data leakage

Correct Response: 1

Explanation: The first step in managing the risk associated with the leakage of confidential data is to conduct a data classification assessment. This involves identifying and categorizing data based on its sensitivity and criticality. By understanding the value and sensitivity of data, organizations can prioritize their protection efforts and implement appropriate access controls, encryption measures, and data handling policies.

Knowledge Area: Real_Life_Exam_Sim

Question Number: 322

Question: Which of the following BEST ensures that a firewall is configured in compliance with an enterprise's security policy?

Option 1: Regularly review and update the firewall configuration

Option 2: Conduct periodic penetration testing

Option 3: Implement change control procedures

Option 4: Perform regular security audits

Correct Response: 1

Explanation: The best approach to ensure that a firewall is configured in compliance with an enterprise's security policy is to regularly review and update the firewall configuration. Regular reviews help to ensure that the firewall rules and settings align with the organization's security policy and requirements. By keeping the configuration up to date, organizations can address emerging threats, vulnerabilities, and compliance requirements effectively.

Knowledge Area: Real_Life_Exam_Sim

Question Number: 323

Question: Which of the following methods involves the use of predictive or diagnostic analytical tools for exposing risk factors?

Option 1: Data mining

Option 2: Penetration testing

Option 3: Business process modeling

Option 4: Gap analysis

Correct Response: 1

Explanation: The method that involves the use of predictive or diagnostic analytical tools for exposing risk factors is data mining. Data mining involves analyzing large datasets to identify patterns, correlations, and anomalies that may indicate potential risks. By applying data mining techniques, organizations can gain insights into risk factors and make informed decisions to mitigate those risks.

Knowledge Area: Real_Life_Exam_Sim

Question Number: 324

Question: When updating the risk register after a risk assessment, what is the most important information to include?

Option 1: Identified risks and their likelihood and impact

Option 2: Actions taken to mitigate risks

Option 3: Current risk levels and trends

Option 4: Roles and responsibilities of risk owners

Correct Response: 1

Explanation: The most important information to include when updating the risk register after a risk assessment is the identified risks and their likelihood and impact. This information provides a comprehensive overview of the risks the organization faces and allows for informed decision-making regarding risk treatment and mitigation strategies. It helps prioritize resources and efforts to address the most significant risks.

Knowledge Area: Real_Life_Exam_Sim

Question Number: 325

Question: When determining which control deficiencies are most significant, what provides the most useful information?

Option 1: Impact analysis

Option 2: Risk assessment reports

Option 3: Control testing results

Option 4: Incident reports

Correct Response: 2

Explanation: When determining which control deficiencies are most significant, risk assessment reports provide the most useful information. Risk assessment reports offer insights into the likelihood and potential impact of identified control deficiencies. They enable organizations to prioritize remediation efforts based on the level of risk exposure and ensure that resources are allocated effectively to address the most significant control deficiencies.

Knowledge Area: Real_Life_Exam_Sim

Question Number: 326

Question: Which approach would most effectively enable a business operations manager to identify events exceeding risk thresholds?

Option 1: Establishing key risk indicators (KRIs)

Option 2: Implementing robust internal controls

Option 3: Conducting regular risk assessments

Option 4: Enhancing business continuity planning

Correct Response: 1

Explanation: Establishing key risk indicators (KRIs) would most effectively enable a business operations manager to identify events exceeding risk thresholds. KRIs are measurable metrics that provide early warning signs of potential risks and allow for proactive risk management. By monitoring KRIs, the manager can identify deviations from acceptable risk levels and take timely actions to mitigate risks.

Knowledge Area: Real_Life_Exam_Sim

Question Number: 327

Question: When reviewing existing controls during a risk assessment, what should raise concerns about potential ineffectiveness in mitigating risks?

Option 1: Manual processes

Option 2: Frequency of testing

Option 3: Limited automation

Option 4: Gaps in coverage

Correct Response: 4

Explanation: Control gaps and weak enforcement indicate risk mitigation deficiencies.

Knowledge Area: Real_Life_Exam_Sim

Question Number: 328

Question: When monitoring a client-facing application, what is most important to ensure continually?

Option 1: Costs stay within budget

Option 2: Vulnerability scans performed

Option 3: Audit logs are reviewed

Option 4: Performance is analyzed

Correct Response: 4

Explanation: Proactive monitoring ensures availability and user experience.

Knowledge Area: Real_Life_Exam_Sim

Question Number: 329

Question: What is the highest risk of having inadequately defined data and system ownership?

Option 1: Non-compliance

Option 2: Difficulty integrating acquisitions

Option 3: Excessive privilege creep

Option 4: Gaps in responsibilities

Correct Response: 4

Explanation: Undefined owners lead to responsibility gaps and actions not taken.

Knowledge Area: Real_Life_Exam_Sim

Question Number: 330

Question: What is the best practice for identifying changes in an organization's overall risk profile?

Option 1: Review static risk register

Option 2: Conduct audits on known issues

Option 3: Monitor existing KRIs

Option 4: Perform refreshed risk assessments

Correct Response: 4

Explanation: Updated risk assessments reliably detect evolving profiles.

Knowledge Area: Real_Life_Exam_Sim

Question Number: 331

Question: The greatest concern with an incident response plan is lack of testing and validation of its effectiveness in actual response situations requiring activation.

Option 1: Incomplete documentation

Option 2: Untrained staff

Option 3: No third-party integration

Option 4: Lack of testing

Correct Response: 4

Explanation: Untested plans risk failure in response.

Knowledge Area: Real_Life_Exam_Sim

Question Number: 332

Question: Comparing residual risk levels before and after a control plan implementation quantifies resulting risk reduction to indicate effectiveness.

Option 1: Stakeholder feedback

Option 2: Cost-benefit analysis

Option 3: Audit results

Option 4: Residual risk metrics

Correct Response: 4

Explanation: Reduced residual risk shows impact.

Knowledge Area: Real_Life_Exam_Sim

Question Number: 333

Question: Reviewing a cloud provider's independent audit results and security certifications helps evaluate the effectiveness of implemented controls.

Option 1: Penetration testing

Option 2: Contract clauses

Option 3: On-site assessments

Option 4: Third-party audits

Correct Response: 4

Explanation: External validations demonstrate cloud controls.

Knowledge Area: Real_Life_Exam_Sim

Question Number: 334

Question: Which of the following would BEST help identify the owner for each risk scenario in a risk register?

Option 1: Risk assessment interviews

Option 2: Stakeholder analysis

Option 3: Organizational chart review

Option 4: Risk appetite assessment

Correct Response: 1

Explanation: Risk assessment interviews would best help identify the owner for each risk scenario in a risk register. By conducting interviews with relevant stakeholders, including subject matter experts and individuals with knowledge of the organization's operations and processes, the ownership of specific risk scenarios can be determined. These interviews provide insights into the individuals or departments responsible for managing or mitigating the identified risks, ensuring accountability and clear ownership within the risk register.

Knowledge Area: Real_Life_Exam_Sim

Question Number: 335

Question: Which of the following MUST be assessed before considering risk treatment options for a scenario with significant impact?

Option 1: Risk likelihood

Option 2: Risk tolerance

Option 3: Risk appetite

Option 4: Risk consequences

Correct Response: 1

Explanation: Risk consequences must be assessed before considering risk treatment options for a scenario with significant impact. Understanding the potential consequences of a risk scenario is crucial for making informed decisions about appropriate risk treatment measures. By assessing the potential impact and severity of the consequences, organizations can prioritize their risk treatment efforts and allocate resources effectively to address risks with significant potential impact.

Knowledge Area: Real_Life_Exam_Sim

Question Number: 336

Question: Implementing which of the following controls would BEST reduce the impact of a vulnerability that has been exploited?

Option 1: Compensating controls

Option 2: Detective controls

Option 3: Corrective controls

Option 4: Preventive controls

Correct Response: 3

Explanation: Implementing corrective controls would best reduce the impact of a vulnerability that has been exploited. Corrective controls are designed to mitigate or eliminate the root cause of vulnerabilities or weaknesses in the system or process. By addressing the underlying cause, corrective controls help prevent the recurrence of the vulnerability and reduce its impact on the organization's security and operations.

Knowledge Area: Real_Life_Exam_Sim

Question Number: 337

Question: Which of the following is a PRIMARY benefit of engaging the risk owner during the risk assessment process?

Option 1: Ensuring accurate risk identification

Option 2: Facilitating risk transfer activities

Option 3: Enhancing risk communication and understanding

Option 4: Defining risk acceptance criteria

Correct Response: 3

Explanation: A primary benefit of engaging the risk owner during the risk assessment process is enhancing risk communication and understanding. By involving the risk owner, there is a direct line of communication between the risk assessor and the individual responsible for managing or mitigating the identified risks. This engagement facilitates a better understanding of the risks, their potential impact, and the necessary risk response actions. It also helps ensure that risk assessment findings and recommendations are effectively communicated to the risk owner, fostering a shared understanding and alignment on risk management decisions and actions.

Knowledge Area: Real_Life_Exam_Sim

Question Number: 338

Question: If one says that the particular control or monitoring tool is sustainable, then it refers to what ability?

Option 1: Long-term viability

Option 2: Scalability

Option 3: Flexibility

Option 4: Effectiveness

Correct Response: 1

Explanation: When one says that a particular control or monitoring tool is sustainable, it refers to its long-term viability. The sustainability of a control or monitoring tool means that it is capable of being maintained, supported, and operated effectively over an extended period. It considers factors such as ongoing resource availability, adaptability to changing requirements, and the ability to address emerging risks and challenges.

Knowledge Area: Real_Life_Exam_Sim

Question Number: 339

Question: Which of the following is the BEST metric to demonstrate the effectiveness of an organization's change management process?

Option 1: Time to implement changes

Option 2: Number of approved changes

Option 3: Customer satisfaction with changes

Option 4: Impact of changes on system performance

Correct Response: 3

Explanation: Customer satisfaction with changes is the best metric to demonstrate the effectiveness of an organization's change management process. It measures the level of satisfaction or acceptance of changes implemented by the organization among its customers or stakeholders. High customer satisfaction indicates that the changes are meeting their needs, expectations, and requirements, reflecting the effectiveness of the change management process in delivering successful and customer-focused changes.

Knowledge Area: Real_Life_Exam_Sim

Question Number: 340

Question: Implementing which of the following will BEST help ensure that systems comply with an established baseline before deployment?

Option 1: Configuration management processes

Option 2: Change management processes

Option 3: Incident management processes

Option 4: Risk management processes

Correct Response: 1

Explanation: Implementing configuration management processes will best help ensure that systems comply with an established baseline before deployment. Configuration management processes involve establishing and maintaining a standard baseline configuration for systems and ensuring that any changes or deviations from the baseline are properly controlled, documented, and authorized. By implementing robust configuration management processes, organizations can ensure that systems are deployed and maintained in accordance with established standards, reducing the risk of configuration-related issues and non-compliance.

Knowledge Area: Real_Life_Exam_Sim

Question Number: 341

Question: What is the BEST information to present to business control owners when justifying costs related to controls?

Option 1: Demonstrated value of the controls

Option 2: Regulatory requirements for controls

Option 3: Cost breakdown of control implementation

Option 4: Comparison of control costs with industry benchmarks

Correct Response: 1

Explanation: The best information to present to business control owners when justifying costs related to controls is the demonstrated value of the controls. Demonstrating the value of controls involves highlighting the benefits and positive outcomes that the controls provide to the organization. This may include improved operational efficiency, risk reduction, compliance with regulatory requirements, and protection of critical assets. Demonstrating the value helps stakeholders understand the importance of investing in controls and supports the business case for control implementation.

Knowledge Area: Real_Life_Exam_Sim

Question Number: 342

Question: Which of the following role carriers is accounted for analyzing risks, maintaining risk profile, and risk-aware decisions?

Option 1: Risk manager

Option 2: Business analyst

Option 3: Project manager

Option 4: Chief risk officer (CRO)

Correct Response: 1

Explanation: The role carrier accounted for analyzing risks, maintaining the risk profile, and making risk-aware decisions is the risk manager. The risk manager is responsible for identifying, assessing, and managing risks within an organization. They analyze risks, maintain the risk profile, and make risk-aware decisions to ensure effective risk management across the organization. The risk manager plays a crucial role in maintaining risk awareness, implementing risk mitigation strategies, and facilitating risk-informed decision-making processes.

Knowledge Area: Real_Life_Exam_Sim

Question Number: 343

Question: Which of the following nodes of the decision tree analysis represents the start point of the decision tree?

Option 1: Root node

Option 2: Leaf node

Option 3: Branch node

Option 4: Terminal node

Correct Response: 1

Explanation: The root node represents the start point of the decision tree analysis. It is the topmost node from which all other nodes and branches originate. The root node represents the initial decision or condition that leads to subsequent branches and nodes in the decision tree, ultimately guiding the decision-making process.

Knowledge Area: Real_Life_Exam_Sim

Question Number: 344

Question: Out of several risk responses, which of the following risk responses is used for negative risk events?

Option 1: Mitigate

Option 2: Exploit

Option 3: Accept

Option 4: Enhance

Correct Response: 1

Explanation: The risk response used for negative risk events is to mitigate. Risk mitigation involves taking actions or implementing measures to reduce the likelihood or impact of identified risks. When faced with negative risk events, organizations typically aim to mitigate the risks by implementing controls, contingency plans, or other risk mitigation strategies to minimize their potential adverse effects.

Knowledge Area: Real_Life_Exam_Sim

Question Number: 345

Question: The BEST way to determine the likelihood of a system availability risk scenario is by assessing the:

Option 1: Historical occurrence of similar events

Option 2: Impact of the risk scenario

Option 3: Control effectiveness in mitigating the risk scenario

Option 4: Frequency of the risk scenario occurring

Correct Response: 1

Explanation: The best way to determine the likelihood of a system availability risk scenario is by assessing the historical occurrence of similar events. By reviewing historical data or incidents related to system availability, organizations can gain insights into the frequency or recurrence of such events. This assessment helps in estimating the likelihood of the risk scenario occurring in the future and informs risk management decisions.

Knowledge Area: Real_Life_Exam_Sim

Question Number: 346

Question: A risk practitioner's PRIMARY focus when validating a risk response action plan should be that the risk response:

Option 1: Addresses the identified risk appropriately

Option 2: Aligns with regulatory requirements

Option 3: Mitigates all potential risks completely

Option 4: Has the lowest possible cost impact on the organization

Correct Response: 1

Explanation: A risk practitioner's primary focus when validating a risk response action plan should be that the risk response addresses the identified risk appropriately. The validation process ensures that the selected risk response aligns with the risk management objectives and effectively mitigates or manages the identified risk. The focus is on evaluating the adequacy and suitability of the risk response in addressing the specific risk event.

Knowledge Area: Real_Life_Exam_Sim

Question Number: 347

Question: Which of the following baselines identifies the specifications required by the resource that meet the approved requirements?

Option 1: Functional baseline

Option 2: Technical baseline

Option 3: Performance baseline

Option 4: Security baseline

Correct Response: 2

Explanation: The technical baseline identifies the specifications required by the resource that meet the approved requirements. It outlines the technical specifications, configurations, and standards that must be met by the resource or system. The technical baseline ensures that the resource is designed, implemented, and operated in accordance with the specified technical requirements.

Knowledge Area: Real_Life_Exam_Sim

Question Number: 348

Question: When reviewing a business continuity plan (BCP), which of the following would be the MOST significant deficiency?

Option 1: Inadequate backup procedures

Option 2: Outdated contact information

Option 3: Unclear communication channels

Option 4: Lack of alternative work locations

Correct Response: 1

Explanation: The most significant deficiency when reviewing a business continuity plan (BCP) would be inadequate backup procedures. Backup procedures are critical for ensuring the availability and recovery of essential systems, data, and resources during a disruptive event. Without proper backup procedures, the organization may face challenges in restoring operations and recovering critical data, significantly impacting its ability to maintain business continuity.

Knowledge Area: Real_Life_Exam_Sim

Question Number: 349

Question: After mapping generic risk scenarios to organizational security policies, the NEXT course of action should be to:

Option 1: Conduct a risk assessment

Option 2: Develop a risk mitigation plan

Option 3: Implement controls and safeguards

Option 4: Communicate the findings to stakeholders

Correct Response: 1

Explanation: The next course of action after mapping generic risk scenarios to organizational security policies should be to conduct a risk assessment. Mapping risk scenarios to security policies provides a basis for identifying and evaluating the specific risks faced by the organization. Conducting a risk assessment involves assessing the likelihood, impact, and potential consequences of identified risks to prioritize and inform the development of a risk mitigation plan and the implementation of appropriate controls and safeguards.

Knowledge Area: Real_Life_Exam_Sim

Question Number: 350

Question: Which of the following BEST describes the role of the IT risk profile in strategic IT-related decisions?

Option 1: It informs decision-making by identifying and assessing IT-related risks.

Option 2: It provides a framework for prioritizing IT projects and investments.

Option 3: It establishes criteria for evaluating IT vendors and service providers.

Option 4: It guides the development of IT policies and procedures.

Correct Response: 1

Explanation: The IT risk profile informs decision-making by identifying and assessing IT-related risks. By understanding the organization's IT risk landscape, decision-makers can evaluate the potential risks associated with strategic IT-related decisions. The IT risk profile provides insights into the likelihood and potential impact of risks, enabling informed decision-making and the development of risk-informed strategies and actions.

Knowledge Area: Real_Life_Exam_Sim

Question Number: 351

Question: The BEST metric to monitor the risk associated with changes deployed to production is the percentage of:

Option 1: Successful changes

Option 2: Failed changes

Option 3: Emergency changes

Option 4: Backlogged changes

Correct Response: 2

Explanation: The best metric to monitor the risk associated with changes deployed to production is the percentage of failed changes. Tracking the percentage of failed changes helps identify potential issues, weaknesses, or risks associated with the change management process. A high percentage of failed changes may indicate inadequate testing, poor coordination, or other factors that can increase the risk of disruptions or negative impacts to the production environment.

Knowledge Area: Real_Life_Exam_Sim

Question Number: 352

Question: The primary role of a data custodian in risk management is classifying data by sensitivity and criticality to guide protection priorities aligned to risk appetite.

Option 1: Enforcing retention policies

Option 2: Granting access

Option 3: Managing backups

Option 4: Classifying data

Correct Response: 4

Explanation: Custodians classify data for protections.

Knowledge Area: Real_Life_Exam_Sim

Question Number: 353

Question: Promoting a risk-aware culture aims to embed risk considerations into daily behaviors and decisions across the organization through reinforced messaging and leadership modeling.

Option 1: Meet compliance mandates

Option 2: Reduce operational surprises

Option 3: Lessen audit findings

Option 4: Align behaviors to goals

Correct Response: 4

Explanation: Culture links risk to decisions and actions.

Knowledge Area: Real_Life_Exam_Sim

Question Number: 354

Question: Input validation controls preventing invalid data entry mitigate risks associated with transactions processing inaccurate data.

Option 1: Encryption

Option 2: Access controls

Option 3: Data loss prevention

Option 4: Input validation

Correct Response: 4

Explanation: Validation mitigates bad data risks.

Knowledge Area: Real_Life_Exam_Sim

Question Number: 355

Question: Documented approvals matching access requests indicate account provisioning aligns with authorized needs, providing effective control.

Option 1: Permission change logs

Option 2: Access certification

Option 3: password resets

Option 4: Documented approvals

Correct Response: 4

Explanation: Approvals validate provisioning.

Knowledge Area: Real_Life_Exam_Sim

Question Number: 356

Question: Justifying risk response recommendations with cost-benefit analyses quantifying expected loss reductions best supports investment decisions.

Option 1: Stakeholder consensus

Option 2: Qualitative impacts

Option 3: Compliance alignment

Option 4: Cost-benefit analysis

Correct Response: 4

Explanation: Cost-benefit analysis justifies actions.

Knowledge Area: Real_Life_Exam_Sim

Question Number: 357

Question: Risk-based vendor questionnaires assessing controls around security, resilience, and privacy help evaluate vendors' control environments.

Option 1: Contract clauses

Option 2: Site visits

Option 3: Financial stability review

Option 4: Risk questionnaires

Correct Response: 3

Explanation: Questionnaires assess vendor controls.

Knowledge Area: Real_Life_Exam_Sim

Question Number: 358

Question: Internal reviewers focus on improving risk management while external reviewers provide independent assurance of effectiveness to meet compliance mandates.

Option 1: Tools and techniques

Option 2: Risk identification

Option 3: Risk monitoring

Option 4: Objectives

Correct Response: 3

Explanation: Internal vs. external reviewers have different focuses.

Knowledge Area: Real_Life_Exam_Sim

Question Number: 359

Question: Ongoing monitoring of key performance indicators tied to control objectives best indicates efficiency by tracking metrics like uptime, defects, or delays.

Option 1: Capacity analysis

Option 2: Risk assessments

Option 3: Vulnerability scans

Option 4: KPI monitoring

Correct Response: 4

Explanation: KPIs signal control efficiency.

Question Number: 360

Question: A risk practitioner would be interested in internal audit findings to identify control gaps or risk exposures potentially requiring additional mitigation.

Option 1: Assess budget needs

Option 2: Guide resource allocation

Option 3: Inform risk strategies

Option 4: Highlight control gaps

Correct Response: 4

Explanation: Audits expose issues for mitigation.

Question Number: 361

Question: The MOST effective way to increase the likelihood that risk responses will be implemented is to:

Option 1: Clearly communicate the rationale for risk responses

Option 2: Assign responsibility to multiple individuals

Option 3: Increase the frequency of risk assessments

Option 4: Provide financial incentives for risk response implementation

Correct Response: 1

Explanation: The most effective way to increase the likelihood that risk responses will be implemented is to clearly communicate the rationale for risk responses. When individuals understand the reasons behind risk responses, including the potential impact and benefits, they are more likely to proactively implement the recommended actions. Clear communication helps create awareness, understanding, and ownership of risk response activities, increasing their likelihood of implementation.

Knowledge Area: Real_Life_Exam_Sim

Question Number: 362

Question: Which of the following is the MOST important data source for monitoring key risk indicators (KRIs)?

Option 1: Internal incident reports

Option 2: External benchmarking data

Option 3: Historical risk assessment results

Option 4: Real-time monitoring systems

Correct Response: 4

Explanation: Real-time monitoring systems are the most important data source for monitoring key risk indicators (KRIs). Real-time monitoring provides immediate and ongoing visibility into the organization's risk landscape, allowing for timely detection and response to potential risk events. By collecting and analyzing real-time data, organizations can track and monitor KRIs in a proactive and dynamic manner, enabling timely risk management interventions.

Knowledge Area: Real_Life_Exam_Sim

Question Number: 363

Question: Which of the following tools is MOST effective in identifying trends in the IT risk profile?

Option 1: Risk assessment software

Option 2: Data analytics tools

Option 3: Vulnerability scanning tools

Option 4: Incident management systems

Correct Response: 2

Explanation: Data analytics tools are the most effective in identifying trends in the IT risk profile. These tools can analyze large volumes of data from various sources, identify patterns, correlations, and trends, and provide insights into the organization's IT risk landscape. By leveraging data analytics, organizations can gain a deeper understanding of emerging risks, patterns of vulnerabilities, and potential areas of concern, enabling proactive risk management and mitigation.

Knowledge Area: Real_Life_Exam_Sim

Question Number: 364

Question: Which of the following should be the PRIMARY consideration when assessing the automation of control monitoring?

Option 1: Cost-effectiveness

Option 2: Regulatory requirements

Option 3: Scalability

Option 4: Effectiveness and efficiency of control monitoring

Correct Response: 4

Explanation: The effectiveness and efficiency of control monitoring should be the primary consideration when assessing the automation of control monitoring. Automation should enhance the ability to monitor controls effectively and efficiently, providing timely and accurate information about control performance and deviations. The goal is to ensure that automated control monitoring enables reliable and comprehensive monitoring of control effectiveness while optimizing resources and minimizing the potential for human error.

Knowledge Area: Real_Life_Exam_Sim

Question Number: 365

Question: Materialization of a risk into an issue or problem would most likely require updating the risk register to document the event and any next steps for response.

Option 1: New control implementation

Option 2: Improved KRI metric

Option 3: Completed risk assessment

Option 4: Risk becoming an issue

Correct Response: 4

Explanation: Issues mean registering impacts and responses.

Knowledge Area: Real_Life_Exam_Sim

Question Number: 366

Question: To maintain effectiveness, risk registers should be regularly reviewed and updated to reflect emerging risks, completed responses, risk owners, and lessons learned.

Option 1: Detailed risk descriptions

Option 2: Mitigation initiatives

Option 3: Impact estimates

Option 4: Regular reviews and updates

Correct Response: 4

Explanation: Updating sustains relevance.

Knowledge Area: Real_Life_Exam_Sim

Question Number: 367

Question: When a risk event appears likely to occur, it transitions to being called an issue requiring response.

Option 1: Vulnerability

Option 2: Threat event

Option 3: Near miss

Option 4: Issue

Correct Response: 4

Explanation: Likely risks become issues needing response.

Knowledge Area: Real_Life_Exam_Sim

Question Number: 368

Question: Input validation controls that check for authorized values on changes made by the DBA provide the best detection of unauthorized data modification.

Option 1: Log reviews

Option 2: Job rotation

Option 3: Access reviews

Option 4: Input validation

Correct Response: 4

Explanation: Validation identifies unauthorized changes.

Knowledge Area: Real_Life_Exam_Sim

Question Number: 369

Question: Consistently achieving target residual risk levels across critical risk types indicates effective IT risk management processes.

Option 1: No audit findings

Option 2: High risk awareness

Option 3: Positive audit results

Option 4: Meeting residual targets

Correct Response: 4

Explanation: Residuals show effectiveness.

Knowledge Area: Real_Life_Exam_Sim

Question Number: 370

Question: Which of the following will BEST quantify the risk associated with malicious users in an organization?

Option 1: Incident response time

Option 2: Number of security controls

Option 3: Frequency of security awareness training

Option 4: Threat intelligence reports

Correct Response: 2

Explanation: The number of security controls will best quantify the risk associated with malicious users in an organization. Security controls are measures put in place to prevent, detect, and respond to security incidents. The presence of a higher number of effective security controls indicates a greater level of protection against malicious user activities, reducing the overall risk associated with them.

Knowledge Area: Real_Life_Exam_Sim

Question Number: 371

Question: Which of the following tasks should be completed prior to creating a disaster recovery plan (DRP)?

Option 1: Conducting a business impact analysis (BI

Option 2: Defining recovery time objectives (RTOs)

Option 3: Developing a risk management plan

Option 4: Establishing a crisis management team

Correct Response: 1

Explanation: Conducting a business impact analysis (BIA) should be completed prior to creating a disaster recovery plan (DRP). A BIA helps identify critical business functions, dependencies, and the impact of disruptions. This information is essential for developing an effective DRP that aligns with the organization's recovery priorities and objectives. The BIA provides insights into the potential financial, operational, and reputational consequences of disruptive events, guiding the development of appropriate recovery strategies.

Knowledge Area: Real_Life_Exam_Sim

Question Number: 372

Question: Which of the following is the BEST indication of the effectiveness of a business continuity program?

Option 1: Successful recovery from a major incident

Option 2: Minimal disruption to operations

Option 3: Compliance with regulatory requirements

Option 4: Positive feedback from customers

Correct Response: 1

Explanation: Successful recovery from a major incident is the best indication of the effectiveness of a business continuity program. The ability to recover and resume critical business functions and operations following a significant disruption demonstrates that the business continuity program is effective in minimizing the impact of disruptive events. Successful recovery validates the preparedness, planning, and effectiveness of the program in ensuring business continuity and resilience.

Knowledge Area: Real_Life_Exam_Sim

Question Number: 373

Question: As part of an overall IT risk management plan, an IT risk register BEST helps management:

Option 1: Prioritize risk response activities

Option 2: Track the status of risk events

Option 3: Allocate resources for risk mitigation

Option 4: Identify emerging risk trends

Correct Response: 1

Explanation: An IT risk register best helps management prioritize risk response activities. The IT risk register provides a comprehensive overview of identified risks, their potential impact, and likelihood. By reviewing the risk register, management can prioritize the most critical risks based on their potential impact on the organization's objectives. This prioritization allows for the allocation of appropriate resources and the implementation of targeted risk response activities to address the most significant risks.

Knowledge Area: Real_Life_Exam_Sim

Question Number: 374

Question: Which of the following should be done FIRST when a new risk scenario has been identified?

Option 1: Assess the risk impact and likelihood

Option 2: Communicate the risk scenario to stakeholders

Option 3: Develop a risk response plan

Option 4: Document the risk scenario

Correct Response: 1

Explanation: Assessing the risk impact and likelihood should be done first when a new risk scenario has been identified. This step involves evaluating the potential consequences and likelihood of the risk event occurring. Assessing the risk impact and likelihood provides a foundation for further risk management activities, such as developing a risk response plan and determining the appropriate risk mitigation strategies.

Knowledge Area: Real_Life_Exam_Sim

Question Number: 375

Question: To reduce risks from penetration testing, obtained signed approval specifying scope and authorizing access before starting provides the best control.

Option 1: Using vetted tools

Option 2: Reviewing results after

Option 3: Having audit monitor

Option 4: Getting signed approval

Correct Response: 4

Explanation: Approval reduces unauthorized access risks.

Knowledge Area: Real_Life_Exam_Sim

Question Number: 376

Question: Periodically reviewing the risk register helps maintain an updated inventory of risks to support risk-based decisions, ensure monitoring, and confirm response ownership.

Option 1: Satisfy auditors

Option 2: Assess team performance

Option 3: Track mitigation initiatives

Option 4: Enable risk-aware choices

Correct Response: 3

Explanation: Updated registers sustain risk management.

Knowledge Area: Real_Life_Exam_Sim

Question Number: 377

Question: Meeting defined risk appetite levels through executed responses best indicates risk management effectiveness.

Option 1: No issues

Option 2: High awareness

Option 3: Peer benchmarks

Option 4: Within appetite

Correct Response: 4

Explanation: Appetite alignment signals effectiveness.

Knowledge Area: Real_Life_Exam_Sim

Question Number: 378

Question: Using maturity models enables assessing the current state to identify and prioritize capability improvements for more effective risk management.

Option 1: Enable certification

Option 2: Clarify metrics

Option 3: Simplify reporting

Option 4: Highlight improvements

Correct Response: 4

Explanation: Maturity aids strengthening capabilities.

Knowledge Area: Real_Life_Exam_Sim

Question Number: 379

Question: A changing risk landscape is best identified through refreshed risk assessments revealing new or shifted exposures compared to the previous risk profile.

Option 1: Loss reviews

Option 2: KRI trends

Option 3: Audit results

Option 4: Risk assessments

Correct Response: 4

Explanation: New assessments identify profile changes.

Knowledge Area: Real_Life_Exam_Sim

Question Number: 380

Question: Business impact analysis determining critical assets and processes should be performed to forecast disaster effects.

Option 1: Acquire backup systems

Option 2: Review continuity plans

Option 3: Purchase insurance

Option 4: Impact analysis

Correct Response: 4

Explanation: Impact analysis forecasts disaster effects.

Knowledge Area: Real_Life_Exam_Sim

Question Number: 381

Question: The PRIMARY objective of testing the effectiveness of a new control before implementation is to:

Option 1: Identify control weaknesses

Option 2: Ensure regulatory compliance

Option 3: Validate control design

Option 4: Measure control performance

Correct Response: 3

Explanation: The primary objective of testing the effectiveness of a new control before implementation is to validate control design. Testing ensures that the control is designed correctly and capable of achieving its intended purpose. By testing the control, organizations can identify any design flaws or gaps and make necessary adjustments before its implementation. This helps ensure that the control will function as intended and effectively mitigate the associated risks.

Knowledge Area: Real_Life_Exam_Sim

Question Number: 382

Question: Which of the following is the PRIMARY consideration when establishing an organization's risk management methodology?

Option 1: Organizational culture

Option 2: Industry standards

Option 3: Budget constraints

Option 4: Regulatory requirements

Correct Response: 1

Explanation: The primary consideration when establishing an organization's risk management methodology is organizational culture. The risk management methodology should align with the organization's values, attitudes, and beliefs regarding risk. By considering the organizational culture, organizations can develop a risk management methodology that is practical, relevant, and supported by key stakeholders. This facilitates effective implementation and integration of risk management practices throughout the organization.

Knowledge Area: Real_Life_Exam_Sim

Question Number: 383

Question: Which of the following is the BEST indicator of an effective IT security awareness program?

Option 1: Decrease in security incidents

Option 2: Increase in security training hours

Option 3: Compliance with security policies

Option 4: Positive feedback from employees

Correct Response: 1

Explanation: A decrease in security incidents is the best indicator of an effective IT security awareness program. An effective program should enhance employees' understanding of security risks and encourage behavior that minimizes security incidents. When employees are more aware and knowledgeable about security best practices, they are more likely to identify and respond appropriately to potential threats, leading to a decrease in security incidents.

Knowledge Area: Real_Life_Exam_Sim

Question Number: 384

Question: Which of the following would BEST help minimize the risk associated with social engineering threats?

Option 1: Security awareness training

Option 2: Implementation of biometric authentication

Option 3: Regular vulnerability scanning

Option 4: Encryption of sensitive data

Correct Response: 1

Explanation: Security awareness training would best help minimize the risk associated with social engineering threats. Social engineering relies on manipulating individuals to gain unauthorized access or sensitive information. By providing security awareness training, organizations can educate employees about common social engineering techniques, how to recognize and respond to them, and the importance of following security protocols. This empowers employees to be vigilant and less susceptible to social engineering attacks.

Knowledge Area: Real_Life_Exam_Sim

Question Number: 385

Question: Which of the following would be MOST helpful when estimating the likelihood of negative events?

Option 1: Historical data

Option 2: Employee opinions

Option 3: External expert advice

Option 4: Intuition or gut feeling

Correct Response: 1

Explanation: Historical data would be most helpful when estimating the likelihood of negative events. By analyzing past events and their frequencies, organizations can gain insights into the likelihood of similar events occurring in the future. Historical data provides a factual basis for estimating probabilities and helps inform decision-making and risk mitigation strategies.

Knowledge Area: Real_Life_Exam_Sim

Question Number: 386

Question: When reviewing a risk response strategy, senior management's PRIMARY focus should be placed on the:

Option 1: Alignment with organizational objectives

Option 2: Cost-effectiveness of the strategy

Option 3: Inclusion of all identified risks

Option 4: Detailed implementation plan

Correct Response: 1

Explanation: When reviewing a risk response strategy, senior management's primary focus should be placed on the alignment with organizational objectives. The risk response strategy should be in line with the organization's overall goals and objectives, ensuring that the response measures contribute to the achievement of desired outcomes. By prioritizing alignment with organizational objectives, senior management can ensure that risk response efforts are targeted, effective, and supportive of the organization's strategic direction.

Knowledge Area: Real_Life_Exam_Sim

Question Number: 387

Question: Encryption of confidential data both at rest and in transit is most effective at protecting against external threats aiming to improperly access sensitive organizational information.

Option 1: Access controls

Option 2: Firewall rules

Option 3: Endpoint protection

Option 4: Encryption

Correct Response: 4

Explanation: Encryption secures data from external access.

Knowledge Area: Real_Life_Exam_Sim

Question Number: 388

Question: A data protection plan should first classify information by sensitivity and criticality to determine appropriate safeguards and align to risk appetite.

Option 1: Evaluate legal requirements

Option 2: Assess vendor contracts

Option 3: Inventory retention policies

Option 4: Classify data

Correct Response: 4

Explanation: Sensitivity classification guides data protections.

Knowledge Area: Real_Life_Exam_Sim

Question Number: 389

Question: Earned value management is used to measure project performance rather than critical success factors.

Option 1: Customer satisfaction

Option 2: ROI

Option 3: Product quality

Option 4: EVM

Correct Response: 3

Explanation: EVM measures project progress, not CSFs.

Knowledge Area: Real_Life_Exam_Sim

Question Number: 390

Question: Risk should be reduced to the acceptable level defined by organizational policies and risk appetite to accomplish effective management.

Option 1: Zero

Option 2: As low as reasonably practicable

Option 3: Insignificant

Option 4: Acceptable level

Correct Response: 4

Explanation: Reducing risk to appetite is the goal.

Knowledge Area: Real_Life_Exam_Sim

Question Number: 391

Question: Analyzing security alerts and system behavior anomalies helps identify suspicious activities that require investigation and response.

Option 1: Access request trends

Option 2: Policy attestations

Option 3: Control maturity

Option 4: Threat monitoring

Correct Response: 3

Explanation: Anomaly detection identifies suspicious events.

Knowledge Area: Real_Life_Exam_Sim

Question Number: 392

Question: When developing a risk taxonomy, the most important focus should be utilizing categories and terminology aligning to business objectives and priorities.

Option 1: Maximizing granularity

Option 2: Enabling calculations

Option 3: Satisfying regulators

Option 4: Matching to strategy

Correct Response: 4

Explanation: Alignment with business goals empowers risk conversations.

Knowledge Area: Real_Life_Exam_Sim

Question Number: 393

Question: Accepting control costs exceeding risk exposure often represents an availability bias overestimating risk likelihood and underestimating response impacts.

Option 1: Management override

Option 2: Insufficient data

Option 3: Inadequate resources

Option 4: Cognitive bias

Correct Response: 4

Explanation: Overspending on controls frequently stems from bias.

Knowledge Area: Real_Life_Exam_Sim

Question Number: 394

Question: Which of the following would MOST likely result in updates to an IT risk profile?

Option 1: Changes in technology trends

Option 2: Employee training programs

Option 3: Routine system maintenance

Option 4: Financial audits

Correct Response: 1

Explanation: Changes in technology trends would most likely result in updates to an IT risk profile. As technology evolves, new risks may emerge, and existing risks may change in nature or significance. Updating the IT risk profile ensures that the organization remains aware of and prepared for the evolving risk landscape associated with the use of technology.

Knowledge Area: Real_Life_Exam_Sim

Question Number: 395

Question: When defining thresholds for control key performance indicators (KPIs), it is MOST helpful to align:

Option 1: Organizational objectives

Option 2: Regulatory requirements

Option 3: Industry benchmarks

Option 4: Internal policies and procedures

Correct Response: 1

Explanation: When defining thresholds for control key performance indicators (KPIs), it is most helpful to align them with organizational objectives. KPI thresholds should be set in a way that reflects the desired outcomes and aligns with the strategic objectives of the organization. By ensuring alignment with organizational objectives, KPIs become more meaningful and effective in measuring the performance and effectiveness of controls.

Knowledge Area: Real_Life_Exam_Sim

Question Number: 396

Question: Which one of the following is the only output for the qualitative risk analysis process?

Option 1: Risk register

Option 2: Risk assessment report

Option 3: Risk mitigation plan

Option 4: Risk response strategy

Correct Response: 1

Explanation: The risk register is the only output for the qualitative risk analysis process. The risk register is a comprehensive document that captures all identified risks, their descriptions, assessments, and other relevant information. It serves as a central repository of project risks and provides a foundation for further risk analysis, response planning, and monitoring.

Knowledge Area: Real_Life_Exam_Sim

Question Number: 397

Question: Which of the following phases is involved in the Data Extraction, Validation, Aggregation, and Analysis?

Option 1: Risk identification

Option 2: Risk assessment

Option 3: Risk response planning

Option 4: Risk monitoring and control

Correct Response: 2

Explanation: The phase involved in the Data Extraction, Validation, Aggregation, and Analysis is the risk assessment phase. In this phase, data is gathered from various sources, validated for accuracy and completeness, aggregated to provide a holistic view, and analyzed to assess the likelihood and impact of identified risks. This analysis helps in prioritizing risks and developing appropriate risk response strategies.

Knowledge Area: Real_Life_Exam_Sim

Question Number: 398

Question: To help ensure the success of a major IT project, it is MOST important to:

Option 1: Define clear project objectives

Option 2: Allocate sufficient budget

Option 3: Follow established project management methodologies

Option 4: Engage stakeholders throughout the project lifecycle

Correct Response: 1

Explanation: To help ensure the success of a major IT project, it is most important to define clear project objectives. Clear objectives provide a clear direction and purpose for the project, guiding decision-making, resource allocation, and project execution. Well-defined objectives help align project activities with the desired outcomes and facilitate effective project management and stakeholder engagement.

Knowledge Area: Real_Life_Exam_Sim

Question Number: 399

Question: Which of the following provides the BEST measurement of an organization's risk management maturity level?

Option 1: Risk assessment results

Option 2: Regulatory compliance status

Option 3: Incident response time

Option 4: Maturity model assessment

Correct Response: 4

Explanation: A maturity model assessment provides the best measurement of an organization's risk management maturity level. Maturity models evaluate an organization's risk management practices, processes, and capabilities against established criteria to determine their maturity level. This assessment helps identify strengths, weaknesses, and areas for improvement, enabling organizations to enhance their risk management practices and achieve higher levels of maturity.

Knowledge Area: Real_Life_Exam_Sim

Question Number: 400

Question: The BEST reason to classify IT assets during a risk assessment is to determine the:

Option 1: Potential impact of asset loss

Option 2: Frequency of asset usage

Option 3: Cost of asset maintenance

Option 4: Availability of asset backups

Correct Response: 1

Explanation: The best reason to classify IT assets during a risk assessment is to determine the potential impact of asset loss. Classifying IT assets helps identify their importance, criticality, and value to the organization. By understanding the potential impact of asset loss, organizations can prioritize their risk mitigation efforts, allocate resources effectively, and implement appropriate controls to protect valuable assets.

Knowledge Area: Real_Life_Exam_Sim

WHAT'S YOUR

FEEDBACK?

TELL US WHAT YOU THINK

Amazing!

You have been studying very hard to this stage.

How is your exam preparation so far? Can the practice test meet your needs and expectation? I desperately desire your voice.

Please kindly consider

1. Visiting my exam practice test books and consider purchasing them to assist you to pass your target exam, though the direct links provided at the beginning of this book
2. Visiting my exam practice test courses held at Udemy though the direct links provided at the beginning of this book
3. Leaving a positive review and feedback to me though the direct book review links provided at the next page.

Keep going! See you at the end of the book.

Warm regards,

Walter

Direct URLs to visit all Walter's Practice Tests at Amazon

Visit Walter's author page:
http://WalterEducation.com

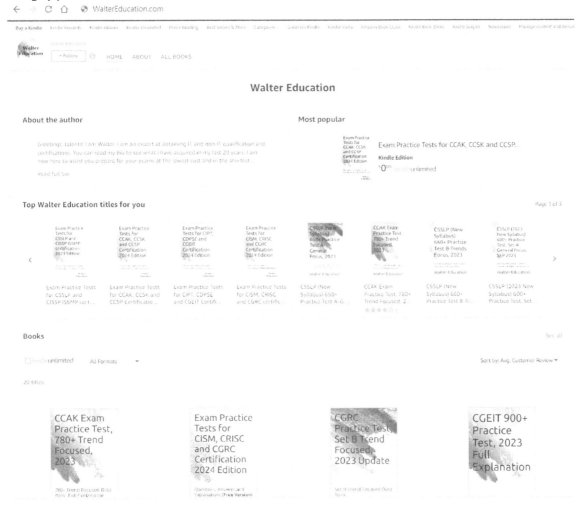

Or the **Links at Amazon Book Store:**

CCAK Exam Practice Test, 780+ Trend Focused, 2023	
Paperback Review URL:	- https://www.amazon.com/review/create-review?&asin=B0CJSXPYM7
Kindle eBook Review URL:	- https://www.amazon.com/review/create-review?&asin=B0CK9QQ44B

CERTIFIED DATA PRIVACY SOLUTIONS ENGINEER (CDPSE) 900+ PRACTICE TEST, 2023, FULL EXPLANATION	
Paperback Review URL:	- https://www.amazon.com/review/create-review?&asin=B0CGL3S5BH
Kindle eBook Review URL:	- https://www.amazon.com/review/create-review?&asin=B0CGL91NQ9

CGEIT 900+ Practice Test, 2023

Paperback Review URL:	- https://www.amazon.com/review/create-review?&asin=B0CGW1Y1X9
Kindle eBook Review URL:	- https://www.amazon.com/review/create-review?&asin=B0CJ8388ZB

CIPT, Certified Information Privacy Technologists, Practice Test

Paperback Review URL:	- https://www.amazon.com/review/create-review?&asin=B0CJ4DLHG2
Kindle eBook Review URL:	- https://www.amazon.com/review/create-review?&asin=B0CJ72MR4M

CRISC 1200+ Practice Test, 2023 (Exam Simulation and Core & Advanced Knowledge)

Paperback Review URL:	- https://www.amazon.com/review/create-review?&asin=B0CJ43R78T
Kindle eBook Review URL:	- https://www.amazon.com/review/create-review?&asin=B0CJ72JJLY

CISM 1050+ Practice Test,2023 Updated, Set B - Trends Focused, ISACA

Paperback Review URL:	- https://www.amazon.com/review/create-review?&asin=B0CJSNR5Z2
Kindle eBook Review URL:	- https://www.amazon.com/review/create-review?&asin=B0CJVWHJHW

CISM 1050+ Practice Test A - Core Focus, ISACA

Paperback Review URL:	- https://www.amazon.com/review/create-review?&asin=B0CJL2HD1R
Kindle eBook Review URL:	- https://www.amazon.com/review/create-review?&asin=B0CJVSQ6Z6

CCSKv4 900+ Practice Test 2023, Full Explanation

Paperback Review URL:	- https://www.amazon.com/review/create-review?&asin=B0CFX2S7D8
Kindle eBook Review URL:	- https://www.amazon.com/review/create-review?&asin=B0CFVLS8ZH

CSSLP (2023 New Syllabus) 600+ Practice Test, Set A General Focus

Paperback Review URL:	- https://www.amazon.com/review/create-review?&asin=B0CK3VTR9D
Kindle eBook Review URL:	- https://www.amazon.com/review/create-review?&asin=PENDING

CSSLP (New Syllabus) 660+ Practice Test B-Trends Focus, SEP 2023

Paperback Review URL:	- https://www.amazon.com/review/create-review?&asin=B0CK3XGCBN
Kindle eBook Review URL:	- https://www.amazon.com/review/create-review?&asin=PENDING

CISSP-ISSMP 650+ Practice Test, 2023 New syllabus, Set A Core Focused

Paperback Review URL:	- https://www.amazon.com/review/create-review?&asin=B0CJLLL4HP
Kindle eBook Review URL:	- https://www.amazon.com/review/create-review?&asin=B0CK2Y6XR7

CISSP-ISSMP 650+ Practice Test, 2023 New syllabus, Set B Trends Focused, ISC2

Paperback Review URL:	- https://www.amazon.com/review/create-review?&asin=B0CJLMV48G
Kindle eBook Review URL:	- https://www.amazon.com/review/create-review?&asin=B0CK2X7CLL

Practice Test for Certified Cloud Security Professional (CCSP): 900+ Practice Test

Paperback Review URL:	- https://www.amazon.com/review/create-review?&asin=B0CFCLW7HJ
Kindle eBook Review URL:	- https://www.amazon.com/review/create-review?&asin=B0CFKSVKSS

CGRC Practice Test, Set A Data Bank, Learn & Exam, 2023 Update

Paperback Review URL:	- https://www.amazon.com/review/create-review?&asin=B0CJBC5MX1
Kindle eBook Review URL:	- https://www.amazon.com/review/create-review?&asin=B0CJYQVM22

CGRC Practice Test, Set B Trend Focused, 2023

Paperback Review URL:	- https://www.amazon.com/review/create-review?&asin=B0CJ43Z8N6
Kindle eBook Review URL:	- https://www.amazon.com/review/create-review?&asin=B0CJ72HWY2

How to give a Review and Rating:

1. Click Here

Create Review

CCAK Exam Practice Test, 780+ Trend Focused, 2023: 780+ Trend Focused Data Bank, Full Expla...

Overall rating

Add a headline

Add a photo or video

Add a written review

2. Tell me anything about the course

Walter Education

Submit

3. Submit

Question Number: 401

Question: Which of the following should be the PRIMARY focus of an IT risk awareness program?

Option 1: Understanding risk management concepts

Option 2: Identifying and reporting risks

Option 3: Mitigating risks through controls

Option 4: Aligning risks with business objectives

Correct Response: 1

Explanation: The primary focus of an IT risk awareness program should be on understanding risk management concepts. It is crucial to educate employees and stakeholders about the fundamentals of risk management, including risk identification, assessment, and mitigation. By building a strong foundation of risk management knowledge, individuals can become active participants in identifying, assessing, and addressing risks in their respective roles and responsibilities.

Knowledge Area: Real_Life_Exam_Sim

Question Number: 402

Question: Which of the following is MOST important to update when an organization's risk appetite changes?

Option 1: Risk assessment methodologies

Option 2: Risk response strategies

Option 3: Risk monitoring procedures

Option 4: Risk appetite statement

Correct Response: 4

Explanation: When an organization's risk appetite changes, the risk appetite statement is the most important element to update. The risk appetite statement outlines the organization's willingness to accept and manage risk within defined boundaries. By updating the risk appetite statement, organizations ensure that decision-making and risk management align with the new risk appetite, guiding actions and strategies to achieve the organization's objectives within the revised risk tolerance levels.

Knowledge Area: Real_Life_Exam_Sim

Question Number: 403

Question: Which of the following is the MOST effective key performance indicator (KPI) for change management?

Option 1: Percentage of successful changes implemented

Option 2: Average time for change approval

Option 3: Number of change requests received

Option 4: Stakeholder satisfaction with changes implemented

Correct Response: 1

Explanation: The most effective key performance indicator (KPI) for change management is the percentage of successful changes implemented. This KPI measures the efficiency and effectiveness of the change management process by assessing the proportion of changes that are implemented successfully without adverse impacts or disruptions. It reflects the organization's ability to plan, execute, and manage changes in a controlled and reliable manner.

Knowledge Area: Real_Life_Exam_Sim

Question Number: 404

Question: Which of the following helps ensure compliance with a non-repudiation policy requirement for electronic transactions?

Option 1: Digital signatures

Option 2: Firewalls

Option 3: Intrusion detection systems

Option 4: Encryption

Correct Response: 1

Explanation: Digital signatures help ensure compliance with a non-repudiation policy requirement for electronic transactions. Digital signatures provide a cryptographic mechanism to verify the integrity and authenticity of electronic documents or transactions, preventing the sender from denying their involvement or the validity of the transaction. They provide strong evidence of the origin and integrity of the data, ensuring non-repudiation and supporting the enforceability of electronic contracts or agreements.

Knowledge Area: Real_Life_Exam_Sim

Question Number: 405

Question: Data owners' top priority when establishing risk mitigation should be reducing intolerable risks to critical assets to align with organizational risk appetite.

Option 1: Meeting compliance mandates

Option 2: Enabling monitoring

Option 3: Optimizing resources

Option 4: Maximizing data access

Correct Response: 1

Explanation: Owners mitigate risks to critical data.

Knowledge Area: Real_Life_Exam_Sim

Question Number: 406

Question: A vulnerability scanner that checks for weak passwords exposed on the network is .

Option 1: Nessus

Option 2: Snort

Option 3: Wireshark

Option 4: NetFlow

Correct Response: 1

Explanation: Nessus scans for vulnerabilities like weak passwords.

Knowledge Area: Real_Life_Exam_Sim

Question Number: 407

Question: An organization's risk management maturity level provides the best measurement of the degree of formality, sophistication, and effectiveness of risk practices.

Option 1: Audit results

Option 2: KRI trends

Option 3: Threat intelligence

Option 4: Training attendance

Correct Response: 1

Explanation: Maturity level reflects risk program sophistication.

Knowledge Area: Real_Life_Exam_Sim

Question Number: 408

Question: Classifying IT assets by criticality and value best determines the potential business impact if an asset is compromised to focus responses on highest risks.

Option 1: System interconnections

Option 2: Data retention needs

Option 3: Backup requirements

Option 4: Access permissions

Correct Response: 1

Explanation: Asset classification evaluates potential impact.

Knowledge Area: Real_Life_Exam_Sim

Question Number: 409

Question: The organization's risk appetite statement should be updated when tolerance for key risk exposures changes to realign risk management priorities.

Option 1: Business strategy

Option 2: Technology landscape

Option 3: Regulatory environment

Option 4: Risk maturity level

Correct Response: 1

Explanation: Changing appetite changes risk priorities.

Knowledge Area: Real_Life_Exam_Sim

Question Number: 410

Question: Which of the following attributes of a key risk indicator (KRI) is MOST important?

Option 1: Relevance to business objectives

Option 2: Availability of data sources

Option 3: Frequency of measurement

Option 4: Alignment with industry benchmarks

Correct Response: 1

Explanation: The most important attribute of a key risk indicator (KRI) is its relevance to business objectives. KRIs should directly reflect the critical risks that impact the achievement of business objectives. By focusing on relevant KRIs, organizations can effectively monitor and manage the risks that are most crucial to their success. Relevance ensures that KRIs provide meaningful insights and drive informed decision-making.

Knowledge Area: Real_Life_Exam_Sim

Question Number: 411

Question: Which of the following is the MOST effective inhibitor of relevant and efficient communication?

Option 1: Lack of transparency

Option 2: Inadequate communication channels

Option 3: Language barriers

Option 4: Poor listening skills

Correct Response: 1

Explanation: Lack of transparency is the most effective inhibitor of relevant and efficient communication. When information is not transparently shared or withheld, it hinders effective communication. Transparency fosters open and honest communication, ensuring that relevant information is accessible to all stakeholders. Without transparency, misunderstandings, misalignment, and inefficiencies can arise, impeding effective risk communication and decision-making.

Knowledge Area: Real_Life_Exam_Sim

Question Number: 412

Question: Which of the following is the BEST course of action to reduce risk impact?

Option 1: Implementing risk mitigation controls

Option 2: Transferring risk to a third party

Option 3: Accepting the risk as unavoidable

Option 4: Avoiding the activities associated with the risk

Correct Response: 1

Explanation: Implementing risk mitigation controls is the best course of action to reduce risk impact. Risk mitigation involves taking specific actions to minimize the likelihood or impact of identified risks. By implementing effective controls, organizations can reduce the potential negative consequences associated with risks and enhance their ability to achieve objectives while minimizing the impact of uncertainties.

Knowledge Area: Real_Life_Exam_Sim

Question Number: 413

Question: Which of the following is MOST helpful in aligning IT risk with business objectives?

Option 1: Regular risk assessments and audits

Option 2: Collaboration between IT and business units

Option 3: Implementing advanced cybersecurity measures

Option 4: Utilizing risk management software

Correct Response: 2

Explanation: Collaboration between IT and business units is most helpful in aligning IT risk with business objectives. By fostering communication, cooperation, and shared understanding between IT and business stakeholders, organizations can ensure that IT risks are identified, assessed, and managed in a manner that supports and aligns with the overarching business objectives. This collaboration enables effective risk-informed decision-making and the integration of risk management into business processes.

Knowledge Area: Real_Life_Exam_Sim

Question Number: 414

Question: Documenting risk response strategies with assigned owners, steps, timeframes, and resource requirements in the risk register helps ensure efficient risk management through clarity.

Option 1: Sorting by priority

Option 2: Tracking with a risk board

Option 3: Weekly analysis meetings

Option 4: Monthly risk training

Correct Response: 1

Explanation: Documented responses enable efficient execution.

Knowledge Area: Real_Life_Exam_Sim

Question Number: 415

Question: Implementing a defense-in-depth strategy with preventive controls like firewalls, detection controls like IDS, and response plans provides the most effective recommendation for preventing cyber intrusions.

Option 1: Threat modeling

Option 2: Password complexity

Option 3: Annual penetration testing

Option 4: Cyber insurance

Correct Response: 1

Explanation: Layered controls prevent, detect, and respond.

Knowledge Area: Real_Life_Exam_Sim

Question Number: 416

Question: Enforcing password changes and access revocation when privileged users change roles best decreases exposure from compromised privileged credentials.

Option 1: Longer password expirations

Option 2: Increased complexity requirements

Option 3: Multi-factor authentication

Option 4: Permission recertification

Correct Response: 2

Explanation: Revocation on role changes limits exposure.

Knowledge Area: Real_Life_Exam_Sim

Question Number: 417

Question: Conducting disaster recovery exercises and tests to validate recovery readiness provides assurance that business resilience and continuity plans will be effective when needed.

Option 1: Documenting response procedures

Option 2: Securing backup facilities

Option 3: Reviewing insurance policies

Option 4: Training staff on plans

Correct Response: 1

Explanation: Tests prove recoverability capabilities.

Knowledge Area: Real_Life_Exam_Sim

Question Number: 418

Question: When developing a risk response, the highest priority should be selecting options that reduce risk to acceptable levels while supporting business objectives and resource constraints.

Option 1: Lowest cost options

Option 2: Fastest implementation

Option 3: Maximum risk reduction

Option 4: Consensus agreement

Correct Response: 1

Explanation: Responding must balance risk reduction with business needs.

Knowledge Area: Real_Life_Exam_Sim

Question Number: 419

Question: The inherent risk associated with an asset before controls reflects the potential impact and likelihood absent any mitigating measures.

Option 1: Residual risk

Option 2: Secondary risk

Option 3: Qualitative risk

Option 4: Inherent risk

Correct Response: 4

Explanation: Inherent risk is pre-control exposure.

Knowledge Area: Real_Life_Exam_Sim

Question Number: 420

Question: The application's business owner is ultimately accountable for managing risks associated with high-risk application vulnerabilities.

Option 1: Security team

Option 2: Software vendor

Option 3: Project manager

Option 4: CISO

Correct Response: 1

Explanation: The business owner owns application risks.

Knowledge Area: Real_Life_Exam_Sim

Question Number: 421

Question: Changes should be promoted to production only after being tested, approved, and scheduled to minimize unplanned impacts.

Option 1: Requested by users

Option 2: Code is optimized

Option 3: Business case approved

Option 4: Vendor validated

Correct Response: 2

Explanation: Testing, approval, scheduling assure production readiness.

Knowledge Area: Real_Life_Exam_Sim

Question Number: 422

Question: An up-to-date risk register helps inform risk-based decisions and establish accountability through defined risk owners and response plans.

Option 1: Satisfy auditors

Option 2: Validate risk model

Option 3: Justify budgets

Option 4: Limit exposures

Correct Response: 2

Explanation: The register enables risk-aware decisions and ownership.

Knowledge Area: Real_Life_Exam_Sim

Question Number: 423

Question: Strong change control processes that require justified scope changes best mitigate risks associated with uncontrolled project scope creep.

Option 1: Project manager discretion

Option 2: Progress tracking

Option 3: Status reporting

Option 4: Change control

Correct Response: 4

Explanation: Change control prevents uncontrolled scope changes.

Knowledge Area: Real_Life_Exam_Sim

Question Number: 424

Question: Which of the following is the most accurate definition of a project risk?

Option 1: An uncertain event or condition that, if it occurs, may have a positive or negative effect on project objectives

Option 2: An unexpected event that always has a negative impact on project objectives

Option 3: A known event that always has a positive impact on project objectives

Option 4: A potential issue that may arise during project execution

Correct Response: 1

Explanation: The most accurate definition of a project risk is that it is an uncertain event or condition that, if it occurs, may have a positive or negative effect on project objectives. Risks can be both positive (opportunities) and negative (threats), and their occurrence is uncertain. Effective risk management involves identifying, assessing, and responding to these potential events to minimize their impact and maximize project success.

Knowledge Area: Real_Life_Exam_Sim

Question Number: 425

Question: Which of the following BEST measures the operational effectiveness of risk management capabilities?

Option 1: Number of identified risks

Option 2: Percentage of risks mitigated

Option 3: Timeliness of risk response actions

Option 4: Reduction in risk impact and likelihood over time

Correct Response: 4

Explanation: The operational effectiveness of risk management capabilities is best measured by the reduction in risk impact and likelihood over time. This indicates that the organization's risk management efforts are successfully identifying, assessing, and responding to risks, resulting in a reduced potential impact and likelihood of negative events. It demonstrates the effectiveness of risk management processes and controls in managing risks proactively.

Knowledge Area: Real_Life_Exam_Sim

Question Number: 426

Question: Which of the following is the final step in the policy development process?

Option 1: Policy implementation

Option 2: Policy review

Option 3: Policy approval

Option 4: Policy dissemination

Correct Response: 4

Explanation: The final step in the policy development process is policy dissemination. Once a policy has been approved, it needs to be effectively communicated and shared with all relevant stakeholders and individuals within the organization. Dissemination ensures that everyone is aware of the policy, understands its requirements, and can adhere to it in their respective roles and responsibilities.

Knowledge Area: Real_Life_Exam_Sim

Question Number: 427

Question: Which of the following is MOST important when developing key performance indicators (KPIs)?

Option 1: Alignment with organizational goals and objectives

Option 2: Availability of data sources

Option 3: Benchmarks with industry standards

Option 4: Inclusion of all project stakeholders

Correct Response: 1

Explanation: The most important factor when developing key performance indicators (KPIs) is their alignment with organizational goals and objectives. KPIs should be directly linked to the desired outcomes and success factors of the organization. By aligning KPIs with organizational goals, it ensures that they measure the critical areas that contribute to the overall success and effectiveness of the organization.

Knowledge Area: Real_Life_Exam_Sim

Question Number: 428

Question: Which of the following would BEST ensure that identified risk scenarios are addressed?

Option 1: Risk mitigation plan

Option 2: Risk identification checklist

Option 3: Risk register

Option 4: Risk assessment matrix

Correct Response: 1

Explanation: A risk mitigation plan would best ensure that identified risk scenarios are addressed. A risk mitigation plan outlines specific actions and measures to be taken to reduce the likelihood or impact of identified risks. It provides a structured approach to addressing risks, ensuring that appropriate risk response strategies are developed and implemented to manage and mitigate the identified risk scenarios effectively.

Knowledge Area: Real_Life_Exam_Sim

Question Number: 429

Question: Which of the following should be PRIMARILY considered while designing information systems controls?

Option 1: Regulatory compliance

Option 2: User convenience

Option 3: Cost-effectiveness

Option 4: Security and risk management

Correct Response: 4

Explanation: While all options are important, security and risk management should be primarily considered while designing information systems controls. Information systems controls aim to safeguard the confidentiality, integrity, and availability of data and systems, as well as mitigate risks associated with unauthorized access, data breaches, and system vulnerabilities. Security and risk management considerations are crucial to ensure the effectiveness and resilience of controls in protecting organizational assets.

Knowledge Area: Real_Life_Exam_Sim

Question Number: 430

Question: Entity-based risks under the COSO ERM framework fall under the Governance and Culture risk dimension focused on behaviors, integrity, and oversight.

Option 1: Strategy

Option 2: Operations

Option 3: Reporting

Option 4: Compliance

Correct Response: 1

Explanation: Entity risks relate to governance and culture.

Knowledge Area: Real_Life_Exam_Sim

Question Number: 431

Question: Formally integrating risk management responsibilities into job descriptions and processes would best facilitate effective risk practices across the organization.

Option 1: Centralized reporting tools

Option 2: External risk consultants

Option 3: Quarterly risk training

Option 4: Timely issue escalation

Correct Response: 1

Explanation: Integrated responsibilities drive broad adoption.

Knowledge Area: Real_Life_Exam_Sim

Question Number: 432

Question: A key benefit of well-designed key risk indicators is providing early warnings of emerging risk conditions through correlation to risk factors before impacts fully materialize.

Option 1: Automated tracking

Option 2: Quantified measures

Option 3: Dashboard visualization

Option 4: Response guidance

Correct Response: 2

Explanation: Early warnings from correlations to risk is critical.

Question Number: 433

Question: The greatest advantage of implementing risk management is enabling informed decisions aligned to organizational risk appetite to drive performance while protecting value.

Option 1: Reduced uncertainties

Option 2: Improved budgeting

Option 3: Compliance assurance

Option 4: Audit readiness

Correct Response: 1

Explanation: Enables risk-aware decision making.

Knowledge Area: Real_Life_Exam_Sim

Question Number: 434

Question: Focusing discussions on how risks relate to strategy helps provide purpose and focus for risk conversations to drive meaningful decisions and actions.

Option 1: Reporting structures

Option 2: Monitoring metrics

Option 3: Historical losses

Option 4: Compliance impacts

Correct Response: 1

Explanation: Strategic relevance gives risk discussions purpose.

Knowledge Area: Real_Life_Exam_Sim

Question Number: 435

Question: Natural disasters like floods, storms, or earthquakes pose physical and environmental risks that can damage assets and disrupt operations.

Option 1: Financial

Option 2: Regulatory

Option 3: Strategic

Option 4: External

Correct Response: 4

Explanation: Natural disasters are external environmental risks.

Knowledge Area: Real_Life_Exam_Sim

Question Number: 436

Question: A strong ethical culture driven by executive commitment to integrity and accountability fosters a robust internal control environment.

Option 1: External audits

Option 2: Process automation

Option 3: Staff training

Option 4: System security controls

Correct Response: 1

Explanation: Culture and tone set by leadership enable controls.

Knowledge Area: Real_Life_Exam_Sim

Question Number: 437

Question: A disruption of operations that impacts the organization's ability to accomplish business objectives is considered a/an:

Option 1: Financial risk

Option 2: Strategic risk

Option 3: Compliance risk

Option 4: Operational risk

Correct Response: 4

Explanation: Business productivity loss is an operational risk.

Knowledge Area: Real_Life_Exam_Sim

Question Number: 438

Question: For large software projects, risk assessments are most effective when performed iteratively and continuously throughout the project lifecycle rather than just once at the start.

Option 1: At project closure

Option 2: During planning

Option 3: At design reviews

Option 4: After implementation

Correct Response: 2

Explanation: Continuous iterative assessments maximize risk insights.

Knowledge Area: Real_Life_Exam_Sim

Question Number: 439

Question: What is the process for selecting and implementing measures to impact risk called?

Option 1: Risk identification

Option 2: Risk assessment

Option 3: Risk mitigation

Option 4: Risk monitoring

Correct Response: 3

Explanation: The process for selecting and implementing measures to impact risk is called risk mitigation. Risk mitigation involves identifying potential risks, assessing their likelihood and impact, and then selecting and implementing appropriate actions or measures to reduce the probability or impact of those risks. It aims to proactively manage risks and minimize their potential negative consequences.

Knowledge Area: Real_Life_Exam_Sim

Question Number: 440

Question: Which of the following is an acceptable method for handling positive project risk?

Option 1: Risk avoidance

Option 2: Risk transference

Option 3: Risk acceptance

Option 4: Risk exploitation

Correct Response: 4

Explanation: Risk exploitation is an acceptable method for handling positive project risk. It involves identifying and taking advantage of opportunities that can bring positive outcomes or benefits to the project. By actively pursuing and exploiting these opportunities, organizations can enhance project success and achieve desired objectives.

Knowledge Area: Real_Life_Exam_Sim

Question Number: 441

Question: What is the value of the exposure factor if the asset is lost completely?

Option 1: 0%

Option 2: 25%

Option 3: 50%

Option 4: 100%

Correct Response: 4

Explanation: The value of the exposure factor is 100% if the asset is lost completely. Exposure factor represents the percentage of loss that would occur if a risk event materializes. In this scenario, the loss of the asset is total, resulting in a 100% exposure factor.

Knowledge Area: Real_Life_Exam_Sim

Question Number: 442

Question: Which of the following would require updates to an organization's IT risk register?

Option 1: Changes in regulatory requirements

Option 2: Employee training programs

Option 3: Routine system maintenance

Option 4: Annual financial audits

Correct Response: 1

Explanation: Changes in regulatory requirements would require updates to an organization's IT risk register. RegulatoryApologies for the incomplete response.

Knowledge Area: Real_Life_Exam_Sim

Question Number: 443

Question: Which of the following would prompt changes in key risk indicator (KRI) thresholds?

Option 1: Annual financial audits

Option 2: Technology upgrades

Option 3: Compliance with regulatory requirements

Option 4: Employee training programs

Correct Response: 3

Explanation: Compliance with regulatory requirements would prompt changes in key risk indicator (KRI) thresholds. Regulatory changes can impact the risk landscape and may require adjustments to the organization's risk management approach. Adapting KRI thresholds ensures that they reflect the evolving regulatory environment and help monitor and assess risks in accordance with the updated requirements. Compliance with regulatory standards is crucial for effective risk management and governance.

Knowledge Area: Real_Life_Exam_Sim

Question Number: 444

Question: What is the main reason to continuously monitor IT risk?

Option 1: Validate control design

Option 2: Identify emerging issues

Option 3: Assess training needs

Option 4: Demonstrate diligence

Correct Response: 2

Explanation: Monitoring rapidly detects new risk issues.

Knowledge Area: Real_Life_Exam_Sim

Question Number: 445

Question: What should primarily guide IT control design?

Option 1: Industry standards

Option 2: Auditor recommendations

Option 3: Legal requirements

Option 4: Business needs

Correct Response: 4

Explanation: Controls should align to business needs and objectives.

Knowledge Area: Real_Life_Exam_Sim

Question Number: 446

Question: Quantifying a single asset's value helps determine the:

Option 1: Total risk exposure

Option 2: Control testing scope

Option 3: Policy exceptions needed

Option 4: Potential loss impact

Correct Response: 4

Explanation: Single asset value quantifies potential loss.

Knowledge Area: Real_Life_Exam_Sim

Question Number: 447

Question: An organization's policies should foremost reflect:

Option 1: Management risk appetite

Option 2: Industry best practices

Option 3: Regulator expectations

Option 4: Company values and objectives

Correct Response: 4

Explanation: Policies should align with organizational goals.

Knowledge Area: Real_Life_Exam_Sim

Question Number: 448

Question: Why perform ongoing risk assessments?

Option 1: Audit requirements

Option 2: Benchmark comparisons

Option 3: Issue validation

Option 4: Identify profile changes

Correct Response: 4

Explanation: Assessments identify risk profile shifts.

Knowledge Area: Real_Life_Exam_Sim

Question Number: 449

Question: When establishing enterprise risk management, the most important focus is:

Option 1: Funding

Option 2: Staffing

Option 3: Executive alignment

Option 4: Technology solutions

Correct Response: 3

Explanation: Executive alignment enables embedded ERM practices.

Knowledge Area: Real_Life_Exam_Sim

Question Number: 450

Question: What best determines software license compliance?

Option 1: Vendor attestations

Option 2: Purchase requisitions

Option 3: Installation tracking

Option 4: Automated discovery scans

Correct Response: 4

Explanation: Automated scans validate installed vs. purchased licenses.

Knowledge Area: Real_Life_Exam_Sim

Question Number: 451

Question: Why test new controls before deployment?

Option 1: Meet project deadlines

Option 2: Set implementation priority

Option 3: Demonstrate value

Option 4: Identify design issues

Correct Response: 4

Explanation: Testing uncovers control weaknesses to address pre-release.

Knowledge Area: Real_Life_Exam_Sim

Question Number: 452

Question: Where are project risks and responses documented?

Option 1: Lessons learned

Option 2: Project management plan

Option 3: Risk register

Option 4: Status reports

Correct Response: 3

Explanation: The risk register centralizes risk details.

Knowledge Area: Real_Life_Exam_Sim

Question Number: 453

Question: Which of the following is NOT a method used in Qualitative risk analysis?

Option 1: Risk probability and impact assessment

Option 2: Risk categorization

Option 3: Risk scoring

Option 4: Monte Carlo simulation

Correct Response: 4

Explanation: Monte Carlo simulation is not a method used in Qualitative risk analysis. While it is a valuable technique for Quantitative risk analysis, it involves statistical modeling and simulation to analyze the impact of uncertainty on project objectives. In Qualitative risk analysis, the focus is on assessing risks qualitatively based on their probability and impact without involving complex simulations.

Knowledge Area: Real_Life_Exam_Sim

Question Number: 454

Question: Which of the following would BEST help an enterprise prioritize risk scenarios?

Option 1: Risk impact assessment

Option 2: Risk likelihood assessment

Option 3: Risk urgency assessment

Option 4: Risk tolerance assessment

Correct Response: 1

Explanation: Risk impact assessment would best help an enterprise prioritize risk scenarios. By assessing the potential impact of each risk scenario, the enterprise can understand the magnitude of the consequences and prioritize risks based on their potential impact on organizational objectives. This allows for the allocation of resources and efforts to address the most critical and impactful risks.

Knowledge Area: Real_Life_Exam_Sim

Question Number: 455

Question: Calculation of the recovery time objective (RTO) is necessary to determine the:

Option 1: Maximum tolerable downtime

Option 2: Recovery point objective (RPO)

Option 3: Mean time between failures (MTBF)

Option 4: Business impact analysis (BI

Correct Response: 1

Explanation: Calculation of the recovery time objective (RTO) is necessary to determine the maximum tolerable downtime. The RTO represents the duration within which a business process or system must be restored after an incident to avoid unacceptable consequences. It helps in setting recovery time targets and planning the necessary resources and strategies to minimize downtime and resume normal operations.

Knowledge Area: Real_Life_Exam_Sim

Question Number: 456

Question: The MOST important reason for implementing change control procedures is to ensure:

Option 1: Stakeholder engagement

Option 2: Scope creep prevention

Option 3: Consistency in project deliverables

Option 4: Effective management of project changes

Correct Response: 4

Explanation: The most important reason for implementing change control procedures is to ensure effective management of project changes. Change control procedures provide a structured approach to evaluate, assess, and approve changes to project scope, objectives, and deliverables. By following change control procedures, organizations can assess the impact of proposed changes, evaluate their feasibility, and make informed decisions to approve or reject changes, ensuring that only authorized and beneficial changes are implemented.

Knowledge Area: Real_Life_Exam_Sim

Question Number: 457

Question: NIST SP 800-53 identifies controls in three primary classes. What are they?

Option 1: Administrative, physical, and technical

Option 2: Preventive, detective, and corrective

Option 3: Strategic, operational, and tactical

Option 4: Internal, external, and hybrid

Correct Response: 1

Explanation: NIST SP 800-53 identifies controls in three primary classes: administrative, physical, and technical. Administrative controls encompass policies, procedures, and guidelines that guide and govern the organization's security framework. Physical controls involve physical safeguards and measures to protect assets and facilities. Technical controls include technical safeguards, mechanisms, and configurations to secure IT systems and infrastructure.

Knowledge Area: Real_Life_Exam_Sim

Question Number: 458

Question: Which of the following is the BEST defense against successful phishing attacks?

Option 1: Regular security awareness training

Option 2: Strong password policies

Option 3: Multi-factor authentication

Option 4: Robust antivirus software

Correct Response: 3

Explanation: Multi-factor authentication is the best defense against successful phishing attacks. Phishing attacks often rely on stolen credentials to gain unauthorized access to sensitive information or systems. By implementing multi-factor authentication, which requires additional verification beyond a username and password, organizations can add an extra layer of security and significantly reduce the risk of successful phishing attacks.

Knowledge Area: Real_Life_Exam_Sim

Question Number: 459

Question: What compliance regulation mandates controls around patient healthcare information privacy and security?

Option 1: SOX

Option 2: GLBA

Option 3: FISMA

Option 4: HIPAA

Correct Response: 4

Explanation: HIPAA regulates protected health information privacy and security.

Knowledge Area: Real_Life_Exam_Sim

Question Number: 460

Question: When would an organization initiate a pre-defined risk response plan?

Option 1: After a schedule change

Option 2: When new risks are identified

Option 3: When risk appetite is exceeded

Option 4: During a project retrospective

Correct Response: 3

Explanation: Triggers like risk materialization require executing planned responses.

Knowledge Area: Real_Life_Exam_Sim

Question Number: 461

Question: What technique helps identify unnecessary controls to remove?

Option 1: Internal audits

Option 2: Risk indicators

Option 3: Process modeling

Option 4: Gap/duplication analysis

Correct Response: 4

Explanation: Gap analysis exposes redundant or unnecessary controls.

Knowledge Area: Real_Life_Exam_Sim

Question Number: 462

Question: What effectively communicates risk summary data to executives?

Option 1: Total risks by department

Option 2: Qualitative analysis results

Option 3: Overdue risk lists

Option 4: Heat maps showing impact and likelihood

Correct Response: 4

Explanation: Heat maps concisely communicate risk profiles.

Knowledge Area: Real_Life_Exam_Sim

Question Number: 463

Question: Why define controls during system design?

Option 1: Enables user access control

Option 2: Limits scope creep

Option 3: Lowers licensing costs

Option 4: Avoids costly rework later

Correct Response: 4

Explanation: Designing controls early prevents expensive fixes.

Knowledge Area: Real_Life_Exam_Sim

Question Number: 464

Question: What indicates security awareness training effectiveness?

Option 1: Time between refreshers

Option 2: Training budget utilization

Option 3: Training materials created

Option 4: Test scores showing retention

Correct Response: 4

Explanation: Scores demonstrate improved behaviors.

Knowledge Area: Real_Life_Exam_Sim

Question Number: 465

Question: What is the first step in business continuity planning?

Option 1: Train staff on plans

Option 2: Acquire backup facilities

Option 3: Insure against losses

Option 4: Conduct impact analysis

Correct Response: 4

Explanation: Impact analysis identifies critical processes and needs.

Knowledge Area: Real_Life_Exam_Sim

Question Number: 466

Question: What helps validate that controls are functioning as intended?

Option 1: Vulnerability scans

Option 2: Compliance audits

Option 3: Penetration testing

Option 4: Control testing

Correct Response: 4

Explanation: Control testing specifically evaluates whether controls are operating effectively.

Knowledge Area: Real_Life_Exam_Sim

Question Number: 467

Question: What helps assign accountability for managing a particular risk?

Option 1: Risk matrix

Option 2: Risk register

Option 3: Risk appetite

Option 4: Risk owner

Correct Response: 4

Explanation: The risk owner is responsible for managing the response to an assigned risk.

Knowledge Area: Real_Life_Exam_Sim

Question Number: 468

Question: Which control would detect unauthorized changes to production data?

Option 1: Access logs

Option 2: IDS

Option 3: DLP

Option 4: File integrity monitoring

Correct Response: 4

Explanation: File integrity monitoring detects and alerts on unexpected data modifications.

Knowledge Area: Real_Life_Exam_Sim

Question Number: 469

Question: Most important for incident response is:

Option 1: Blocking attacks

Option 2: Timely recognition

Option 3: Data logging

Option 4: Tracing source

Correct Response: 2

Explanation: Quick recognition limits damage.

Knowledge Area: Real_Life_Exam_Sim

Question Number: 470

Question: Anti-malware effectiveness is best indicated by:

Option 1: Staff hours lost

Option 2: Software patches

Option 3: Successful attacks

Option 4: Server downtime

Correct Response: 3

Explanation: Fewer successful attacks mean better protection.

Knowledge Area: Real_Life_Exam_Sim

Question Number: 471

Question: When evaluating IT risk management, most important is confirming:

Option 1: Risk appetite/tolerance

Option 2: New control processes

Option 3: Risk reporting

Option 4: Investment alignment

Correct Response: 1

Explanation: Appetite sets risk expectations.

Knowledge Area: Real_Life_Exam_Sim

Question Number: 472

Question: A risk assessment output is:

Option 1: Residual risk

Option 2: Control identification

Option 3: Risk identification

Option 4: Mitigated risk

Correct Response: 4

Explanation: Assessments reveal risks.

Knowledge Area: Real_Life_Exam_Sim

Question Number: 473

Question: The first security monitoring step is:

Option 1: Implement monitoring

Option 2: Prioritize risks

Option 3: Identify controls

Option 4: Report results

Correct Response: 3

Explanation: Monitoring depends on identified controls.

Knowledge Area: Real_Life_Exam_Sim

Question Number: 474

Question: Management has requested a routine information security risk report. Which format would BEST ensure the risks are understood by the audience?

Option 1: Detailed risk assessment

Option 2: Heat map of critical risks

Option 3: Technical vulnerability scan results

Option 4: Executive dashboard highlighting trends

Correct Response: 4

Explanation: Executive dashboards effectively communicate key risk information to management.

Knowledge Area: Real_Life_Exam_Sim

Question Number: 475

Question: Risk thresholds are specified in a:

Option 1: Impact matrix

Option 2: Probability matrix

Option 3: Risk indicator matrix

Option 4: Scenario matrix

Correct Response: 3

Explanation: A risk indicator matrix sets thresholds.

Knowledge Area: Real_Life_Exam_Sim

Question Number: 476

Question: The most important risk response factor is:

Option 1: Implementation capability

Option 2: Response efficiency

Option 3: Response cost

Option 4: Risk importance

Correct Response: 3

Explanation: Feasibility determines viability.

Knowledge Area: Real_Life_Exam_Sim

Question Number: 477

Question: Effective risk analysis should:

Option 1: Limit scope

Option 2: Focus on likelihood

Option 3: Assume equal protection

Option 4: Address loss potential

Correct Response: 4

Explanation: Potential loss insight guides responses.

Knowledge Area: Real_Life_Exam_Sim

Question Number: 478

Question: The greatest reporting risk is to data:

Option 1: Availability

Option 2: Integrity

Option 3: Confidentiality

Option 4: Reliability

Correct Response: 2

Explanation: Integrity is critical for accurate reporting.

Knowledge Area: Real_Life_Exam_Sim

Question Number: 479

Question: Classifying assets is most important for:

Option 1: Access rights

Option 2: Risk ownership

Option 3: Security objectives

Option 4: Control identification

Correct Response: 4

Explanation: Classification guides required controls.

Knowledge Area: Real_Life_Exam_Sim

Question Number: 480

Question: What is most critical when designing controls?

Option 1: Process owner involvement

Option 2: Internal audit involvement

Option 3: KRI identification

Option 4: Risk impact

Correct Response: 1

Explanation: Involving the process owner is key.

Knowledge Area: Real_Life_Exam_Sim

Question Number: 481

Question: The primary objective in selecting responses is to:

Option 1: Identify compensating controls

Option 2: Reduce risk factors

Option 3: Minimize residual risk

Option 4: Reduce risk to acceptable levels

Correct Response: 3

Explanation: The goal is to reach acceptable risk.

Knowledge Area: Real_Life_Exam_Sim

Question Number: 482

Question: Which is NOT true about risk governance?

Option 1: Seeks to fill risk gaps

Option 2: Requires annual reporting

Option 3: Enables risk management

Option 4: Is a systemic approach

Correct Response: 2

Explanation: Reporting is not necessarily annual.

Knowledge Area: Real_Life_Exam_Sim

Question Number: 483

Question: A cloud provider contract must include:

Option 1: Financial statements

Option 2: Recovery plan

Option 3: Source code escrow

Option 4: Responsibility ownership

Correct Response: 2

Explanation: It should define accountability.

Knowledge Area: Real_Life_Exam_Sim

Question Number: 484

Question: The greatest concern with a risk register is:

Option 1: No executive reviews

Option 2: Excluding risk changes

Option 3: Unlinked IT risks

Option 4: Qualitative impacts

Correct Response: 2

Explanation: Excluding risk factor changes is most concerning.

Knowledge Area: Real_Life_Exam_Sim

Question Number: 485

Question: Accountability for a risk is best shown in a:

Option 1: Risk scenario

Option 2: Risk catalog

Option 3: RACI matrix

Option 4: Risk register

Correct Response: 3

Explanation: A RACI matrix clarifies accountability.

Knowledge Area: Real_Life_Exam_Sim

Question Number: 486

Question: For effective business support, a risk register must:

Option 1: Reflect assessments

Option 2: Support maturity models

Option 3: Be reviewed by IT steering

Option 4: Be available to risk groups

Correct Response: 1

Explanation: It must reflect current assessment results.

Knowledge Area: Real_Life_Exam_Sim

Question Number: 487

Question: Who should implement security controls?

Option 1: Data custodian

Option 2: Internal auditor

Option 3: Data owner

Option 4: End user

Correct Response: 3

Explanation: The data owner is responsible.

Knowledge Area: Real_Life_Exam_Sim

Question Number: 488

Question: Which statement about risk evaluation is true?

Option 1: Only after significant change

Option 2: Annually for all processes

Option 3: Annually or after change

Option 4: Every 4-6 months for critical

Correct Response: 3

Explanation: Evaluation should happen annually or after major change.

Knowledge Area: Real_Life_Exam_Sim

Question Number: 489

Question: IT risk assessments are best used by management:

Option 1: To show compliance

Option 2: As cost-benefit input

Option 3: To measure success

Option 4: To inform decisions

Correct Response: 4

Explanation: Assessments provide decision-making insights.

Knowledge Area: Real_Life_Exam_Sim

Question Number: 490

Question: A risk owner should be accountable for:

Option 1: Managing controls

Option 2: Implementing actions

Option 3: Risk management process

Option 4: Business process

Correct Response: 4

Explanation: The risk owner governs the business process.

Knowledge Area: Real_Life_Exam_Sim

Question Number: 491

Question: Which would be considered a vulnerability?

Option 1: Delayed access removal

Option 2: Malware corruption

Option 3: Authorized access

Option 4: Downtime from DoS

Correct Response: 1

Explanation: Delayed access removal is a vulnerability.

Knowledge Area: Real_Life_Exam_Sim

Question Number: 492

Question: Prudent practice requires risk appetite not exceed which level?

Option 1: Residual risk

Option 2: Inherent risk

Option 3: Risk tolerance

Option 4: Risk capacity

Correct Response: 4

Explanation: Appetite should not surpass capacity.

Knowledge Area: Real_Life_Exam_Sim

Question Number: 493

Question: What are the primary control objectives?

Option 1: Detect, recover, attack

Option 2: Prevent, respond, log

Option 3: Prevent, control, attack

Option 4: Prevent, recover, detect

Correct Response: 4

Explanation: Key goals are to prevent, recover and detect.

Knowledge Area: Real_Life_Exam_Sim

Question Number: 494

Question: Which statement describes policy?

Option 1: Minimum controls required

Option 2: Steps to ensure security

Option 3: Overall security direction

Option 4: Technology best practices

Correct Response: 3

Explanation: Policy sets overall security direction.

Knowledge Area: Real_Life_Exam_Sim

Question Number: 495

Question: What provides the most valuable input for assessing disaster recovery capabilities?

Option 1: Higher % systems meeting RTOs

Option 2: Fewer systems needing plans

Option 3: More systems tested annually

Option 4: Lower % systems with long RTOs

Correct Response: 4

Explanation: Fewer systems with lengthy recovery times indicates stronger DR readiness.

Knowledge Area: Real_Life_Exam_Sim

Question Number: 496

Question: Before adopting a new SaaS application, what activity provides the most risk insights?

Option 1: Review provider's uptime history

Option 2: Analyze provider's security architecture

Option 3: Assess provider's backup procedures

Option 4: Compare to industry standards

Correct Response: 3

Explanation: Assessing the provider's security controls is critical to manage SaaS risks.

Question Number: 497

Question: How should management utilize IT risk assessment results?

Option 1: Demonstrate compliance

Option 2: Justify expenditures

Option 3: Measure success metrics

Option 4: Inform risk decisions

Correct Response: 4

Explanation: Risk assessments provide valuable insights to inform management decisions.

Knowledge Area: Real_Life_Exam_Sim

Question Number: 498

Question: To optimize risk management resource allocation, what should drive the focus areas?

Option 1: Regulatory requirements

Option 2: Senior management concerns

Option 3: Industry benchmarks

Option 4: Assessed risk appetite

Correct Response: 4

Explanation: Aligning efforts with the organization's risk appetite directs optimal focus.

Knowledge Area: Real_Life_Exam_Sim

Question Number: 499

Question: What is the most effective option to mitigate supply chain disruption risks?

Option 1: Increase inventory levels

Option 2: Improve demand forecasting

Option 3: Dual source critical components

Option 4: Negotiate volume discounts

Correct Response: 3

Explanation: Dual sourcing key items through alternate suppliers reduces risk.

Knowledge Area: Real_Life_Exam_Sim

Question Number: 500

Question: Per best practices, risk appetite should not surpass which level?

Option 1: Residual risk

Option 2: Inherent risk

Option 3: Risk tolerance

Option 4: Risk capacity

Correct Response: 4

Explanation: Risk appetite should not exceed the organization's overall risk capacity.

Knowledge Area: Real_Life_Exam_Sim

What do you think about our book?

Don't hesitate to help us improve it!

So-so   Good   Perfect

WalterEducation.com

Amazing!

You have been studying very hard to this stage.

How is your exam preparation so far? Can the practice test meet your needs and expectation? I desperately desire your voice.

Please kindly consider

1. Visiting my exam practice test books and consider purchasing them to assist you to pass your target exam, though the direct links provided at the beginning of this book
2. Visiting my exam practice test courses held at Udemy though the direct links provided at the beginning of this book
3. Leaving a positive review and feedback to me though the direct book review links provided at the next page.

Keep going! See you at the end of the book.

Warm regards,

Walter

Direct URLs to visit all Walter's Practice Tests at Amazon

Visit Walter's author page:
http://WalterEducation.com

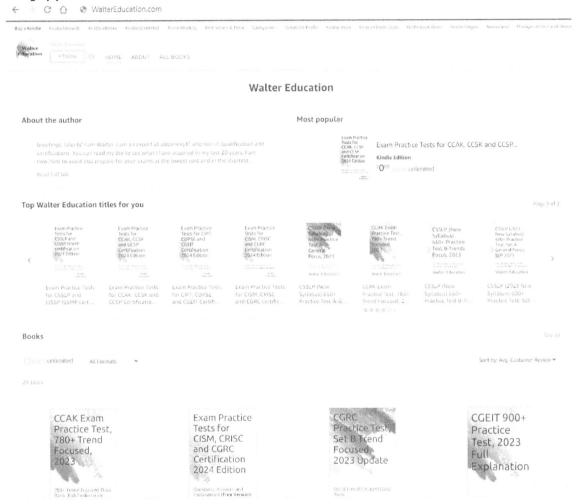

Or the **Links at Amazon Book Store:**

CCAK Exam Practice Test, 780+ Trend Focused, 2023	
Paperback Review URL:	- https://www.amazon.com/review/create-review?&asin=B0CJSXPYM7
Kindle eBook Review URL:	- https://www.amazon.com/review/create-review?&asin=B0CK9QQ44B

CERTIFIED DATA PRIVACY SOLUTIONS ENGINEER (CDPSE) 900+ PRACTICE TEST, 2023, FULL EXPLANATION	
Paperback Review URL:	- https://www.amazon.com/review/create-review?&asin=B0CGL3S5BH
Kindle eBook Review URL:	- https://www.amazon.com/review/create-review?&asin=B0CGL91NQ9

CGEIT 900+ Practice Test, 2023

Paperback Review URL:	- https://www.amazon.com/review/create-review?&asin=B0CGW1Y1X9
Kindle eBook Review URL:	- https://www.amazon.com/review/create-review?&asin=B0CJ8388ZB

CIPT, Certified Information Privacy Technologists, Practice Test

Paperback Review URL:	- https://www.amazon.com/review/create-review?&asin=B0CJ4DLHG2
Kindle eBook Review URL:	- https://www.amazon.com/review/create-review?&asin=B0CJ72MR4M

CRISC 1200+ Practice Test, 2023 (Exam Simulation and Core & Advanced Knowledge)

Paperback Review URL:	- https://www.amazon.com/review/create-review?&asin=B0CJ43R78T
Kindle eBook Review URL:	- https://www.amazon.com/review/create-review?&asin=B0CJ72JJLY

CISM 1050+ Practice Test,2023 Updated, Set B - Trends Focused, ISACA

Paperback Review URL:	- https://www.amazon.com/review/create-review?&asin=B0CJSNR5Z2
Kindle eBook Review URL:	- https://www.amazon.com/review/create-review?&asin=B0CJVWHJHW

CISM 1050+ Practice Test A - Core Focus, ISACA

Paperback Review URL:	- https://www.amazon.com/review/create-review?&asin=B0CJL2HD1R
Kindle eBook Review URL:	- https://www.amazon.com/review/create-review?&asin=B0CJVSQ6Z6

CCSKv4 900+ Practice Test 2023, Full Explanation

Paperback Review URL:	- https://www.amazon.com/review/create-review?&asin=B0CFX2S7D8
Kindle eBook Review URL:	- https://www.amazon.com/review/create-review?&asin=B0CFVLS8ZH

CSSLP (2023 New Syllabus) 600+ Practice Test, Set A General Focus

Paperback Review URL:	- https://www.amazon.com/review/create-review?&asin=B0CK3VTR9D
Kindle eBook Review URL:	- https://www.amazon.com/review/create-review?&asin=PENDING

CSSLP (New Syllabus) 660+ Practice Test B-Trends Focus, SEP 2023

Paperback Review URL:	- https://www.amazon.com/review/create-review?&asin=B0CK3XGCBN
Kindle eBook Review URL:	- https://www.amazon.com/review/create-review?&asin=PENDING

CISSP-ISSMP 650+ Practice Test, 2023 New syllabus, Set A Core Focused

Paperback Review URL:	- https://www.amazon.com/review/create-review?&asin=B0CJLLL4HP
Kindle eBook Review URL:	- https://www.amazon.com/review/create-review?&asin=B0CK2Y6XR7

CISSP-ISSMP 650+ Practice Test, 2023 New syllabus, Set B Trends Focused, ISC2

| Paperback Review URL: | - https://www.amazon.com/review/create-review?&asin=B0CJLMV48G |
| Kindle eBook Review URL: | - https://www.amazon.com/review/create-review?&asin=B0CK2X7CLL |

Practice Test for Certified Cloud Security Professional (CCSP): 900+ Practice Test

| Paperback Review URL: | - https://www.amazon.com/review/create-review?&asin=B0CFCLW7HJ |
| Kindle eBook Review URL: | - https://www.amazon.com/review/create-review?&asin=B0CFKSVKSS |

CGRC Practice Test, Set A Data Bank, Learn & Exam, 2023 Update

| Paperback Review URL: | - https://www.amazon.com/review/create-review?&asin=B0CJBC5MX1 |
| Kindle eBook Review URL: | - https://www.amazon.com/review/create-review?&asin=B0CJYQVM22 |

CGRC Practice Test, Set B Trend Focused, 2023

| Paperback Review URL: | - https://www.amazon.com/review/create-review?&asin=B0CJ43Z8N6 |
| Kindle eBook Review URL: | - https://www.amazon.com/review/create-review?&asin=B0CJ72HWY2 |

How to give a Review and Rating:

1. Click Here

Create Review

CCAK Exam Practice Test, 780+ Trend Focused, 2023 780+ Trend Focused Data Bank, Full Expla...

Overall rating   Clear

⭐⭐⭐⭐⭐

Add a headline

What's most important to know?

Add a photo or video

Shoppers find images and videos more helpful than text alone.

Add a written review

What did y...

2.
Tell me anything about the course

3. Submit

Question Number: 501

Question: A vendor identified a new project risk. The risk register and responses were updated. What else should the project manager update?

Option 1: Project scope statement

Option 2: Project communications plan

Option 3: Project contractual agreements

Option 4: Project management plan

Correct Response: 4

Explanation: The project management plan should reflect new risk information.

Knowledge Area: Real_Life_Exam_Sim

Question Number: 502

Question: A director demands a late change to the project scope. What should the project manager do with the verbal change request?

Option 1: Implement the change immediately

Option 2: Direct the team to add it if possible

Option 3: Do not act without written request

Option 4: Report the director to the sponsor

Correct Response: 3

Explanation: Verbal direction should not dictate a change.

Knowledge Area: Real_Life_Exam_Sim

Question Number: 503

Question: A scope change request may impact cost, schedule, and other areas. What process evaluates the overall change impact?

Option 1: Risk analysis

Option 2: Configuration management

Option 3: Project change control

Option 4: Integrated change control

Correct Response: 4

Explanation: Integrated change control assesses all impacts.

Knowledge Area: Real_Life_Exam_Sim

Question Number: 504

Question: A machine will overheat and shutdown above 500 degrees. At 450 degrees it will pause to cool. What is 450 degrees called in this context?

Option 1: Risk identification

Option 2: Risk event

Option 3: Risk trigger

Option 4: Risk response

Correct Response: 3

Explanation: 450 degrees is the defined risk trigger point.

Knowledge Area: Real_Life_Exam_Sim

Question Number: 505

Question: A project finds a cheaper way to complete work, saving $65,000 for a $25,000 cost. What response was used?

Option 1: Avoiding

Option 2: Accepting

Option 3: Exploiting

Option 4: Enhancing

Correct Response: 3

Explanation: The opportunity was exploited for project savings.

Knowledge Area: Real_Life_Exam_Sim

Question Number: 506

Question: For a high-impact project, management wants early risk information to support avoidance. What determines avoidance preference?

Option 1: Mitigation-ready PM

Option 2: Risk-reward mentality

Option 3: Risk utility function

Option 4: Risk aversion

Correct Response: 4

Explanation: A risk utility function measures avoidance desire.

Knowledge Area: Real_Life_Exam_Sim

Question Number: 507

Question: What communicates approval or denial of a proposed change request?

Option 1: Configuration management system

Option 2: Integrated change control

Option 3: Change log

Option 4: Scope change control

Correct Response: 2

Explanation: Integrated change control governs changes.

Knowledge Area: Real_Life_Exam_Sim

Question Number: 508

Question: Where should risks from new technology be documented for tracking?

Option 1: Project scope statement

Option 2: Project charter

Option 3: Watch list

Option 4: Risk register

Correct Response: 4

Explanation: The risk register tracks and manages risks.

Knowledge Area: Real_Life_Exam_Sim

Question Number: 509

Question: What process evaluates a change to reduce status reports from weekly to biweekly?

Option 1: Configuration management

Option 2: Communications management

Option 3: Integrated change control

Option 4: Project change control

Correct Response: 3

Explanation: Integrated change control governs changes.

Knowledge Area: Real_Life_Exam_Sim

Question Number: 510

Question: The IRGC risk governance framework aims to:

Option 1: Evaluate secondary impacts

Option 2: Enhance organizational resilience

Option 3: Integrate risk disciplines

Option 4: Build robust models

Correct Response: 4

Explanation: IRGC integrates risk disciplines into robust governance models.

Knowledge Area: Real_Life_Exam_Sim

Question Number: 511

Question: During risk identification, all documents are used EXCEPT the:

Option 1: Requirements checklist

Option 2: Risk register

Option 3: Stakeholder analysis

Option 4: Cost baseline

Correct Response: 2

Explanation: The risk register tracks identified risks and is not an input.

Knowledge Area: Real_Life_Exam_Sim

Question Number: 512

Question: When a vendor's costs increase, the change should pass through:

Option 1: Scope control

Option 2: Schedule control

Option 3: Cost control

Option 4: No control

Correct Response: 3

Explanation: Cost changes go through cost change control processes.

Knowledge Area: Real_Life_Exam_Sim

Question Number: 513

Question: Risk analysis can be improved by:

Option 1: Focusing on critical risks

Option 2: Involving select stakeholders

Option 3: Rushing qualitative assessments

Option 4: Using subject matter experts

Correct Response: 4

Explanation: Experts provide insights into risks and responses.

Knowledge Area: Real_Life_Exam_Sim

Question Number: 514

Question: A system not fulfilling needs and being unused reflects:

Option 1: Project risk

Option 2: Residual risk

Option 3: Business risk

Option 4: Inherent risk

Correct Response: 3

Explanation: This demonstrates ineffective business risk management.

Knowledge Area: Real_Life_Exam_Sim

Question Number: 515

Question: Risk of unauthorized website modification falls under:

Option 1: FTP bounce attacks

Option 2: Web defacing

Option 3: Ping flooding

Option 4: Denial of service

Correct Response: 2

Explanation: Web defacing is an unauthorized change risk.

Knowledge Area: Real_Life_Exam_Sim

Question Number: 516

Question: An alarm that triggers machine shutdown at high temperatures serves as:

Option 1: Risk identification

Option 2: Risk trigger

Option 3: Risk indicator

Option 4: Risk response

Correct Response: 2

Explanation: The temperature trigger initiates a shutdown response.

Knowledge Area: Real_Life_Exam_Sim

Question Number: 517

Question: To test disaster recovery, a project manager should review:

Option 1: Risk tolerance

Option 2: Incident response

Option 3: Recovery time

Option 4: Risk appetite

Correct Response: 3

Explanation: Recovery time shows disaster preparedness.

Knowledge Area: Real_Life_Exam_Sim

Question Number: 518

Question: Which type of analysis examines the extent to which the uncertainty of each element affects the object under consideration when all other uncertain elements are held at their baseline values?

Option 1: Sensitivity analysis

Option 2: Monte Carlo simulation

Option 3: Root cause analysis

Option 4: Scenario analysis

Correct Response: 1

Explanation: The type of analysis described in this scenario is sensitivity analysis. Sensitivity analysis examines the impact of changing one variable while keeping all other variables at their baseline values. It helps identify which elements or factors have the highest potential to affect the object under consideration. By understanding these sensitivities, organizations can focus their risk management efforts on critical areas and make informed decisions.

Knowledge Area: Real_Life_Exam_Sim

Question Number: 519

Question: In rating project risks based on probability and impact, who is correct in the scenario where the project manager rates each risk separately, and a team member suggests creating an accumulative risk score?

Option 1: The project manager is correct

Option 2: The team member is correct

Option 3: Both approaches are valid

Option 4: Neither approach is valid

Correct Response: 1

Explanation: In this scenario, the project manager is correct. Rating each risk separately based on probability and impact allows for a more comprehensive understanding of the risks. It enables the project manager to prioritize risks and allocate resources accordingly. Creating an accumulative risk score may overlook specific risks that require specific attention and mitigation efforts.

Knowledge Area: Real_Life_Exam_Sim

Question Number: 520

Question: Mary, a project manager, is using a facilitator to help generate ideas about project risks. What risk identification method is Mary likely using?

Option 1: Delphi technique

Option 2: Brainstorming

Option 3: SWOT analysis

Option 4: Checklist analysis

Correct Response: 2

Explanation: Mary is likely using the risk identification method of brainstorming. Brainstorming involves a facilitated session where project team members and stakeholders generate ideas and identify potential risks. It encourages open discussion and creativity, allowing for a wide range of risks to be identified. The involvement of a facilitator helps in guiding and managing the brainstorming session effectively.

Knowledge Area: Real_Life_Exam_Sim

Question Number: 521

Question: To configure a monitoring tool to report only when alerts are marked as "critical," what should be done?

Option 1: Adjust the alert thresholds

Option 2: Increase the monitoring frequency

Option 3: Modify the reporting format

Option 4: Define the alert severity levels

Correct Response: 1

Explanation: To configure a monitoring tool to report only when alerts are marked as "critical," the alert thresholds should be adjusted. By setting the thresholds specifically for critical alerts, the monitoring tool will generate reports only when the alerts meet the predefined criteria. This ensures that the focus is on critical events, allowing for efficient monitoring and response to significant risks.

Knowledge Area: Real_Life_Exam_Sim

Question Number: 522

Question: From a business perspective, what is the most important objective of a disaster recovery test?

Option 1: Validate the effectiveness of backup and recovery procedures

Option 2: Assess the performance of technical infrastructure components

Option 3: Identify gaps and areas for improvement in the recovery process

Option 4: Ensure minimal disruption and timely recovery of business operations

Correct Response: 4

Explanation: From a business perspective, the most important objective of a disaster recovery test is to ensure minimal disruption and timely recovery of business operations. The test aims to validate the organization's ability to recover critical processes and systems in the event of a disaster. By conducting the test, organizations can identify any gaps or areas forI apologize for the incomplete response.

Knowledge Area: Real_Life_Exam_Sim

Question Number: 523

Question: You are managing a project to develop a new system interface. You've identified all possible risks. What is needed next to prioritize the risks?

Option 1: Mitigation strategies

Option 2: Qualitative analysis

Option 3: Probability and impact assessment

Option 4: Risk categorization

Correct Response: 3

Explanation: Prioritization requires probability and impact analysis of identified risks.

Knowledge Area: Real_Life_Exam_Sim

Question Number: 524

Question: Your project has external stakeholders. What plan provides guidance on appropriately communicating risks?

Option 1: Risk management plan

Option 2: Communications management plan

Option 3: Stakeholder engagement plan

Option 4: Procurement management plan

Correct Response: 2

Explanation: The communications plan covers appropriate risk reporting.

Knowledge Area: Real_Life_Exam_Sim

Question Number: 525

Question: Identifying project risks requires inputs. Which is NOT an input to risk identification?

Option 1: Activity cost estimates

Option 2: Project documents

Option 3: Enterprise risk databases

Option 4: Lessons learned

Correct Response: 1

Explanation: Cost estimates are not an input to identifying risks.

Knowledge Area: Real_Life_Exam_Sim

Question Number: 526

Question: In qualitative analysis, you grouped risks by common causes. What is the primary advantage of this?

Option 1: Simplifies quantitative modeling

Option 2: Highlights correlation and impacts

Option 3: Satisfies governance requirements

Option 4: Aids risk monitoring

Correct Response: 2

Explanation: Grouping shows how risks interconnect.

Knowledge Area: Real_Life_Exam_Sim

Question Number: 527

Question: You refuse to accept risks threatening injury, so you hired vendors to remove the risk. What response is this?

Option 1: Mitigate

Option 2: Exploit

Option 3: Accept

Option 4: Avoid

Correct Response: 4

Explanation: Transferring the work avoids the risk fully.

Knowledge Area: Real_Life_Exam_Sim

Question Number: 528

Question: As a project manager, you must identify risks that could impact your project. What inputs help identify risks related to activity durations?

Option 1: Project budget

Option 2: Requirements docs

Option 3: Activity duration estimates

Option 4: Lessons learned

Correct Response: 3

Explanation: Duration estimates help highlight timing risks.

Knowledge Area: Real_Life_Exam_Sim

Question Number: 529

Question: You are the risk professional of your enterprise. You need to calculate the potential revenue loss if a specific risk occurs. Your enterprise has an e-commerce website that generates US $1 million of revenue each day. If a denial-of-service (DoS) attack occurs that lasts half a day, what is the potential loss?

Option 1: US $0.5 million

Option 2: US $0.25 million

Option 3: US $1 million

Option 4: US $2 million

Correct Response: 2

Explanation: The potential loss due to the DoS attack can be calculated by multiplying the revenue generated per day ($1 million) by the duration of the attack (half a day or 0.5). Therefore, the potential loss would be US $1 million * 0.5 = US $0.25 million. Hence, the correct option is b) US $0.25 million.

Knowledge Area: Real_Life_Exam_Sim

Question Number: 530

Question: Billy, the project manager of the HAR Project, is in month six of the project, which is scheduled to last for 18 months. Management asks Billy about the frequency of project team participation in risk reassessment. What should Billy tell management if he's following the best practices for risk management?

Option 1: Risk reassessment should be done monthly

Option 2: Risk reassessment should be done quarterly

Option 3: Risk reassessment should be done annually

Option 4: Risk reassessment should be done on an ad-hoc basis

Correct Response: 2

Explanation: Following the best practices for risk management, Billy should tell management that risk reassessment should be done quarterly. Regular risk reassessment helps ensure that risks are monitored and evaluated periodically, taking into account any changes in the project's context, risks, or risk responses. It allows for timely identification of emerging risks and reassessment of existing risks to ensure effective risk management.

Knowledge Area: Real_Life_Exam_Sim

Question Number: 531

Question: A delay is hurting your project's schedule. With approval, you fast track work to finish faster. What will likely increase?

Option 1: Risk identification

Option 2: Project costs

Option 3: Schedule flexibility

Option 4: Project risks

Correct Response: 4

Explanation: Fast tracking compresses the schedule but increases risks.

Knowledge Area: Real_Life_Exam_Sim

Question Number: 532

Question: You are identifying stakeholders to communicate requirements and risks. Using a salience model involves which activity?

Option 1: Assessing reporting needs

Option 2: Grouping stakeholders by roles

Option 3: Mapping influence and impact

Option 4: Developing a communications matrix

Correct Response: 3

Explanation: Salience models map stakeholder influence/impact.

Knowledge Area: Real_Life_Exam_Sim

Question Number: 533

Question: To determine risk probability and impacts, you could conduct an expected monetary value (EMV) analysis of potential costs.

Option 1: Decision tree analysis

Option 2: Risk urgency assessment

Option 3: RBS development

Option 4: Stakeholder analysis

Correct Response: 1

Explanation: EMV analysis evaluates risk impacts and likelihood.

Knowledge Area: Real_Life_Exam_Sim

Question Number: 534

Question: What tool will help you measure the probability, impact, and risk exposure?

Option 1: Risk probability and impact assessment matrix

Option 2: Risk breakdown structure

Option 3: Risk register

Option 4: Risk assessment questionnaire

Correct Response: 1

Explanation: The tool that will help you measure the probability, impact, and risk exposure is the risk probability and impact assessment matrix. This tool allows you to assess the likelihood and consequences of identified risks and calculate their overall risk exposure. By using the matrix, you can prioritize risks based on their probability and impact, helping you focus on those with higher risk exposure.

Knowledge Area: Real_Life_Exam_Sim

Question Number: 535

Question: In which project management process group will you implement risk response plans for the ABC project?

Option 1: Initiating

Option 2: Planning

Option 3: Executing

Option 4: Monitoring and controlling

Correct Response: 2

Explanation: The project management process group in which risk response plans will be implemented for the GHY project is the planning process group. During the planning phase, the project manager identifies risks, assesses their impacts and likelihood, and develops risk response plans to address them. Implementing risk response plans involves executing the planned risk mitigation and contingency actions to reduce the impact or likelihood of identified risks.

Knowledge Area: Real_Life_Exam_Sim

Question Number: 536

Question: As an experienced Project Manager working on a project to develop a machine for producing auto components, you schedule meetings with the project team and key stakeholders to identify risks. What is a key output of this process?

Option 1: Risk management plan

Option 2: Risk register

Option 3: Risk breakdown structure

Option 4: Risk identification checklist

Correct Response: 2

Explanation: A key output of the risk identification process is the risk register. The risk register is a comprehensive document that captures all identified risks, their descriptions, potential impacts, and initial assessments. It serves as a central repository of project risks and provides a foundation for further risk analysis, response planning, and monitoring.

Knowledge Area: Real_Life_Exam_Sim

Question Number: 537

Question: Executives feel IT should own IT risks in an IT scenario review. How should you address this?

Option 1: Agree that IT owns the risks

Option 2: Explain all stakeholders own a share of risk

Option 3: Let executives delegate all IT risks to IT

Option 4: Focus only on non-IT risks

Correct Response: 2

Explanation: Explain that all stakeholders share responsibility for mitigating risks.

Knowledge Area: Real_Life_Exam_Sim

Question Number: 538

Question: Why include the cost management plan in quantitative risk analysis?

Option 1: It calculates the project ROI

Option 2: It estimates activity costs for impacts

Option 3: It outlines the risk budget

Option 4: It defines risk reporting formats

Correct Response: 2

Explanation: Cost estimates support quantifying risk impacts.

Knowledge Area: Real_Life_Exam_Sim

Question Number: 539

Question: After monitoring occurred risks, what is the next risk management step?

Option 1: Risk identification

Option 2: Qualitative analysis

Option 3: Risk response

Option 4: Control enhancements

Correct Response: 4

Explanation: Improve controls through learned lessons.

Knowledge Area: Real_Life_Exam_Sim

Question Number: 540

Question: To identify potential schedule delay risks, you compare planned and actual progress to date. What technique is this?

Option 1: Risk urgency assessment

Option 2: Schedule analysis

Option 3: Cost-benefit analysis

Option 4: Risk categorization

Correct Response: 2

Explanation: Schedule analysis exposes risks around activity timelines.

Knowledge Area: Real_Life_Exam_Sim

Question Number: 541

Question: Which technique helps identify risks posed by changes to an IT system?

Option 1: Regression testing

Option 2: Impact analysis

Option 3: User acceptance testing

Option 4: Load testing

Correct Response: 2

Explanation: Impact analysis studies how changes affect related processes and technologies to identify potential risks.

Knowledge Area: Real_Life_Exam_Sim

Question Number: 542

Question: An employee lost a laptop containing sensitive data. What should be done FIRST?

Option 1: Locate the laptop

Option 2: Identify the data lost

Option 3: Suspend the employee

Option 4: Invoke incident response

Correct Response: 4

Explanation: Following incident response ensures an orderly and effective response to the data loss event.

Knowledge Area: Real_Life_Exam_Sim

Question Number: 543

Question: What helps assign accountability for responding to a particular risk?

Option 1: Risk register

Option 2: Risk matrix

Option 3: Risk appetite

Option 4: Risk owner

Correct Response: 4

Explanation: The risk owner is responsible for managing the response to a given risk.

Knowledge Area: Real_Life_Exam_Sim

Question Number: 544

Question: Which control helps detect unauthorized changes to production environments?

Option 1: Change requests

Option 2: Access controls

Option 3: Vulnerability scans

Option 4: File integrity monitoring

Correct Response: 4

Explanation: File integrity monitoring detects and alerts on unexpected modifications to files.

Knowledge Area: Real_Life_Exam_Sim

Question Number: 545

Question: Where should root causes of operational disruptions be documented?

Option 1: Risk register

Option 2: Incident reports

Option 3: Audit reports

Option 4: Business impact assessments

Correct Response: 2

Explanation: Incident reports detail the root causes found during an investigation of operational events.

Knowledge Area: Real_Life_Exam_Sim

Question Number: 546

Question: Many policy exceptions indicate:

Option 1: Risk owners want efficiency

Option 2: Risk approaches tolerance

Option 3: Policies need reviewing

Option 4: Vulnerabilities persist

Correct Response: 2

Explanation: Exceptions increase aggregate risk exposure.

Knowledge Area: Real_Life_Exam_Sim

Question Number: 547

Question: To augment ransomware awareness, the next priority is:

Option 1: Multifactor authentication

Option 2: Encryption in motion

Option 3: Encryption at rest

Option 4: Continuous backup

Correct Response: 4

Explanation: Backups enable recovery after an attack.

Knowledge Area: Real_Life_Exam_Sim

Question Number: 548

Question: To augment ransomware awareness, the next priority is:

Option 1: Inclusion of all resources

Option 2: External log sources

Option 3: Time synchronization

Option 4: Access permissions

Correct Response: 2

Explanation: Time sync enables event correlation.

Knowledge Area: Real_Life_Exam_Sim

Question Number: 549

Question: When a provider says hacking risk is low, you should:

Option 1: Accept the risk assessment

Option 2: Perform your own assessment

Option 3: Implement more controls

Option 4: Audit the provider

Correct Response: 4

Explanation: An independent assessment is needed.

Knowledge Area: Real_Life_Exam_Sim

Question Number: 550

Question: To reduce residual risk, the best step is to:

Option 1: Develop new actions

Option 2: Recommend risk acceptance

Option 3: Prioritize remediation

Option 4: Add controls

Correct Response: 3

Explanation: Focusing on remediation is most effective.

Knowledge Area: Real_Life_Exam_Sim

Question Number: 551

Question: New website payments will likely increase:

Option 1: Inherent risk

Option 2: Risk tolerance

Option 3: Residual risk

Option 4: Risk appetite

Correct Response: 3

Explanation: More activity creates more residual risk exposure.

Knowledge Area: Real_Life_Exam_Sim

Question Number: 552

Question: With a computer center on an earthquake fault, most important is:

Option 1: Hot site readiness

Option 2: Offsite backup media

Option 3: Avoiding shared sites

Option 4: Remote location

Correct Response: 4

Explanation: Immediate processing resumption is critical.

Knowledge Area: Real_Life_Exam_Sim

Question Number: 553

Question: For a new CRM system, who should own data leakage risk?

Option 1: CRO

Option 2: Controls manager

Option 3: CISO

Option 4: Business owner

Correct Response: 4

Explanation: The business process owner is accountable.

Knowledge Area: Real_Life_Exam_Sim

Question Number: 554

Question: A company is implementing a new cloud-based ERP system. What approach would BEST protect business objectives?

Option 1: Perform real-time transaction monitoring

Option 2: Utilize the cloud provider's security controls

Option 3: Implement redundant ERP instances

Option 4: Negotiate comprehensive SLA terms

Correct Response: 4

Explanation: Strong SLAs help ensure ERP availability and performance.

Knowledge Area: Real_Life_Exam_Sim

Question Number: 555

Question: A hospital is deploying a new MRI machine. What should the risk practitioner recommend to support objectives?

Option 1: Conduct mandatory staff training

Option 2: Perform scans in a Faraday cage

Option 3: Follow manufacturer maintenance procedures

Option 4: Activate built-in authentication controls

Correct Response: 3

Explanation: Proper maintenance protects availability and reduces downtime.

Knowledge Area: Real_Life_Exam_Sim

Question Number: 556

Question: A risk assessment of an accounting system determined the Oracle database is out of support. The BEST response would be to:

Option 1: Migrate to a supported version after testing

Option 2: Implement additional database monitoring

Option 3: Rely on the application vendor for support

Option 4: Accept the risk until next year's budget

Correct Response: 1

Explanation: Migrating to a supported version after thorough testing protects the accounting system while minimizing disruptions.

Knowledge Area: Real_Life_Exam_Sim

Question Number: 557

Question: An organization faces regulatory compliance risk from an outdated legacy system. Which risk treatment option would be BEST?

Option 1: Accept the risk

Option 2: Implement controls to protect legacy system

Option 3: Migrate applications to a supported platform

Option 4: Insure compliance-related losses

Correct Response: 3

Explanation: Migrating to supported platforms reduces inherent risk.

Knowledge Area: Real_Life_Exam_Sim

Question Number: 558

Question: A hospital faces the risk of medical device malfunctions during surgeries. Which option would be optimal for managing this risk?

Option 1: Increase staff training on devices

Option 2: Purchase additional spare parts inventory

Option 3: Implement preventive maintenance procedures

Option 4: Outsource surgeries to external facilities

Correct Response: 3

Explanation: Preventive maintenance reduces probability of medical device failures.

Knowledge Area: Real_Life_Exam_Sim

Question Number: 559

Question: An organization is concerned about intellectual property theft and wants to implement a data loss prevention program to better protect sensitive information. Which approach would provide the MOST value?

Option 1: Conduct periodic user security awareness training

Option 2: Disable external storage devices via group policy

Option 3: Implement network monitoring to detect abnormal data transfers

Option 4: Install endpoint DLP agents to scan and block confidential data exfiltration

Correct Response: 4

Explanation: Installing DLP agents provides automated scanning and blocking of confidential data extraction, preventing exploitation of authorized access for IP theft.

Knowledge Area: Real_Life_Exam_Sim

Question Number: 560

Question: An organization wants to identify potential causes leading to missed customer delivery dates. Which approach would be MOST useful?

Option 1: Fault tree analysis

Option 2: Regression testing

Option 3: Fishbone diagram

Option 4: Failure modes analysis

Correct Response: 3

Explanation: A fishbone diagram can map out causes of an effect like missed deliveries.

Knowledge Area: Real_Life_Exam_Sim

Question Number: 561

Question: A hospital is trying to reduce surgery delays. Which technique would effectively analyze contributing factors?

Option 1: Control charts

Option 2: Pareto analysis

Option 3: Ishikawa diagram

Option 4: Decision tree

Correct Response: 3

Explanation: A fishbone diagram can trace surgery delays back to root causes for analysis.

Knowledge Area: Real_Life_Exam_Sim

Question Number: 562

Question: A retailer is concerned about cyber risks to a new e-commerce platform. Which approach would allow modeling different attack scenarios?

Option 1: Bowtie diagram

Option 2: Failure tree analysis

Option 3: Actuarial data modeling

Option 4: Bayesian network analysis

Correct Response: 4

Explanation: Bayesian networks can probabilistically model cyber attack scenarios and effects.

Knowledge Area: Real_Life_Exam_Sim

Question Number: 563

Question: An organization is adopting a BYOD policy and wants to evaluate the likelihood and impact of security risks associated with employee-owned devices accessing corporate resources. Which quantitative risk analysis method would provide the MOST accurate assessment?

Option 1: Threat surveys

Option 2: Vulnerability scans

Option 3: Annualized loss expectancies

Option 4: Monte Carlo simulations

Correct Response: 4

Explanation: Monte Carlo simulations using probability distributions for threat frequency and statistical loss data provides a quantitative risk estimate.

Knowledge Area: Real_Life_Exam_Sim

Question Number: 564

Question: A hospital is upgrading its EHR system and wants to assess the likelihood and impact of patient record availability and integrity risks during the transition. Which technique would enable statistically modeling this risk scenario?

Option 1: Key risk indicators

Option 2: Failure modes analysis

Option 3: Sensitivity analysis

Option 4: Bayesian network diagrams

Correct Response: 4

Explanation: Bayesian network analysis incorporates probabilities for risk event likelihoods and statistical impact distributions.

Knowledge Area: Real_Life_Exam_Sim

Question Number: 565

Question: A hospital assessed its controls for hazardous chemical management and found several vulnerabilities that could result in improper handling and environmental discharges. Which approach would enable focusing risk treatment plans on the MOST critical gaps?

Option 1: Fishbone diagram of causes

Option 2: Industry best practice reviews

Option 3: Risk register integration

Option 4: Risk analysis quantifying environmental and safety impacts

Correct Response: 4

Explanation: Quantitatively estimating potential safety and environmental impacts from control gaps guides priority for risk treatment.

Knowledge Area: Real_Life_Exam_Sim

Question Number: 566

Question: A company needs to prioritize information security risks for remediation. Which technique would provide the MOST value?

Option 1: Threat trend analysis

Option 2: Vulnerability scan results

Option 3: Risk register scoring

Option 4: Risk heat map visualization

Correct Response: 4

Explanation: A risk heat map graphically identifies high priority risks based on likelihood and impact.

Knowledge Area: Real_Life_Exam_Sim

Question Number: 567

Question: An organization wants to visually represent key cybersecurity risks for the board of directors to provide clear risk rankings and priorities for treatment. Which risk analysis output would provide the MOST effective visualization of significant risks requiring remediation?

Option 1: Risk likelihood and impact matrix

Option 2: Threat trend analysis

Option 3: Vulnerability scan results

Option 4: Risk heat map with color-coded severity indicators

Correct Response: 4

Explanation: A risk heat map provides graphical color-coded visualization of risk likelihood vs impact comparisons to identify high priority risks for treatment.

Knowledge Area: Real_Life_Exam_Sim

Question Number: 568

Question: A hospital is conducting an enterprise risk assessment of patient safety hazards and desires a technique to effectively communicate key risks to executive leadership for risk treatment prioritization. Which approach would provide the BEST visualization of the most critical patient safety risks?

Option 1: Bowtie analysis diagrams

Option 2: Failure modes analysis

Option 3: Risk register scoring

Option 4: Risk heat map illustrating color-coded criticality levels

Correct Response: 4

Explanation: A risk heat map vividly highlights patient safety risks requiring priority attention through color-coded criticality indicators.

Knowledge Area: Real_Life_Exam_Sim

Question Number: 569

Question: An organization wants to be notified when operational risks exceed acceptable levels and require intervention. Which risk management technique would be MOST effective for setting thresholds and identifying exceeded risk appetite conditions?

Option 1: Annual risk assessments

Option 2: Industry benchmarking

Option 3: Key risk indicators with triggers

Option 4: Risk register reporting

Correct Response: 3

Explanation: Implementing key risk indicators with defined thresholds identifies when risks exceed accepted levels per risk appetite.

Knowledge Area: Real_Life_Exam_Sim

Question Number: 570

Question: Which group is responsible for establishing and implementing risk management policies and controls as the SECOND line of defense?

Option 1: External auditors

Option 2: The board of directors

Option 3: Business unit managers

Option 4: The risk management function

Correct Response: 4

Explanation: The risk management function is the second line of defense for managing policies and controls.

Knowledge Area: Real_Life_Exam_Sim

Question Number: 571

Question: An organization needs to determine whether its security awareness training is effectively improving employee behavior and reducing related risks like phishing and social engineering. Which approach would provide the BEST evaluation?

Option 1: Conduct surveys on training satisfaction

Option 2: Assess training completion rates

Option 3: Measure phishing click rates before and after training

Option 4: Compare to industry security training benchmarks

Correct Response: 3

Explanation: Measuring changes in phishing click rates through simulated tests before and after training evaluates its effectiveness in improving security behavior.

Knowledge Area: Real_Life_Exam_Sim

Question Number: 572

Question: An organization wants to model different cyber attack scenarios against a new system. Which technique would provide the MOST thorough analysis?

Option 1: Threat modeling

Option 2: Vulnerability scanning

Option 3: Penetration testing

Option 4: Attack tree analysis

Correct Response: 4

Explanation: Attack trees trace paths through different attack steps enabling thorough scenario analysis.

Knowledge Area: Real_Life_Exam_Sim

Question Number: 573

Question: What method enables real-time monitoring of controls and alerts when results exceed defined risk tolerances?

Option 1: Ad hoc reporting

Option 2: Control self-assessment

Option 3: Continuous monitoring

Option 4: Predictive analytics

Correct Response: 3

Explanation: Continuous monitoring provides real-time tracking of controls against risk thresholds.

Knowledge Area: Real_Life_Exam_Sim

Question Number: 574

Question: What technique involves personnel performing evaluations of the existence and effectiveness of controls within their business unit?

Option 1: Key risk indicators

Option 2: Continuous auditing

Option 3: Control self-assessment

Option 4: Regression analysis

Correct Response: 3

Explanation: Control self-assessment engages staff in evaluating controls.

Knowledge Area: Real_Life_Exam_Sim

Question Number: 575

Question: An organization wants to understand the regulatory environment it operates in. Which of the following would provide the BEST source for identifying applicable laws and regulations?

Option 1: Interviews with business management

Option 2: Review of contracts with customers

Option 3: Examination of HR policies

Option 4: Analysis of legal and compliance department materials

Correct Response: 4

Explanation: Legal/compliance materials outline relevant regulatory requirements the organization must adhere to.

Knowledge Area: SUPPORTING TASKS

Question Number: 576

Question: Which of the following techniques would BEST identify impacts of IT risks on business objectives?

Option 1: Reviewing security logs

Option 2: Conducting breach simulations

Option 3: Surveying business management

Option 4: Analyzing vulnerability scan results

Correct Response: 2

Explanation: Breach simulations model realistic threat scenarios to assess potential business impacts.

Knowledge Area: SUPPORTING TASKS

Question Number: 577

Question: A new CIO has been hired and wants to understand how IT risks could affect business goals. What artifact should be reviewed?

Option 1: IT policies

Option 2: Risk register

Option 3: Asset inventory

Option 4: Threat intelligence reports

Correct Response: 2

Explanation: The risk register outlines identified IT risks and their potential effects on business operations.

Knowledge Area: SUPPORTING TASKS

Question Number: 578

Question: Which technique would help identify vulnerabilities in an organization's public cloud environment?

Option 1: Review security logs

Option 2: Conduct penetration testing

Option 3: Analyze threat intelligence

Option 4: Interview staff

Correct Response: 2

Explanation: Penetration testing attempts to actually exploit cloud vulnerabilities.

Knowledge Area: SUPPORTING TASKS

Question Number: 579

Question: A new video conferencing platform has been implemented. What is the GREATEST threat to assess?

Option 1: Malware infection

Option 2: DDoS attacks

Option 3: Data leakage

Option 4: Password cracking

Correct Response: 3

Explanation: Video conferencing introduces risks of accidental data leakage.

Knowledge Area: SUPPORTING TASKS

Question Number: 580

Question: An organization has identified a threat of DDoS attacks and a vulnerability of limited network bandwidth. What is the resulting risk scenario?

Option 1: Excessive ping requests saturate available bandwidth

Option 2: Attackers gain access to sensitive data

Option 3: New malware bypasses antivirus software

Option 4: Users fall for phishing emails

Correct Response: 1

Explanation: The threat and vulnerability combine to create a DDoS bandwidth saturation risk.

Knowledge Area: SUPPORTING TASKS

Question Number: 581

Question: Which threat-vulnerability pair could result in data theft by rogue employees?

Option 1: Weak access controls - Disgruntled employee

Option 2: SQL injection - Poor input validation

Option 3: DDoS attack - Underprovisioned network

Option 4: Password reuse - Phishing attack

Correct Response: 1

Explanation: Weak access controls and rogue employees pose an insider data theft risk.

Knowledge Area: SUPPORTING TASKS

Question Number: 582

Question: Which role would be BEST to assign as the risk owner for cloud security threats?

Option 1: CIO

Option 2: CISO

Option 3: Cloud provider

Option 4: Business manager

Correct Response: 2

Explanation: The CISO has relevant cloud security expertise to manage this risk.

Knowledge Area: SUPPORTING TASKS

Question Number: 583

Question: A new online payment system is being implemented. Who should own the related data security risk?

Option 1: IT manager

Option 2: CFO

Option 3: COO

Option 4: Payment processor

Correct Response: 3

Explanation: The COO oversees payment operations and should own associated data risks.

Knowledge Area: SUPPORTING TASKS

Question Number: 584

Question: A key regulatory compliance risk was supposed to be addressed. However, the work was never started. What is the MOST likely reason?

Option 1: Insufficient budget

Option 2: Lack of skills

Option 3: Poor risk analysis

Option 4: Unassigned risk ownership

Correct Response: 4

Explanation: Unassigned ownership allowed accountability gaps for managing the risk.

Knowledge Area: SUPPORTING TASKS

Question Number: 585

Question: What action should be taken to incorporate identified risks into the IT risk register?

Option 1: Assigning risk owners and developing response strategies

Option 2: Conducting cost-benefit analysis of the risks

Option 3: Transferring risks to external parties through insurance

Option 4: Accepting risks without proactive measures

Correct Response: 1

Explanation: To incorporate identified risks into the IT risk register, the appropriate action is assigning risk owners and developing response strategies. This ensures accountability, proactive risk management, and the implementation of measures to mitigate or respond to identified risks.

Knowledge Area: SUPPORTING TASKS

Question Number: 586

Question: Which technique helps guide discussions to establish risk tolerance with business leaders?

Option 1: Control testing

Option 2: Process flow analysis

Option 3: Risk assessment workshops

Option 4: Cost-benefit analysis

Correct Response: 3

Explanation: Interactive workshops facilitate risk dialogues with stakeholders.

Knowledge Area: SUPPORTING TASKS

Question Number: 587

Question: A risk practitioner is meeting with system owners to define risk appetite. What metric would be MOST useful?

Option 1: Residual risk ratings

Option 2: Threat levels

Option 3: Inherent risk scores

Option 4: Loss expectancy

Correct Response: 4

Explanation: Loss expectancy metrics quantify risk appetite in financial terms.

Knowledge Area: SUPPORTING TASKS

Question Number: 588

Question: Which scenario reflects ineffective facilitation of risk appetite dialogues?

Option 1: Exceeding risk tolerance

Option 2: Universal risk avoidance

Option 3: Perfectly quantified appetite

Option 4: Differing assumptions

Correct Response: 4

Explanation: Misaligned assumptions lead to inconsistent or conflicting risk appetites.

Knowledge Area: SUPPORTING TASKS

Question Number: 589

Question: Interviews with business managers reveal varying levels of acceptable brand reputation risk. What should the risk practitioner do?

Option 1: Default to the most conservative view

Option 2: Report the differences to the board

Option 3: Consolidate the input and average

Option 4: Lead further discussions to align

Correct Response: 4

Explanation: The practitioner should drive consensus on a unified appetite.

Knowledge Area: SUPPORTING TASKS

Question Number: 590

Question: A company wants to improve security awareness. Which training topic would be LEAST impactful?

Option 1: Password hygiene

Option 2: Social engineering

Option 3: VPN protocols

Option 4: Data handling

Correct Response: 3

Explanation: Technical VPN concepts have low relevance to most staff.

Knowledge Area: SUPPORTING TASKS

Question Number: 591

Question: Which metric indicates the greatest success in improving security awareness?

Option 1: Training attendance

Option 2: Phishing click rate

Option 3: Training satisfaction

Option 4: Test scores

Correct Response: 2

Explanation: Reduced phishing susceptibility shows improved awareness.

Knowledge Area: SUPPORTING TASKS

Question Number: 592

Question: How should training effectiveness be evaluated?

Option 1: Trainee feedback surveys

Option 2: Testing comprehension

Option 3: Measuring behavioral change

Option 4: Training expense

Correct Response: 2

Explanation: Testing measures actual improvements in security behaviors

Knowledge Area: SUPPORTING TASKS

Question Number: 593

Question: A risk practitioner is assessing a scenario of disrupted online services due to a DDoS attack. Which would help determine likelihood?

Option 1: Vendor contracts

Option 2: Network traffic patterns

Option 3: Profit margins

Option 4: Incident reports

Correct Response: 2

Explanation: Analyzing network traffic would reveal DDoS vulnerability.

Knowledge Area: SUPPORTING TASKS

Question Number: 594

Question: When analyzing the business impact of a risk scenario, which data point is LESS relevant?

Option 1: RTO

Option 2: Revenue loss

Option 3: Staff hours

Option 4: Incident response costs

Correct Response: 4

Explanation: Incident response costs have lower business impact than disruption.

Knowledge Area: SUPPORTING TASKS

Question Number: 595

Question: An organization experiences frequent security incidents. What does this suggest about their risk assessments?

Option 1: Threats are overestimated

Option 2: Impacts are underestimated

Option 3: Likelihoods are underestimated

Option 4: Vulnerabilities are overlooked

Correct Response: 3

Explanation: The incidents show threat likelihood is higher than initially assessed.

Knowledge Area: SUPPORTING TASKS

Question Number: 596

Question: An organization implements a new cloud access security broker (CASB) to prevent unauthorized SaaS usage. Which action would allow the risk practitioner to MOST accurately evaluate the control?

Option 1: Review CASB training completion

Option 2: Analyze blocked SaaS access attempts

Option 3: Survey employee CASB satisfaction

Option 4: Assess documentation of security features

Correct Response: 2

Explanation: Analyzing instances of blocked unauthorized access evaluates CASB effectiveness.

Knowledge Area: SUPPORTING TASKS

Question Number: 597

Question: To reduce data exfiltration threats, DLP software has been deployed on endpoint devices. What indicates the control is operating as intended?

Option 1: Number of devices with DLP installed

Option 2: Decrease in policy violations

Option 3: Encryption of removable media

Option 4: Blocking of unauthorized email attachments

Correct Response: 2

Explanation: Decline in DLP policy violations demonstrates effectiveness.

Knowledge Area: SUPPORTING TASKS

Question Number: 598

Question: An organization implements MFA to reduce unauthorized account access. What would determine if the control is working properly?

Option 1: Compliance with security standards

Option 2: Complexity of MFA policies

Option 3: Number of accounts requiring MFA

Option 4: Decrease in successful account takeovers

Correct Response: 4

Explanation: A decline in unauthorized access proves MFA is effective.

Knowledge Area: SUPPORTING TASKS

Question Number: 599

Question: A risk analysis identified data theft via unauthorized access as a critical risk. A control analysis shows access management controls are inadequately designed and implemented. What is this an example of?

Option 1: Accepted risk

Option 2: Residual risk

Option 3: Control gap

Option 4: Non-compliance

Correct Response: 3

Explanation: The poor controls represent a gap compared to the desired state of strong access controls.

Knowledge Area: SUPPORTING TASKS

Question Number: 600

Question: Risk analysis identified data leakage via email as high-likelihood with high business impact. However, no DLP controls are implemented for email. What does this signify?

Option 1: Non-compliance

Option 2: Mitigated risk

Option 3: An accepted risk

Option 4: A risk-control gap

Correct Response: 4

Explanation: The lack of email DLP indicates a gap versus desired control state.

Knowledge Area: SUPPORTING TASKS

Question Number: 601

Question: A risk scenario has been assessed as above risk tolerance. Which technique would BEST facilitate selecting an appropriate response with stakeholders?

Option 1: Surveys

Option 2: Cost-benefit analysis

Option 3: Decision trees

Option 4: Focus groups

Correct Response: 2

Explanation: Cost-benefit analysis quantifies response options for decision making.

Knowledge Area: SUPPORTING TASKS

Question Number: 602

Question: When evaluating risk response options, what is the BEST criteria for selection?

Option 1: Cost

Option 2: Speed

Option 3: Risk owner preference

Option 4: Effectiveness

Correct Response: 4

Explanation: Effectiveness in mitigating risk is the most important criteria.

Knowledge Area: SUPPORTING TASKS

Question Number: 603

Question: A risk practitioner is meeting with system owners to discuss response options for a regulatory compliance risk above tolerance. What should be the MAIN focus?

Option 1: Internal audit recommendations

Option 2: Costs of remediation

Option 3: Alignment to risk appetite

Option 4: Solution offered by technology vendors

Correct Response: 3

Explanation: Ensuring alignment to risk appetite drives stakeholder decisions.

Knowledge Area: SUPPORTING TASKS

Question Number: 604

Question: Which response is preferable if a risk is being knowingly accepted?

Option 1: Reduce

Option 2: Transfer

Option 3: Enhance controls

Option 4: Increase monitoring

Correct Response: 4

Explanation: Accepted risks warrant enhanced monitoring and oversight.

Knowledge Area: SUPPORTING TASKS

Question Number: 605

Question: A risk owner is developing a treatment plan for a high priority risk scenario. What should the risk practitioner recommend focusing on first?

Option 1: Budget

Option 2: Vendors

Option 3: Timing

Option 4: Scope

Correct Response: 4

Explanation: The scope of risk treatment must be defined before other details.

Knowledge Area: SUPPORTING TASKS

Question Number: 606

Question: During creation of a risk treatment plan, which topic would the risk practitioner be LEAST involved in?

Option 1: Cost analysis

Option 2: Control selection

Option 3: Implementation roles

Option 4: Training development

Correct Response: 2

Explanation: Control selection is driven primarily by the risk and process owners.

Knowledge Area: SUPPORTING TASKS

Question Number: 607

Question: The CISO drafted a risk treatment plan and sent it to the risk practitioner for review. What would be the BEST course of action?

Option 1: Revise the plan as needed

Option 2: Notify executive leadership of gaps

Option 3: Reject the plan and start over

Option 4: Provide input and recommend changes

Correct Response: 4

Explanation: The practitioner should collaborate with the CISO to enhance the draft plan.

Knowledge Area: SUPPORTING TASKS

Question Number: 608

Question: A risk treatment plan calls for implementation of a new firewall by Q3. It is now Q4, but no firewall is in place. What should the risk practitioner do?

Option 1: Update the risk register

Option 2: Inform executive management

Option 3: Confirm the vendor contract

Option 4: Revise the implementation timeline

Correct Response: 2

Explanation: Leadership should be notified that the planned response was not executed.

Knowledge Area: SUPPORTING TASKS

Question Number: 609

Question: DLP tools were implemented per a risk treatment plan. What validates execution per the plan?

Option 1: Decrease in policy violations

Option 2: Number of endpoints with DLP

Option 3: Measuring mean time to detect

Option 4: Reviewing tool procurement paperwork

Correct Response: 1

Explanation: Seeing fewer DLP violations proves planned implementation and effectiveness.

Knowledge Area: SUPPORTING TASKS

Question Number: 610

Question: What is an advantage of leveraging KRIs for risk monitoring?

Option 1: Faster response

Option 2: Lower costs

Option 3: Higher accuracy

Option 4: Improved reporting

Correct Response: 1

Explanation: KRIs enable quicker responses by providing early signals of increasing risk.

Knowledge Area: SUPPORTING TASKS

Question Number: 611

Question: An organization implements daily malware scan failures as a KRI. What does a spike in failures indicate?

Option 1: Increased likelihood of infection

Option 2: Antivirus software is outdated

Option 3: Scans are being skipped or manipulated

Option 4: More devices are being scanned

Correct Response: 1

Explanation: More failures indicates increased infection risk.

Knowledge Area: SUPPORTING TASKS

Question Number: 612

Question: Which metric could serve as a useful KRI for application security risks?

Option 1: Logins during non-business hours

Option 2: PHP errors in web logs

Option 3: Cloud storage consumption

Option 4: BYOD policy exemptions

Correct Response: 2

Explanation: Increasing PHP errors may reflect emerging web app vulnerabilities.

Knowledge Area: SUPPORTING TASKS

Question Number: 613

Question: A KRI tracking unauthorized WiFi access points detects an upwards trend. What should the risk practitioner do?

Option 1: Report a risk control failure

Option 2: Conduct security awareness training

Option 3: Tune the indicator threshold

Option 4: Perform a wireless survey

Correct Response: 3

Explanation: The threshold may need adjustment if too sensitive to normal fluctuations.

Knowledge Area: SUPPORTING TASKS

Question Number: 614

Question: The risk practitioner notices a KRI for privileged account access exceeding its threshold. What is the BEST next step?

Option 1: Update access control policies

Option 2: Perform an account audit

Option 3: Lower the defined threshold

Option 4: Request added monitoring

Correct Response: 2

Explanation: Analyze and investigate the underlying cause of the spike.

Knowledge Area: SUPPORTING TASKS

Question Number: 615

Question: A new secure email gateway is deployed. Which would be the BEST KPI for it?

Option 1: Template-based phishing reporting rate

Option 2: Policy exception requests

Option 3: Total spam emails stopped

Option 4: Percentage of encrypted emails

Correct Response: 3

Explanation: Total spam blocked measures effectiveness of the control.

Knowledge Area: SUPPORTING TASKS

Question Number: 616

Question: An organization deploys new antivirus software. What provides meaningful data as a KPI?

Option 1: Threat definitions updated

Option 2: Scan frequency and coverage

Option 3: Malware infections quarantined

Option 4: Signature update failures

Correct Response: 3

Explanation: Infections caught proves AV effectiveness.

Knowledge Area: SUPPORTING TASKS

Question Number: 617

Question: An assessment reveals a web application firewall is inconsistently blocking SQL injection attacks. What does this indicate about the control environment?

Option 1: Non-compliance issues exist

Option 2: The environment lacks maturity

Option 3: Risks are being accepted

Option 4: Threats are being underestimated

Correct Response: 2

Explanation: The inconsistent blocking reflects immaturity of the WAF control.

Knowledge Area: SUPPORTING TASKS

Question Number: 618

Question: A phishing test shows a slight decline in clicks over last year. What does this show about the environment?

Option 1: Improved end user behavior

Option 2: Increased training effectiveness

Option 3: Control degradation

Option 4: Complacent leadership

Correct Response: 1

Explanation: The small decline indicates minor behavioral improvements.

Knowledge Area: SUPPORTING TASKS

Question Number: 619

Question: A recent assessment identified several high severity vulnerabilities in customer facing web applications. What should the risk practitioner report to leadership?

Option 1: Underlying threat sources

Option 2: Timelines for remediation

Option 3: Effort required for patching

Option 4: Potential business impact

Correct Response: 4

Explanation: Business impact reporting facilitates risk-based decisions.

Knowledge Area: SUPPORTING TASKS

Question Number: 620

Question: The CTO has requested a risk management report before approving funding for new controls. What should be the focus of the report?

Option 1: Compliance status

Option 2: Description of controls

Option 3: Summary of risks

Option 4: Metrics on control effectiveness

Correct Response: 3

Explanation: Current risks drive decisions on funding new controls.

Knowledge Area: SUPPORTING TASKS

Question Number: 621

Question: A new cloud access security broker (CASB) tool was recently implemented. What reporting would LEAST influence stakeholder risk decisions?

Option 1: User satisfaction results

Option 2: Threats blocked by CASB

Option 3: Reduction in data exposure events

Option 4: Policy compliance improvement

Correct Response: 1

Explanation: Reporting user feedback has little risk management value.

Knowledge Area: SUPPORTING TASKS

Question Number: 622

Question: A risk practitioner is assessing alignment with ISO 27001 controls. Which documentation would provide the LEAST value?

Option 1: Information security policies

Option 2: Risk assessment results

Option 3: Inventory of assets

Option 4: SLAs with vendors

Correct Response: 3

Explanation: An asset inventory provides limited visibility into actual control implementation.

Knowledge Area: SUPPORTING TASKS

Question Number: 623

Question: When evaluating alignment with the CIS Critical Security Controls, which activities provide the MOST value?

Option 1: Surveys to staff

Option 2: Review of network diagrams

Option 3: Control validation testing

Option 4: Comparison of security budgets

Correct Response: 3

Explanation: Testing provides empirical evidence of real-world implementation.

Knowledge Area: SUPPORTING TASKS

Question Number: 624

Question: An organization is reviewing its IT architecture to improve resilience against emerging threats. As the Chief Risk Officer, which of the following alternatives should receive PRIMARY consideration to strengthen the overall security posture in a cost effective manner?

Option 1: Deploying additional firewalls and network segmentation

Option 2: Investing in regular employee security awareness

Option 3: Outsourcing the entire network infrastructure

Option 4: Centrally monitoring all systems and applications for anomalies

Correct Response: 2

Explanation: , Employee training programs help identify and address human vulnerabi

Knowledge Area: IT Enterprise Architecture in Risk Management

----

Question Number: 625

Question: A retailer experienced lengthy website outages during peak holiday shopping seasons due to infrastructure limitations. As a risk consultant, the BEST first step recommendation is to:

Option 1: Seek cloud migration proposals to facilitate scalability

Option 2: Hire additional in-house IT support staff

Option 3: Benchmark uptime indices of rival companies

Option 4: Partition the website across multiple redundant data centers

Correct Response: 4

Explanation: , Distributing digital properties across diverse locations employing redundancy techniques fortifies availability during high demand periods.

Knowledge Area: IT Enterprise Architecture in Risk Management

----

Question Number: 626

Question: A government agency requires its constituent departments standardize on core technologies. As the IT Risk Manager, your priority should be to:

Option 1: Assess interoperability across proposed solutions

Option 2: Socialize change management plans to impacted teams

Option 3: Justify additional budgets to the Finance department

Option 4: Waive procurement policies temporarily for faster deployment

Correct Response: 1

Explanation: , Vetting solution coherence reduces integration vulnerabilities prior to rollout at scale.

Knowledge Area: IT Enterprise Architecture in Risk Management

----

Question Number: 627

Question: A system outage impacted customers for over 3 hours and exposed a weakness in change management processes. The CISO should FIRST implement:

Option 1: Regular risk assessments

Option 2: Documentation standards

Option 3: Testing for all changes

Option 4: Change advisory board reviews,

Correct Response: 3

Explanation: , Testing mitigates unintended impacts from modifications.

Knowledge Area: IT Operations Management (e.g., change management, IT assets, problems, incidents) in Risk Management

----

Question Number: 628

Question: To improve problem resolution oversight, the IT director is evaluating tracking systems. The BEST selection criterion is one that provides:

Option 1: Automated workflows

Option 2: Audit logs

Option 3: Performance dashboards

Option 4: Capacity planning,

Correct Response: 2

Explanation: , Audit trails maintain transparency and accountability in issue handling.

Knowledge Area: IT Operations Management (e.g., change management, IT assets, problems, incidents) in Risk Management

----

Question Number: 629

Question: The CRO must report key risk indicators to the Board. The BEST metric related to availability is:

Option 1: Number of assets

Option 2: Mean time to resolution

Option 3: System uptime percentage

Option 4: Service alerts,

Correct Response: 3

Explanation: , Uptime encapsulates overall digital service delivery.

Knowledge Area: IT Operations Management (e.g., change management, IT assets, problems, incidents) in Risk Management

----

Question Number: 630

Question: An IT project manager is conducting risk management planning for a new software development project. What should be the FIRST step performed?

Option 1: Brainstorm risk sources

Option 2: Review risk management policies

Option 3: Identify risk response strategies

Option 4: Define risk assessment methodologies

Correct Response: 2

Explanation: Policies/standards should first be reviewed when planning project risk management.

Knowledge Area: Project Management in Risk Management

Question Number: 631

Question: An IT project manager is implementing risk responses during a project to address identified risks. Which response would be the LEAST effective for high priority risks?

Option 1: Risk acceptance

Option 2: Risk mitigation

Option 3: Risk avoidance

Option 4: Risk transference

Correct Response: 1

Explanation: High priority project risks warrant active responses like mitigation or transfer.

Knowledge Area: Project Management in Risk Management

Question Number: 632

Question: A complex IT system implementation has several uncertain requirements. What risk management strategy would BEST address this uncertainty?

Option 1: Detailed project planning

Option 2: Progress monitoring

Option 3: Contingency budgeting

Option 4: Flexible scope management

Correct Response: 4

Explanation: An agile, flexible scope approach manages uncertain requirements.

Knowledge Area: Project Management in Risk Management

Question Number: 633

Question: An IT project risk has occurred, causing delays and budget overruns. What is the BEST immediate response?

Option 1: Lessons learned review

Option 2: Status report to sponsor

Option 3: Re-baselining schedule/budget

Option 4: Assess impact and response plans

Correct Response: 4

Explanation: First assess risk impact and response options when a risk occurs.

Knowledge Area: Project Management in Risk Management

Question Number: 634

Question: An organization is developing a disaster recovery plan. What is the FIRST step of the process?

Option 1: Document recovery procedures

Option 2: Implement resilience controls

Option 3: Test the plan

Option 4: Conduct a business impact analysis

Correct Response: 4

Explanation: A BIA identifying critical systems is the first DRM step.

Knowledge Area: Disaster Recovery Management (DRM) in Risk Management

----

Question Number: 635

Question: A company has encountered a cyberattack disrupting operations. What is the HIGHEST priority when invoking disaster recovery plans?

Option 1: Restoring compromised systems

Option 2: Analyzing the attack

Option 3: Communicating with stakeholders

Option 4: Activating critical business processes

Correct Response: 4

Explanation: Recovering critical business operations is the top priority.

Knowledge Area: Disaster Recovery Management (DRM) in Risk Management

----

Question Number: 636

Question: What is the first step in implementing Data Lifecycle Management in risk management?

Option 1: Data classification and categorization

Option 2: Data backup and storage

Option 3: Data disposal and destruction

Option 4: Data encryption and access control

Correct Response: 1

Explanation: The first step in implementing Data Lifecycle Management in risk management is data classification and categorization. This step involves identifying and classifying data based on its sensitivity, criticality, and regulatory requirements. It helps organizations understand the types of data they have and prioritize their risk management efforts accordingly.

Knowledge Area: Data Lifecycle Management in Risk Management

Question Number: 637

Question: Which phase of the data lifecycle involves securely disposing of data at the end of its usefulness?

Option 1: Data disposal and destruction

Option 2: Data backup and storage

Option 3: Data processing and utilization

Option 4: Data classification and categorization

Correct Response: 1

Explanation: The phase of the data lifecycle that involves securely disposing of data at the end of its usefulness is the data disposal and destruction phase. This phase ensures that data is properly and securely disposed of to prevent unauthorized access or retrieval, reducing the risk of data breaches or privacy violations.

Knowledge Area: Data Lifecycle Management in Risk Management

Question Number: 638

Question: What is a primary objective of data lifecycle management in risk management?

Option 1: Mitigate data-related risks throughout its lifecycle

Option 2: Optimize data storage and retrieval processes

Option 3: Ensure data compliance with industry regulations

Option 4: Minimize data backup and retention costs

Correct Response: 1

Explanation: The primary objective of data lifecycle management in risk management is to mitigate data-related risks throughout its lifecycle. This involves implementing appropriate controls, processes, and strategies to identify, assess, and manage risks associated with data collection, storage, processing, and disposal.

Knowledge Area: Data Lifecycle Management in Risk Management

Question Number: 639

Question: Which phase of the System Development Life Cycle (SDLC) is focused on identifying and assessing risks associated with the proposed system?

Option 1: Requirements gathering and analysis

Option 2: Design and development

Option 3: Implementation and testing

Option 4: Maintenance and evaluation

Correct Response: 1

Explanation: The requirements gathering and analysis phase of the SDLC is focused on identifying and assessing risks associated with the proposed system. This phase involves gathering user requirements, analyzing business processes, and identifying potential risks and vulnerabilities that need to be addressed in the system design.

Knowledge Area: System Development Life Cycle (SDLC) in Risk Management

----

Question Number: 640

Question: Which of the following is an example of an emerging technology that can be used in risk management?

Option 1: Artificial Intelligence (AI)

Option 2: Traditional spreadsheet software

Option 3: Legacy mainframe systems

Option 4: Paper-based documentation

Correct Response: 1

Explanation: Artificial Intelligence (AI) is an example of an emerging technology that can be used in risk management. AI can analyze large volumes of data, identify patterns and trends, and provide insights to support risk assessment and decision-making processes.

Knowledge Area: Emerging Technologies in Risk Management

Question Number: 641

Question: How can data analytics contribute to risk management?

Option 1: By analyzing large volumes of data to identify patterns and trends

Option 2: By relying solely on subjective assessments and opinions

Option 3: By avoiding the need for risk assessment and mitigation

Option 4: By eliminating the need for risk management processes

Correct Response: 1

Explanation: Data analytics can contribute to risk management by analyzing large volumes of data to identify patterns and trends. By leveraging data analytics techniques and tools, organizations can gain insights into potential risks, assess their likelihood and impact, and make informed decisions regarding risk mitigation and management strategies.

Knowledge Area: Emerging Technologies in Risk Management

Question Number: 642

Question: Which of the following is a widely recognized information security framework used in risk management?

Option 1: ISO/IEC 27001

Option 2: Six Sigma

Option 3: ITIL (Information Technology Infrastructure Library)

Option 4: COSO (Committee of Sponsoring Organizations of the Treadway Commission)

Correct Response: 1

Explanation: ISO/IEC 27001 is a widely recognized information security framework used in risk management. It provides a systematic approach for establishing, implementing, maintaining, and continually improving an information security management system (ISMS) based on risk management principles and best practices.

Knowledge Area: Information Security Concepts, Frameworks and Standards in Risk Management

----

Question Number: 643

Question: What is the primary goal of implementing information security frameworks, standards, and concepts in risk management?

Option 1: To protect information assets and minimize risks

Option 2: To increase operational efficiency and reduce costs

Option 3: To comply with legal and regulatory requirements

Option 4: To improve customer satisfaction and loyalty

Correct Response: 1

Explanation: The primary goal of implementing information security frameworks, standards, and concepts in risk management is to protect information assets and minimize risks. By adopting best practices and applying appropriate controls, organizations can safeguard their sensitive information, reduce the likelihood and impact of security incidents, and ensure the confidentiality, integrity, and availability of data.

Knowledge Area: Information Security Concepts, Frameworks and Standards in Risk Management

----

Question Number: 644

Question: What is the primary goal of information security awareness training in risk management?

Option 1: To ensure employees are aware of potential risks and their responsibilities in protecting information

Option 2: To enhance technical security controls and measures

Option 3: To transfer risks to external parties through contracts

Option 4: To eliminate all risks associated with information security

Correct Response: 1

Explanation: The primary goal of information security awareness training in risk management is to ensure employees are aware of potential risks and their responsibilities in protecting information. By providing training and education, organizations can empower employees to identify and respond to security threats, follow best practices, and contribute to a culture of security awareness and risk mitigation.

Knowledge Area: Information Security Awareness Training in Risk Management

----

Question Number: 645

Question: What is the first step in implementing an effective information security awareness training program?

Option 1: Assessing training needs and identifying target audience

Option 2: Developing training materials and content

Option 3: Delivering training sessions to employees

Option 4: Evaluating the effectiveness of the training program

Correct Response: 1

Explanation: The first step in implementing an effective information security awareness training program is assessing training needs and identifying the target audience. This involves understanding the organization's specific security risks, identifying the roles and responsibilities of different employees, and determining the knowledge and skills required to address those risks.

Knowledge Area: Information Security Awareness Training in Risk Management

----

Question Number: 646

Question: What is the purpose of conducting business impact analysis in Business Continuity Management (BCM)?

Option 1: To identify critical business functions and their dependencies

Option 2: To eliminate all risks associated with critical business operations

Option 3: To transfer risks to external parties through contracts

Option 4: To accept risks without taking any proactive measures

Correct Response: 1

Explanation: The purpose of conducting business impact analysis in Business Continuity Management (BCM) is to identify critical business functions and their dependencies. This analysis helps organizations understand the potential impacts of disruptions on these functions, prioritize recovery efforts, and allocate resources effectively to ensure the continuity of essential operations.

Knowledge Area: Business Continuity Management in Risk Management

----

Question Number: 647

Question: How does data privacy and data protection contribute to overall risk management efforts?

Option 1: By mitigating the risk of data breaches and regulatory non-compliance

Option 2: By eliminating all risks associated with data processing

Option 3: By transferring risks to external parties through contracts

Option 4: By accepting risks without taking any proactive measures

Correct Response: 1

Explanation: Data privacy and data protection contribute to overall risk management efforts by mitigating the risk of data breaches and regulatory non-compliance. By implementing appropriate safeguards, organizations can protect sensitive data, reduce the likelihood of security incidents, and ensure compliance with applicable data protection laws and regulations.

Knowledge Area: Data Privacy and Data Protection Principles in Risk Management

----

Question Number: 648

Question: A new regulation necessitates improved client data security. Which risk response would BEST address compliance?

Option 1: Insurance purchase

Option 2: Process audits

Option 3: Control implementation

Option 4: Fines budgeting

Correct Response: 3

Explanation: Implementing controls reduces compliance risk exposure.

Knowledge Area: Risk Treatment / Risk Response Options in Risk Management

----

Question Number: 649

Question: Why is third-party risk management important in risk management efforts?

Option 1: Third-party relationships can introduce additional risks to an organization

Option 2: Third-party risk management eliminates all risks associated with third-party relationships

Option 3: Third-party risk management hinders business operations and growth

Option 4: Third-party risk management is not relevant for effective risk management

Correct Response: 1

Explanation: Third-party risk management is important in risk management efforts because third-party relationships can introduce additional risks to an organization. By properly managing these risks, organizations can protect their assets, sensitive information, and reputation while ensuring the continuity of business operations.

Knowledge Area: Third-Party Risk Management in Risk Management

----

Question Number: 650

Question: How does third-party risk management contribute to overall risk management efforts?

Option 1: By identifying and mitigating risks associated with third-party relationships

Option 2: By accepting risks without taking any proactive measures

Option 3: By transferring risks to external parties through contracts

Option 4: By eliminating all risks associated with third-party relationships

Correct Response: 1

Explanation: Third-party risk management contributes to overall risk management efforts by identifying and mitigating risks associated with third-party relationships. By assessing and managing risks related to vendors, suppliers, and business partners, organizations can protect themselves from potential vulnerabilities and disruptions caused by third-party activities.

Knowledge Area: Third-Party Risk Management in Risk Management

----

Question Number: 651

Question: During a risk assessment, a major control gap is identified. What should be the FIRST step?

Option 1: Implement a new control

Option 2: Report finding to management

Option 3: Log issue in tracking system

Option 4: Update risk register

Correct Response: 3

Explanation: The first step is to log the finding in the issue tracking system.

Knowledge Area: Issue, Finding and Exception Management in Risk Management

----

Question Number: 652

Question: What is the MOST important action when remediating a non-compliant issue?

Option 1: Implement tactical fix

Option 2: Report on remediation

Option 3: Diagnose the root cause

Option 4: Verify resolution effectiveness

Correct Response: 3

Explanation: Focus on diagnosing and resolving the root cause first.

Knowledge Area: Issue, Finding and Exception Management in Risk Management

----

Question Number: 653

Question: Scenario: An organization is entering into a strategic partnership with a third-party vendor to outsource certain operations. What is the primary step in managing the risks associated with the partnership?

Option 1: Conducting due diligence and performing a comprehensive vendor assessment

Option 2: Eliminating all risks associated with the partnership through proactive measures

Option 3: Transferring all risks to the third-party vendor through contractual agreements

Option 4: Accepting risks without taking any proactive measures

Correct Response: 1

Explanation: The primary step in managing the risks associated with a strategic partnership with a third-party vendor is conducting due diligence and performing a comprehensive vendor assessment. By thoroughly evaluating the vendor's capabilities, security practices, and compliance with regulations, organizations can mitigate potential risks and ensure a trusted and secure partnership.

Knowledge Area: Management of Emerging Risk in Risk Management

----

Question Number: 654

Question: Regulators have mandated a financial organization implement stricter access controls. Which control standard should they look to first?

Option 1: COBIT

Option 2: PCI DSS

Option 3: ISO 27001

Option 4: NIST SP 800-53

Correct Response: 4

Explanation: NIST SP 800-53 provides guidance on access control standards.

Knowledge Area: Control Types, Standards and Frameworks in Risk Management

----

Question Number: 655

Question: What is the BEST control model for ensuring financial data integrity?

Option 1: COSO

Option 2: CMMI

Option 3: ITIL

Option 4: COBIT

Correct Response: 1

Explanation: COSO provides control principles for financial reporting integrity.

Knowledge Area: Control Types, Standards and Frameworks in Risk Management

----

Question Number: 656

Question: A company is implementing a new cloud-based payroll system. What is the BEST way to evaluate controls before adoption?

Option 1: Review vendor audit report

Option 2: Conduct onsite assessment

Option 3: Examine certification compliance

Option 4: Request test account to validate controls

Correct Response: 4

Explanation: Validating controls with a test account provides best assurance.

Knowledge Area: Control Design, Selection and Analysis in Risk Management

----

Question Number: 657

Question: A company wants to improve security over customer data. Which approach would BEST ensure controls stay effective over time?

Option 1: One-time implementation

Option 2: Monthly control testing

Option 3: Continuous monitoring

Option 4: Annual control audits

Correct Response: 3

Explanation: Continuous monitoring maintains control effectiveness.

Knowledge Area: Control Implementation in Risk Management

Question Number: 658

Question: A new cloud solution did not meet security requirements during testing. What should happen NEXT before deployment?

Option 1: Grant exception

Option 2: Reassess after launch

Option 3: Develop remediation plan

Option 4: Terminate initiative

Correct Response: 3

Explanation: Develop a plan to remediate deficiencies first.

Knowledge Area: Control Implementation in Risk Management

Question Number: 659

Question: An organization wants to evaluate the effectiveness of firewall rules. Which testing approach would BEST meet this objective?

Option 1: Policy review

Option 2: Control self-assessment

Option 3: Penetration testing

Option 4: Vulnerability scanning

Correct Response: 3

Explanation: Penetration testing is best to validate firewall rule effectiveness.

Knowledge Area: Control Testing and Effectiveness Evaluation in Risk Management

----

Question Number: 660

Question: Which technique would provide the MOST accurate assessment of a control's design effectiveness?

Option 1: Process walkthrough

Option 2: Control configuration review

Option 3: Simulation testing

Option 4: Policy review

Correct Response: 3

Explanation: Simulating the control in action assesses design effectiveness.

Knowledge Area: Control Testing and Effectiveness Evaluation in Risk Management

----

Question Number: 661

Question: An application audit identified input validation weaknesses. What should be done FIRST before closing findings?

Option 1: Re-test application post-fix

Option 2: Review remediation plan

Option 3: Inspect code changes

Option 4: Confirm stakeholder sign-off

Correct Response: 1

Explanation: Retest to verify control effectiveness before closure.

Knowledge Area: Control Testing and Effectiveness Evaluation in Risk Management

----

Question Number: 662

Question: What is the primary goal of managing emerging risks in risk management?

Option 1: To identify and assess new and evolving risks

Option 2: To eliminate all risks associated with emerging risks

Option 3: To transfer risks to external parties through contracts

Option 4: To accept risks without taking any proactive measures

Correct Response: 1

Explanation: The primary goal of managing emerging risks in risk management is to identify and assess new and evolving risks. By proactively identifying and assessing emerging risks, organizations can develop appropriate strategies and plans to mitigate their potential impact.

Knowledge Area: Risk Treatment Plans in Risk Management

Question Number: 663

Question: Which of the following is a key component of managing emerging risks?

Option 1: Continuous monitoring and surveillance

Option 2: Risk avoidance and elimination

Option 3: Risk transfer to external parties through contracts

Option 4: Risk acceptance and mitigation

Correct Response: 1

Explanation: Continuous monitoring and surveillance is a key component of managing emerging risks. By continuously monitoring the environment, staying updated on new trends and developments, and conducting proactive surveillance, organizations can identify emerging risks in a timely manner and respond effectively to mitigate their potential impact.

Knowledge Area: Risk Treatment Plans in Risk Management

Question Number: 664

Question: How should the accuracy of risk data be validated before using in reporting?

Option 1: Compare totals to last year

Option 2: Review for reasonableness

Option 3: Spot check source system

Option 4: All of the above

Correct Response: 4

Explanation: Use reasonability checks, spot checks, trending to validate accuracy.

Knowledge Area: Data Collection, Aggregation, Analysis and Validation in Risk Management

----

Question Number: 665

Question: An organization wants to monitor endpoint security controls. Which technique would provide CONTINUOUS monitoring?

Option 1: Annual audits

Option 2: Daily log reviews

Option 3: Periodic testing

Option 4: Automatedensors and analytics

Correct Response: 4

Explanation: Automated sensors and analytics enable continuous monitoring.

Knowledge Area: Risk and Control Monitoring Techniques in Risk Management

----

Question Number: 666

Question: A retailer needs to improve monitoring of POS system controls. Which technique would BEST detect suspicious activity?

Option 1: Code review

Option 2: Penetration testing

Option 3: Transaction analytics

Option 4: Vulnerability scanning

Correct Response: 3

Explanation: Transaction analytics can identify anomalies and misuse.

Knowledge Area: Risk and Control Monitoring Techniques in Risk Management

----

Question Number: 667

Question: The CIO has asked for a routine report on security posture. Which report would provide the MOST meaningful view?

Option 1: Latest penetration test results

Option 2: Compliance audit status

Option 3: Dashboard of key risk metrics

Option 4: Inventory of security controls

Correct Response: 3

Explanation: Key risk metrics quickly communicate security posture.

Knowledge Area: Risk and Control Reporting Techniques (heatmap, scorecards, dashboards) in Risk Management

----

Question Number: 668

Question: A risk committee has asked for a report on resilience. What would be MOST relevant?

Option 1: Recovery procedures

Option 2: Incident response plans

Option 3: Dashboard of resilience KRIs

Option 4: Failover test results

Correct Response: 3

Explanation: Key resilience indicators quickly communicate posture.

Knowledge Area: Risk and Control Reporting Techniques (heatmap, scorecards, dashboards) in Risk Management

----

Question Number: 669

Question: A security team needs to report on malware defense effectiveness. Which metric would be BEST?

Option 1: Anti-virus definition age

Option 2: Malware detection rate

Option 3: Firewall ruleset size

Option 4: Intrusion detection alerts

Correct Response: 2

Explanation: Malware detection rate measures defenses working.

Knowledge Area: Key Performance Indicators in Risk Management

----

Question Number: 670

Question: What metric indicates business continuity program maturity?

Option 1: Recovery time objective

Option 2: Recovery point objective

Option 3: Failed disaster recovery tests

Option 4: Unplanned downtime

Correct Response: 4

Explanation: Unplanned downtime measures resilience.

Knowledge Area: Key Risk Indicators (KRIs) in Risk Management

----

Question Number: 671

Question: A compliance team needs to report on user access controls. Which metric is MOST meaningful?

Option 1: Password complexity enabled

Option 2: Access certification completion rate

Option 3: Privilege entitlement approvals

Option 4: User accounts recertified annually

Correct Response: 2

Explanation: Completion rate shows access oversight.

Knowledge Area: Key Control Indicators (KCIs) in Risk Management

----

Question Number: 672

Question: Scenario: An organization experiences a data breach resulting in the exposure of customer information. What is the primary contributing condition to this risk event?

Option 1: Inadequate cybersecurity controls and vulnerabilities

Option 2: External hacking attempts and malicious activities

Option 3: Insider threat and unauthorized access by employees

Option 4: Natural disasters and physical damage to infrastructure

Correct Response: 1

Explanation: The primary contributing condition to the data breach risk event is inadequate cybersecurity controls and vulnerabilities. Weaknesses in the organization's security measures and systems can expose customer information to unauthorized access and potential data breaches.

Knowledge Area: Risk Events (e.g., contributing conditions, loss result) in Risk Management

----

Question Number: 673

Question: A bank is concerned about emerging cyber threats to new mobile payment applications. What technique would provide the MOST proactive understanding?

Option 1: Vulnerability testing

Option 2: Threat intelligence monitoring

Option 3: Penetration testing after launch

Option 4: Threat modeling before implementation

Correct Response: 4

Explanation: Threat modeling surfaces risks before launch.

Knowledge Area: Threat Modelling and Threat Landscape in Risk Management

----

Question Number: 674

Question: Scenario: An organization experiences a significant control deficiency in its financial reporting process. What is the primary objective of conducting a vulnerability and control deficiency analysis for this deficiency?

Option 1: Identifying the root causes of the control deficiency and developing corrective actions

Option 2: Transferring the control deficiency to an external party through outsourcing

Option 3: Accepting the control deficiency without taking any proactive measures

Option 4: Eliminating all control deficiencies through immediate remediation

Correct Response: 1

Explanation: The primary objective of conducting a vulnerability and control deficiency analysis for the identified control deficiency is identifying the root causes of the control deficiency and developing corrective actions. This analysis helps in understanding the underlying factors contributing to the deficiency, enabling organizations to address the systemic issues, improve their risk management processes, and implement effective controls to mitigate the identified deficiencies.

Knowledge Area: Vulnerability and Control Deficiency Analysis (e.g., root cause analysis) in Risk Management

----

Question Number: 675

Question: Scenario: An organization discovers a critical vulnerability in its web application. What is the primary action to take in response to this vulnerability?

Option 1: Conducting a thorough vulnerability assessment to understand the potential impact

Option 2: Implementing temporary compensating controls until a permanent fix is available

Option 3: Transferring the vulnerability to an external party through outsourcing or insurance

Option 4: Accepting the vulnerability without taking any action

Correct Response: 1

Explanation: The primary action to take in response to the identified vulnerability in the web application is conducting a thorough vulnerability assessment to understand the potential impact. This assessment helps in evaluating the likelihood and severity of the vulnerability, enabling organizations to prioritize their mitigation efforts and implement appropriate measures to address the vulnerability.

Knowledge Area: Vulnerability and Control Deficiency Analysis (e.g., root cause analysis) in Risk Management

----

Question Number: 676

Question: Scenario: An organization experiences a breach in its network security resulting in unauthorized access to sensitive data. What is the primary step in conducting a vulnerability and control deficiency analysis for this breach?

Option 1: Identifying the root causes of the breach and control deficiencies

Option 2: Implementing immediate measures to stop the breach and mitigate the impact

Option 3: Transferring the breach to an external party through legal actions

Option 4: Accepting the breach without taking any action

Correct Response: 1

Explanation: The primary step in conducting a vulnerability and control deficiency analysis for the identified breach is identifying the root causes of the breach and control deficiencies. This analysis helps in understanding how the breach occurred, the weaknesses in the control environment, and developing appropriate measures to prevent future breaches.

Knowledge Area: Vulnerability and Control Deficiency Analysis (e.g., root cause analysis) in Risk Management

----

Question Number: 677

Question: An organization wants to improve its risk assessment by incorporating threat scenarios. What information would be MOST useful in developing scenarios?

Option 1: Recent cyber threats in the news

Option 2: Results of vulnerability scans

Option 3: Outcomes of penetration testing

Option 4: Threat intelligence from CERTs

Correct Response: 4

Explanation: Threat intelligence provides insights into relevant scenarios.

Knowledge Area: Risk Scenario Development in Risk Management

Question Number: 678

Question: A financial firm's risk analysis primarily uses quantitative data. What technique would enhance the risk scenario process?

Option 1: Conduct probabilistic risk modeling

Option 2: Interview business process owners

Option 3: Review threat information from vendors

Option 4: Perform quantitative risk surveys

Correct Response: 2

Explanation: Interviews provide qualitative insights into risk scenarios.

Knowledge Area: Risk Scenario Development in Risk Management

Question Number: 679

Question: An organization performs primarily qualitative risk assessments. What technique would ENHANCE analysis?

Option 1: Brainstorming risk scenarios

Option 2: Incorporating key risk metrics

Option 3: Using Monte Carlo simulations

Option 4: Benchmarking industry loss data

Correct Response: 3

Explanation: Simulations bring quantitative rigor to qualitative assessments.

Knowledge Area: Risk Scenario Development in Risk Management

Question Number: 680

Question: Which of the following is a commonly used risk assessment framework in risk management?

Option 1: ISO 31000: Risk Management Principles and Guidelines

Option 2: COSO Enterprise Risk Management Framework

Option 3: NIST SP 800-30: Risk Management Guide for Information Technology Systems

Option 4: All of the above

Correct Response: 1

Explanation: ISO 31000: Risk Management Principles and Guidelines, COSO Enterprise Risk Management Framework, and NIST SP 800-30: Risk Management Guide for Information Technology Systems are all commonly used risk assessment frameworks in risk management. These frameworks provide guidance and best practices for conducting risk assessments and managing risks effectively.

Knowledge Area: Risk Assessment Concepts, Standards and Frameworks in Risk Management

----

Question Number: 681

Question: Scenario: An organization is planning to conduct a risk assessment for its information technology systems. Which framework would be most suitable for this purpose?

Option 1: NIST SP 800-30: Risk Management Guide for Information Technology Systems

Option 2: ISO 31000: Risk Management Principles and Guidelines

Option 3: COSO Enterprise Risk Management Framework

Option 4: COBIT (Control Objectives for Information and Related Technologies)

Correct Response: 1

Explanation: For conducting a risk assessment specifically for information technology systems, the NIST SP 800-30: Risk Management Guide for Information Technology Systems would be the most suitable framework. It provides a structured approach and guidance for identifying, assessing, and mitigating risks associated specifically with IT systems.

Knowledge Area: Risk Assessment Concepts, Standards and Frameworks in Risk Management

----

Question Number: 682

Question: Which of the following risk assessment concepts emphasizes the importance of considering the likelihood and impact of risks?

Option 1: Risk likelihood

Option 2: Risk severity

Option 3: Risk appetite

Option 4: Risk tolerance

Correct Response: 1

Explanation: The concept of risk likelihood emphasizes the importance of considering the likelihood or probability of risks occurring. It helps in understanding the chances or frequency of risks happening and allows organizations to prioritize their risk management efforts accordingly.

Knowledge Area: Risk Assessment Concepts, Standards and Frameworks in Risk Management

----

Question Number: 683

Question: An organization is creating a risk register. Which components should be included for each risk?

Option 1: Description, rating, response, owner

Option 2: Current status, test results, audit notes

Option 3: Start date, end date, last update, simulator

Option 4: Threat source, annual loss expectancy, control gaps

Correct Response: 1

Explanation: Registers should cover risk description, assessment, response, ownership.

Knowledge Area: Risk Register in Risk Management

Question Number: 684

Question: A company wants to improve its risk register. Which element would enhance visibility into emerging risks?

Option 1: Add threat categories

Option 2: Include risk maps

Option 3: Add leading indicators

Option 4: Expand list of impacts

Correct Response: 3

Explanation: Leading indicators highlight emerging risks.

Knowledge Area: Risk Register in Risk Management

Question Number: 685

Question: A company is performing primarily qualitative risk assessments. What technique would ENHANCE analysis by incorporating financial exposures?

Option 1: Decision tree analysis

Option 2: Key risk indicators

Option 3: Risk surveys and workshops

Option 4: Quantitative risk modeling

Correct Response: 4

Explanation: Quantitative modeling provides financial loss insights.

Knowledge Area: Risk Analysis Methodologies in Risk Management

----

Question Number: 686

Question: An organization relies on risk questionnaires for analysis. What technique would provide MORE insights on emerging risks?

Option 1: Teaming workshops

Option 2: Risk indicator monitoring

Option 3: Financial impact analysis

Option 4: Root cause analysis

Correct Response: 2

Explanation: Risk indicators highlight emerging issues not captured in questionnaires.

Knowledge Area: Risk Analysis Methodologies in Risk Management

----

Question Number: 687

Question: A hospital wants to prioritize information security risks. What analysis would provide MOST meaningful rankings?

Option 1: Threat vulnerability analysis

Option 2: Pareto analysis of risk themes

Option 3: Risks mapped on qualitative scales

Option 4: Analysis of potential financial losses

Correct Response: 4

Explanation: Potential losses quantify business impacts for prioritization.

Knowledge Area: Risk Analysis Methodologies in Risk Management

----

Question Number: 688

Question: Scenario: A company is conducting a business impact analysis (BIA) to assess the potential consequences of a major system failure. What is the first step in conducting a BIA?

Option 1: Identifying critical business functions and their dependencies

Option 2: Assessing the financial impact of the system failure

Option 3: Implementing immediate measures to mitigate the system failure

Option 4: Accepting the system failure without taking any action

Correct Response: 1

Explanation: The first step in conducting a business impact analysis (BIA) is identifying critical business functions and their dependencies. This step helps in understanding the interdependencies between different functions and their importance to the organization. It provides a foundation for prioritizing recovery efforts and allocating resources effectively.

Knowledge Area: Business Impact Analysis in Risk Management

Question Number: 689

Question: Scenario: An organization wants to assess the potential consequences of a natural disaster. What is the primary step in conducting a business impact analysis (BIA) for this situation?

Option 1: Identifying critical business functions and their dependencies

Option 2: Assessing the probability of the natural disaster

Option 3: Implementing immediate measures to mitigate the natural disaster

Option 4: Accepting the natural disaster without taking any action

Correct Response: 1

Explanation: The primary step in conducting a business impact analysis (BIA) for a natural disaster is identifying critical business functions and their dependencies. This step helps in understanding the interdependencies and impact on the organization, forming the basis for prioritizing recovery efforts and resource allocation.

Knowledge Area: Business Impact Analysis in Risk Management

Question Number: 690

Question: A penetration test identified several critical vulnerabilities in an internet-facing ERP application. What type of risk do these findings represent?

Option 1: Residual

Option 2: Compliance

Option 3: Operational

Option 4: Inherent

Correct Response: 1

Explanation: The findings highlight residual risk even after controls were applied.

Knowledge Area: Inherent and Residual Risk in Risk Management

----

Question Number: 691

Question: A company is adopting a new cloud payroll system and wants to perform due diligence. What risk analysis would BEST highlight pre-control risks?

Option 1: Vendor security audit

Option 2: Penetration testing after implementation

Option 3: Review ofInhererent risks prior to adoption

Option 4: Threat modeling after integration

Correct Response: 3

Explanation: Analyzing inherent risks before adoption identifies pre-control issues.

Knowledge Area: Inherent and Residual Risk in Risk Management

----

Question Number: 692

Question: A company's board wants to strengthen risk oversight. What role should be created?

Option 1: Senior risk manager

Option 2: Dedicated risk auditor

Option 3: Chief Risk Officer

Option 4: Risk management committee

Correct Response: 3

Explanation: The Chief Risk Officer leads the risk program at the executive level.

Knowledge Area: Organizational Structure, Roles and Responsibilities in Risk Management

----

Question Number: 693

Question: What is the MAIN benefit of a "three lines of defense" risk model?

Option 1: Clear separation of duties

Option 2: Centralized expertise

Option 3: Holistic risk coverage

Option 4: Greater operational integration

Correct Response: 1

Explanation: The model provides clear separation between risk functions.

Knowledge Area: Organizational Structure, Roles and Responsibilities in Risk Management

----

Question Number: 694

Question: An organization wants to build a stronger risk culture. What is the FIRST step?

Option 1: Establish zero-tolerance conduct policies

Option 2: Implement mandatory risk training

Option 3: Define desired cultural elements

Option 4: Enforce stringent controls

Correct Response: 3

Explanation: Define desired cultural traits and behaviors first.

Knowledge Area: Organizational Culture in Risk Management

Question Number: 695

Question: Senior management wants to improve risk behaviors. What action would be MOST impactful?

Option 1: Publish a code of conduct

Option 2: Increase accountability for violations

Option 3: Reward positive risk behaviors

Option 4: Enforce mandatory training

Correct Response: 2

Explanation: Increased accountability drives cultural change.

Knowledge Area: Organizational Culture in Risk Management

Question Number: 696

Question: An organization is initiating a risk culture transformation. What is MOST important for the risk team?

Option 1: Assessing risk culture maturity

Option 2: Defining risk appetite

Option 3: Monitoring risk metrics

Option 4: Role modeling desired behaviors

Correct Response: 4

Explanation: The risk team should visibly role model desired cultural traits.

Knowledge Area: Organizational Culture in Risk Management

Question Number: 697

Question: What indicates strong risk culture maturity?

Option 1: Mandatory training completion

Option 2: Level of policy enforcement

Option 3: Employee survey engagement scores

Option 4: Individual accountability for behaviors

Correct Response: 4

Explanation: Accountability for actions demonstrates cultural maturity.

Knowledge Area: Organizational Culture in Risk Management

Question Number: 698

Question: An organization wants to implement new risk management policies. What should be done FIRST?

Option 1: Customize industry standard frameworks

Option 2: Conduct a gap assessment

Option 3: Draft new policy documents

Option 4: Obtain executive approval

Correct Response: 2

Explanation: A gap assessment identifies policy needs and priorities.

Knowledge Area: Policies and Standards in Risk Management

Question Number: 699

Question: How should policy exceptions be managed?

Option 1: Zero tolerance of deviations

Option 2: Recorded and approved through exception workflow

Option 3: Allowed unless explicitly prohibited

Option 4: Not tracked unless required for audit

Correct Response: 2

Explanation: Record and approve exceptions through defined workflow.

Knowledge Area: Policies and Standards in Risk Management

Question Number: 700

Question: An organization wants to identify operational risk exposures. Which approach would provide the BROADEST view?

Option 1: Process audits

Option 2: Risk self-assessments

Option 3: Loss event data analysis

Option 4: Risk workshops

Correct Response: 1

Explanation: Analyzing business processes provides an end-to-end view of risks.

Knowledge Area: Business Processes in Risk Management

Question Number: 701

Question: What is an effective way to identify process control gaps?

Option 1: Process walkthroughs

Option 2: Control testing

Option 3: RCSAs

Option 4: Audit findings

Correct Response: 1

Explanation: Process walkthroughs reveal operational vulnerabilities.

Knowledge Area: Business Processes in Risk Management

Question Number: 702

Question: A company wants to improve information security. What should be done FIRST?

Option 1: Classify data by sensitivity

Option 2: Implement encryption controls

Option 3: Perform risk assessment

Option 4: Prevent use of external drives

Correct Response: 1

Explanation: Classify data to drive appropriate controls.

Knowledge Area: Organizational Assets in Risk Management

Question Number: 703

Question: What is an advantage of implementing an ERM framework?

Option 1: Satisfies industry standards for risk management

Option 2: Provides centralized oversight of all risks

Option 3: Ensures holistic coverage of risk disciplines

Option 4: Enforces top-down consistency across silos

Correct Response: 4

Explanation: ERM provides consistent discipline across decentralized units.

Knowledge Area: Enterprise Risk Management and Risk Management Framework in Risk Management

----

Question Number: 704

Question: How does an ERM framework MOST benefit strategic planning?

Option 1: Catalogs assets requiring protection

Option 2: Highlights critical risk interdependencies

Option 3: Enables quantitative risk modeling

Option 4: Identifies threats tied to objectives

Correct Response: 2

Explanation: ERM highlights cross-risk impacts on objectives.

Knowledge Area: Enterprise Risk Management and Risk Management Framework in Risk Management

----

Question Number: 705

Question: What is the PRIMARY purpose of the three lines of defense model?

Option 1: To integrate risk processes

Option 2: To define risk reporting flows

Option 3: To assign risk roles

Option 4: To segregate risk responsibilities

Correct Response: 4

Explanation: The model separates risk duties across lines.

Knowledge Area: Three Lines of Defense in Risk Management

Question Number: 706

Question: Why are risk interdependency analyses useful?

Option 1: Illustrate cross-functional impacts

Option 2: Satisfy regulatory requirements

Option 3: Enable resource optimization

Option 4: Simplify risk reporting

Correct Response: 1

Explanation: Interdependency mapping shows risk correlations.

Knowledge Area: Risk Profile in Risk Management

Question Number: 707

Question: What guides decisions on risk acceptance and responses?

Option 1: Risk appetite statement

Option 2: Risk register

Option 3: Audit findings

Option 4: Threat intelligence

Correct Response: 1

Explanation: The risk appetite statement guides risk acceptance decisions.

Knowledge Area: Risk Appetite and Risk Tolerance in Risk Management

----

Question Number: 708

Question: How can overly restrictive risk tolerance impact an organization?

Option 1: Increased staff turnover

Option 2: Lower revenue opportunities

Option 3: Higher cost of risk management

Option 4: Reduced focus on core objectives

Correct Response: 2

Explanation: Excessive restrictions constrain beneficial opportunities.

Knowledge Area: Risk Appetite and Risk Tolerance in Risk Management

----

Question Number: 709

Question: Scenario: An organization operates in a highly regulated industry and must adhere to specific legal and regulatory requirements. What is the primary consequence of non-compliance with legal and regulatory requirements?

Option 1: Legal and financial penalties

Option 2: Elimination of all risks

Option 3: Transfer of risks to external parties

Option 4: Acceptance of non-compliance without taking any action

Correct Response: 1

Explanation: The primary consequence of non-compliance with legal and regulatory requirements is the risk of legal and financial penalties. Non-compliance can result in fines, sanctions, legal actions, reputational damage, and loss of business opportunities. Adhering to legal and regulatory requirements is crucial for maintaining compliance, protecting the organization's reputation, and mitigating the potential adverse consequences of non-compliance.

Knowledge Area: Legal, Regulatory and Contractual Requirements in Risk Management

----

Question Number: 710

Question: Scenario: A risk management professional is faced with a situation where they discover unethical behavior within their organization. What is the primary action they should take based on professional ethics?

Option 1: Report the unethical behavior to the appropriate authorities or management

Option 2: Ignore the unethical behavior and continue with their regular duties

Option 3: Confront the individuals involved in the unethical behavior

Option 4: Document the unethical behavior for personal records and take no further action

Correct Response: 1

Explanation: The primary action a risk management professional should take based on professional ethics is to report the unethical behavior to the appropriate authorities or management. Upholding professional ethics involves promoting integrity, transparency, and accountability. Reporting unethical behavior helps in maintaining ethical standards, protecting the organization, and ensuring a healthy work environment.

Knowledge Area: Professional Ethics of Risk Management in Risk Management

----

Question Number: 711

Question: Scenario: A risk management professional is faced with a conflict of interest situation where their personal interests may compromise their professional judgment. What is the best course of action based on professional ethics?

Option 1: Disclose the conflict of interest to relevant stakeholders and recuse oneself from the decision-making process

Option 2: Prioritize personal interests over professional obligations

Option 3: Seek personal gain from the conflict of interest situation

Option 4: Ignore the conflict of interest and proceed with the decision-making process

Correct Response: 1

Explanation: The best course of action based on professional ethics is for the risk management professional to disclose the conflict of interest to relevant stakeholders and recuse themselves from the decision-making process. This ensures transparency, avoids bias, and upholds the integrity of the risk management profession.

Knowledge Area: Professional Ethics of Risk Management in Risk Management

----

Question Number: 712

Question: Scenario: A risk management professional receives confidential information from a colleague that could potentially benefit them financially. What is the appropriate action based on professional ethics?

Option 1: Maintain confidentiality and not use the information for personal gain

Option 2: Share the confidential information with others for personal gain

Option 3: Disclose the confidential information to competitors for personal gain

Option 4: Ignore the confidential information and proceed with regular duties

Correct Response: 1

Explanation: The appropriate action based on professional ethics is for the risk management professional to maintain confidentiality and not use the confidential information for personal gain. Upholding professional ethics involves respecting confidentiality, safeguarding sensitive information, and acting in the best interests of the organization and stakeholders.

Knowledge Area: Professional Ethics of Risk Management in Risk Management

Review Me

How satisfied are you with our book?

Unsatisfied   Neutral   Satisfied

Thank you for finishing this Book.
Excellent Work!

One Last Thing - Once Again, Walter Need Your Help

You support to Walter and Walter's work is **utmost important**, and it helps the entire profession ecosystem becomes more sustainable, healthier and most importantly more reputable.

Please kindly consider

1. Visiting my exam practice test books and consider purchasing them to assist you to pass your target exam, though the direct links provided at the beginning of this book
2. Visiting my exam practice test courses held at Udemy though the direct links provided at the beginning of this book
3. Leaving a positive review and feedback to me though the direct book review links provided at the next page.

I shall be very grateful if I could have your support to me. Once again, I wish you all the best and good luck in your exam. Thank you.

Warm regards,

Walter

Direct URLs to visit all Walter's Practice Tests at Amazon

Visit Walter's author page:

http://WalterEducation.com

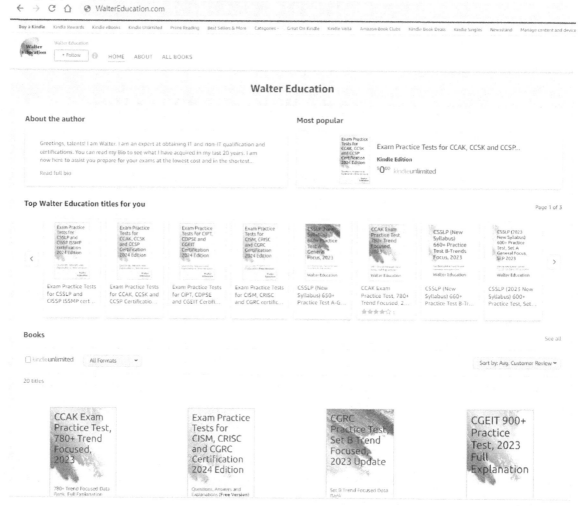

Or the **Links at Amazon Book Store:**

CCAK Exam Practice Test, 780+ Trend Focused, 2023	
Paperback Review URL:	- https://www.amazon.com/review/create-review?&asin=B0CJSXPYM7
Kindle eBook Review URL:	- https://www.amazon.com/review/create-review?&asin=B0CK9QQ44B

CERTIFIED DATA PRIVACY SOLUTIONS ENGINEER (CDPSE) 900+ PRACTICE TEST, 2023, FULL EXPLANATION	
Paperback Review URL:	- https://www.amazon.com/review/create-review?&asin=B0CGL3S5BH
Kindle eBook Review URL:	- https://www.amazon.com/review/create-review?&asin=B0CGL91NQ9

CGEIT 900+ Practice Test, 2023	
Paperback Review URL:	- https://www.amazon.com/review/create-review?&asin=B0CGW1Y1X9
Kindle eBook Review URL:	- https://www.amazon.com/review/create-review?&asin=B0CJ8388ZB

CIPT, Certified Information Privacy Technologists, Practice Test	
Paperback Review URL:	- https://www.amazon.com/review/create-review?&asin=B0CJ4DLHG2
Kindle eBook Review URL:	- https://www.amazon.com/review/create-review?&asin=B0CJ72MR4M

CRISC 1200+ Practice Test, 2023 (Exam Simulation and Core & Advanced Knowledge)	
Paperback Review URL:	- https://www.amazon.com/review/create-review?&asin=B0CJ43R78T
Kindle eBook Review URL:	- https://www.amazon.com/review/create-review?&asin=B0CJ72JJLY

CISM 1050+ Practice Test,2023 Updated, Set B - Trends Focused, ISACA	
Paperback Review URL:	- https://www.amazon.com/review/create-review?&asin=B0CJSNR5Z2
Kindle eBook Review URL:	- https://www.amazon.com/review/create-review?&asin=B0CJVWHJHW

CISM 1050+ Practice Test A - Core Focus, ISACA	
Paperback Review URL:	- https://www.amazon.com/review/create-review?&asin=B0CJL2HD1R
Kindle eBook Review URL:	- https://www.amazon.com/review/create-review?&asin=B0CJVSQ6Z6

CCSKv4 900+ Practice Test 2023, Full Explanation	
Paperback Review URL:	- https://www.amazon.com/review/create-review?&asin=B0CFX2S7D8
Kindle eBook Review URL:	- https://www.amazon.com/review/create-review?&asin=B0CFVLS8ZH

CSSLP (2023 New Syllabus) 600+ Practice Test, Set A General Focus	
Paperback Review URL:	- https://www.amazon.com/review/create-review?&asin=B0CK3VTR9D

Kindle eBook Review URL:	- https://www.amazon.com/review/create-review?&asin=PENDING

CSSLP (New Syllabus) 660+ Practice Test B-Trends Focus, SEP 2023

Paperback Review URL:	- https://www.amazon.com/review/create-review?&asin=B0CK3XGCBN
Kindle eBook Review URL:	- https://www.amazon.com/review/create-review?&asin=PENDING

CISSP-ISSMP 650+ Practice Test, 2023 New syllabus, Set A Core Focused

Paperback Review URL:	- https://www.amazon.com/review/create-review?&asin=B0CJLLL4HP
Kindle eBook Review URL:	- https://www.amazon.com/review/create-review?&asin=B0CK2Y6XR7

CISSP-ISSMP 650+ Practice Test, 2023 New syllabus, Set B Trends Focused, ISC2

Paperback Review URL:	- https://www.amazon.com/review/create-review?&asin=B0CJLMV48G
Kindle eBook Review URL:	- https://www.amazon.com/review/create-review?&asin=B0CK2X7CLL

Practice Test for Certified Cloud Security Professional (CCSP): 900+ Practice Test

Paperback Review URL:	- https://www.amazon.com/review/create-review?&asin=B0CFCLW7HJ
Kindle eBook Review URL:	- https://www.amazon.com/review/create-review?&asin=B0CFKSVKSS

CGRC Practice Test, Set A Data Bank, Learn & Exam, 2023 Update

Paperback Review URL:	- https://www.amazon.com/review/create-review?&asin=B0CJBC5MX1
Kindle eBook Review URL:	- https://www.amazon.com/review/create-review?&asin=B0CJYQVM22

CGRC Practice Test, Set B Trend Focused, 2023

Paperback Review URL:	- https://www.amazon.com/review/create-review?&asin=B0CJ43Z8N6
Kindle eBook Review URL:	- https://www.amazon.com/review/create-review?&asin=B0CJ72HWY2

How to give a Review and Rating:

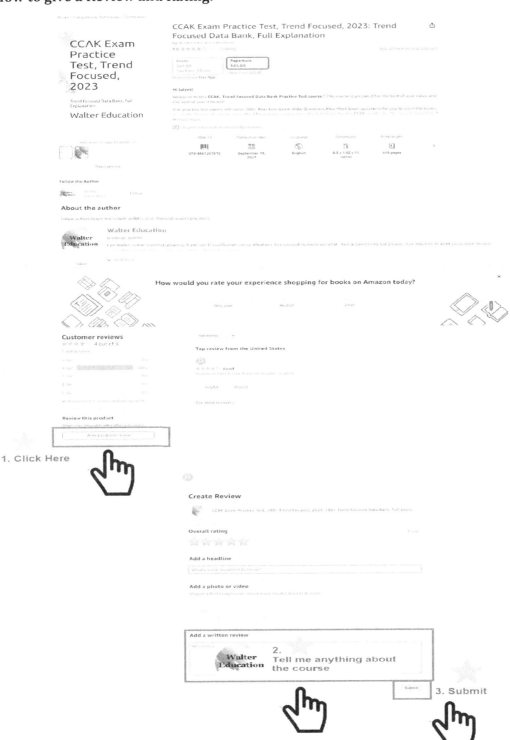

1. Click Here

Create Review

Overall rating

Add a headline

Add a photo or video

Add a written review

Walter Education
2. Tell me anything about the course

Submit

3. Submit

Made in the USA
Middletown, DE
02 April 2024

52501630R00243